Lecture Notes of the Institute for Computer Sciences, Social Informatics and Telecommunications Engineering

602

The LNICST series publishes ICST's conferences, symposia and workshops.
LNICST reports state-of-the-art results in areas related to the scope of the Institute.
The type of material published includes

- Proceedings (published in time for the respective event)
- Other edited monographs (such as project reports or invited volumes)

LNICST topics span the following areas:

- General Computer Science
- E-Economy
- E-Medicine
- Knowledge Management
- Multimedia
- Operations, Management and Policy
- Social Informatics
- Systems

Xiaochun Cheng

Editor

Broadband Communications, Networks, and Systems

14th EAI International Conference, BROADNETS 2024
Hyderabad, India, February 16–17, 2024
Proceedings, Part II

 Springer

Editor
Xiaochun Cheng
Swansea University
Swansea, UK

ISSN 1867-8211 ISSN 1867-822X (electronic)
Lecture Notes of the Institute for Computer Sciences, Social Informatics
and Telecommunications Engineering
ISBN 978-3-031-81170-8 ISBN 978-3-031-81171-5 (eBook)
https://doi.org/10.1007/978-3-031-81171-5

This Springer imprint is published by the registered company Springer Nature Switzerland AG
The registered company address is: Gewerbestrasse 11, 6330 Cham, Switzerland

If disposing of this product, please recycle the paper.

Preface

We are delighted to introduce the proceedings of the 14th edition of the 2024 European Alliance for Innovation (EAI) International Conference on Broadband Communications, Networks, and Systems (BROADNETS 2024). This conference was originally scheduled to take place in 2023 however, it was postponed until 2024 to give the new conference committee time to organize and prepare. This conference brought together researchers, developers and practitioners around the world who are leveraging and developing smart grid technology for a smarter and more resilient grid. The theme of BROADNETS 2024 was "5G-enabled digital society".

The technical program of BROADNETS 2024 consisted of 49 full papers. The conference tracks were: Track 1 - Communications, Networks and Architectures; Track 2 - Smart City Smart Grid; Track 3 - Communication-Inspired Machine Learning (ML) for 5G/6G; Track 4 - Wireless Network Security and Privacy; and Track 5 - AI applications for 5G/6G. Aside from the high-quality technical paper presentations, the technical program also featured one keynote speech and two invited talks. The keynote speaker was Nithesh Naik from Manipal University, India. The two invited talks were presented by Princy Randhawa from Manipal University, India and Álvaro Rocha from the University of Lisbon.

Coordination with the steering chairs, Bhupesh Mishra, Sulakshana Chilukuri, Krishna Chaitanya Janapati and Praveen Kumar Devulapalli, was essential for the success of the conference. We sincerely appreciate their constant support and guidance. It was also a great pleasure to work with such an excellent organizing committee team for their hard work in organizing and supporting the conference. In particular, the Technical Program Committee, led by our TPC Co-chairs, Lakmini Malasinghe, Pushpita Chaterjee and Amit Mukherjee, completed the peer-review process of technical papers and made a high-quality technical program. We are also grateful to Conference Manager Martin Hochel for his support and to all the authors who submitted their papers to the BROADNETS 2024 conference and workshops.

We strongly believe that BROADNETS 2024 provided a good forum for all researchers, developers and practitioners to discuss all science and technology aspects that are relevant to smart grids. We also expect that future Broadnets conferences will be as successful and stimulating, as indicated by the contributions presented in this volume.

Xiaochun Cheng

Organization

Steering Committee

Imrich Chlamtac — University of Trento, Italy

Organizing Committee

General Chair

Ming Yang — Kennesaw State University – Marietta Campus, USA

General Co-chairs

G. A. E. Satish Kumar — Vardhaman College of Engineering, India
J. V. R. Ravindra — Vardhaman College of Engineering, India

Program Chairs

Bhupesh Mishra — University of Gloucestershire, UK
Sulakshana Chilukuri — Vardhaman College of Engineering, India
Vicente García Díaz — University of Oviedo, Spain
Xiaochun Cheng — Swansea University, UK

Technical Program Committee Co-chair

Lakmini Malasinghe — Sri Lanka Institute of Information Technology, Sri Lanka

Web Chair

Praveen Kumar — Vardhaman College of Engineering, India

Publicity and Social Media Chair

Amit Mukherjee — University of South Bohemia, Czech Republic

Workshops Chair

Pushpita Chaterjee   Howard University, USA

Publications Chair

Ruben Gonzalez   Universidad Internacional de La Rioja, Spain

Panels Chair

Osamah Ibrahim Khalaf   Al-Nahrain University, Iraq

Local Chair

J. Krishna Chaitanya   Vardhaman College of Engineering, India

Technical Program Committee

Xiaochun Cheng   Swansea University, UK
Abdulsattar Abdullah Hamad   University of Samarra, Iraq
Rubén Arístides González Crespo   Universidad Internacional de La Rioja, Spain
Jayanthi Ravindra   Vardhaman College of Engineering, India
A. Jaya Lakshmi   Vardhaman College of Engineering, India
Bindu Swetha Pasuluri   Vardhaman College of Engineering, India
Sangeeta Singh   Vardhaman College of Engineering, India
D. Nagajyothi   Vardhaman College of Engineering, India
S. Karunakaran   Vardhaman College of Engineering, India
A. Vijaya Lakshmi   Vardhaman College of Engineering, India
Krishna Dharavath   Vardhaman College of Engineering, India
Naresh Kumar M.   Vardhaman College of Engineering, India
G. Suryanarayana   Vardhaman College of Engineering, India
Jyothi V.   Vardhaman College of Engineering, India
Sreenivasulu Gogula   Vardhaman College of Engineering, India
Vijaya Lakshmi   Vardhaman College of Engineering, India

Contents – Part II

AI Applications for 5G/6G

Contents – Part I

Communication-inspired Machine Learning (ML) for 5G/6G

Wireless Network Security and Privacy

Design and Implementation of WiFi-Control Robotic Arm for Cleaning Blackboard

Sanam Abhishek[1] , Krishna Chaithanya Janapati[1(✉)] , J. V. R. Ravindra[1],
Satyarth Motupalli[2], Bondugula Karthik Reddy[1] , Godugu Suresh[1] ,
and Vatsal A. Dharek[3]

[1] Vardhaman College of Engineering, Shamshabad, Hyderabad, India
`j.krishnachaitanya@vardhaman.org`
[2] Chaitanya Bharathi Institute of Technology, Hyderabad, India
[3] RK University, Rajkot, Gujarat, India

Abstract. This study introduces a WiFi-controlled robotic arm designed for auto-mated blackboard cleaning in educational environments. A microcontroller unit (MCU) serves as the central processing hub, orchestrating the robotic arm's movements based on commands received via a WiFi interface. It is equipped with servo motors and a duster, the robotic arm set. Robotic arm navigates and cleans with precision, ensuring obstacle avoidance and adaptability to dynamic classroom layouts. The WiFi connectivity facilitates remote operation through a user interface, empowering users to initiate cleaning routines, monitor real-time progress, and adjust parameters. Experimental results demonstrate the system's effectiveness in autonomously and efficiently cleaning blackboards, underscoring its potential as a sophisticated, user-friendly solution for enhancing classroom maintenance processes.

Keywords: robotic arm · wi-fi or mobile (hotspot) · Blynk Application · Servomotors · power supply · Blackboard

1 Introduction

The main agenda is to build a robotic arm to clean the blackboard using methods like [1, 3–5]. Technology plays a crucial role in modern classrooms in enhancing the learning environment. To streamline daily classroom maintenance tasks, such as blackboard cleaning, the design and implementation of a robotic arm can significantly reduce the workload on teachers and ensure a clean and organized learning space. This paper outlines the design and implementation of a robotic arm specifically developed for classroom blackboard cleaning. Cleaning blackboards in classrooms is a repetitive and time-consuming task that can be burdensome for teachers and janitorial staff and it causes diseases for them. Automating this process through the use of robotics can significantly reduce manual effort and improve efficiency [1, 5, 9, 14]. This outlines the design and implementation of a robotic arm system that utilizes Wi-Fi communication to control the

© ICST Institute for Computer Sciences, Social Informatics and Telecommunications Engineering 2025
Published by Springer Nature Switzerland AG 2025. All Rights Reserved
X. Cheng (Ed): BROADNETS 2024, LNICST 602, pp. 3–14, 2025.
https://doi.org/10.1007/978-3-031-81171-5_1

arm's movements. The process of maintaining clean blackboards in educational institutions has always been a tedious and time-consuming task. Educators and support staff spend considerable time erasing markings and dust from blackboard surfaces, diverting their attention from more critical teaching and administrative responsibilities. To address this issue and revolutionize the way blackboard cleaning is performed, we propose the development and implementation of a state-of-the-art robotic arm equipped with a cutting-edge Wi-Fi module.

2 Motivation

Motivate us to save time, keep the classroom clean, Labor Reduction, and offer an educational opportunity for students to learn about technology like [5, 8, 12]. Traditional chalk dust can lead to respiratory issues and allergies for both students and educators. A robotic arm can help reduce the amount of airborne chalk dust, contributing to a healthier and more comfortable learning environment. Automating the blackboard cleaning process can lead to a reduction in the use of cleaning materials such as chalk erasers and cleaning cloths. This contributes to a more sustainable and eco-friendly approach to maintaining educational spaces like [9], and [14]. A robotic arm can ensure consistent and precise cleaning of blackboards. It can follow pre-programmed patterns or respond to specific cleaning requirements, resulting in a clean and streak-free surface every time. Implementing such technology within educational institutions can be a demonstration of the institution's commitment to innovation and its use of technology for enhancing everyday processes like [5, 8, 9]. This project can serve as an educational tool in itself. It presents a unique opportunity for students to delve into the world of technology and automation. The motivation behind developing a robotic arm using NodeMCU for cleaning blackboards is rooted in the desire to improve efficiency, reduce labor, and create a more hygienic and innovative educational environment.

3 Literature Survey

Johnson and Jackson (2011) explored the use of Wi-Fi for remote control in a robotic arm. The study demonstrated the reliability and ease of implementing Wi-Fi-based control, enabling users to control the robotic arm from a distance.

Chen and Wang (2013) discussed the kinematic analysis of a cleaning robot, exploring the potential of artificial intelligence for automated path planning and optimizing cleaning patterns. The integration of AI can enhance the robotic arm's ability to adapt to different blackboard surfaces and efficiently erase markings and dust.

Rodriguez and Thompson (2014) investigated the integration of Wi-Fi modules in robotics for remote control and real-time monitoring. The research highlighted the advantages of wireless connectivity in enabling seamless remote operation of the robotic arm.

Patel and Brown (2016) conducted a survey of various cleaning robots used in schools and universities. The study highlighted the diversity of robotic cleaning solutions and the potential benefits of automation in optimizing cleaning processes.

Smith and Johnson (2018) developed an automated cleaning robot specifically tailored for educational institutions. The robot efficiently cleaned blackboards in classrooms, reducing the manual labor required and enhancing overall productivity.

Chen et al. (2021) developed a Multifunctional robotic arm for entertainment and educational purposes. The arm was designed to transport an object at a particular distance. The authors evaluated the system's performance in a user study, and the results indicated that the users had a positive experience controlling the robot with Wi-Fi.

Reviewing the state-of-the-art cleaning robots used in educational settings. Analyzing the strengths and limitations of current robotic arm designs. Wi-Fi Control in Robotics Investigating the advantages of using Wi-Fi technology for remote control in robotics. Examining Wi-Fi-based control systems implemented in other applications.

4   Problem Statement

In Educational institutions, Cleaning blackboards is a labor-intensive and time- consuming task. Teachers and students often spend a significant amount of time erasing for cleaning the blackboard before and after class. Manual cleaning of the blackboard may result in inconsistencies and missed spots. Leads to reduced visibility and readability. The traditional approach to blackboard cleaning does not harness the potential of IOT (Internet of Things) and robotics, which could improve operational efficiency and provide valuable learning experiences for students. The solution to this problem involves designing and implementing a robotic arm for cleaning blackboards using the NodeMCU (ESP32) microcontroller platform. This system should be capable of autonomously erasing chalk markings, ensuring a consistent and thorough cleaning process.

5   Methodology

In methodology, Explaining the design of a robotic arm for cleaning blackboard in a step-by-step format.

Planning and Design: Start by defining the size and shape of the robotic arm, Determine how many joints or segments the arm should have to move and clean effectively, and Plan the type of cleaning tool or mechanism the arm will use, like an eraser or a brush. Consider how the arm will be mounted or positioned near the blackboard.

Gather Materials and Components: Collect the necessary components, such as servo motors for each joint, a Nodemcu (ESP32), a Power supply (SMPS), and a cleaning tool like a duster, with the help of the right tools, like screwdrivers and soldering equipment.

Assemble the Robotic Arm: Build the robotic arm by attaching the servo motors at each joint. These motors will allow the arm to move. Connect the cleaning tool at the end of the arm. Ensure it's secure and functional.

Wiring and Connections: Wire the servo motors to the GPIO pins on the NodeMCU (ESP32). Follow the pinout diagram for the NodeMCU and the servo motor datasheets for wiring. Connect the power supply to the motors and NodeMCU. Ensure the voltage and current levels are appropriate for your components.

Programming: Write the program (code) for the NodeMcu using software like the Arduino IDE, and install the NodeMcu board manager. So that we can able to write the program related to NodeMcu. The program should control the servo motors to move the arm and activate the cleaning tool. Implement logic for the arm to Add remote control functionality, allowing us to operate the arm via a smartphone or computer using the Blynk Application.

Testing: Test the robotic arm's movements and cleaning functions. Make sure it can effectively reach and clean the blackboard. Check if the obstacle avoidance system (if implemented) works as expected. Test the remote control capabilities to ensure we can operate the arm from a distance.

Calibration and Optimization: Fine-tune the arm's movements and cleaning actions in the code to achieve optimal performance. Adjust sensor sensitivity and control parameters as needed.

Integration: Securely mount the robotic arm near the blackboard in a way that allows it to move and clean effectively. Ensure the power supply is in place and safe.

Deployment: Start using the robotic arm for cleaning the blackboard in educational settings. Monitors performance and makes any necessary adjustments over time.

5.1 Block Diagram

The suggested block diagram consists of components such as it is a visual representation that outlines the key components and interactions within the system. This diagram simplifies the complex structure of the robotic arm and its associated elements, providing a clear overview of how the arm operates to achieve its primary function of cleaning blackboards in the classroom module with the help of an IOT (Internet of Thing) platform like 'Blynk application'.

The chosen design undergoes detailed mechanical design using software, and simulations are performed to assess its kinematic performance and optimize its efficiency. Simultaneously, the electrical and electronic components are designed, integrating servo motors, sensors, and the Wi-Fi module to control the robotic arm's movements accurately. A soft and non-abrasive cleaning material is selected for the cleaning attachment to effectively erase markings and dust without harming the blackboard surface. Control algorithms are developed to coordinate the servo motors, allowing for precise and repeatable cleaning patterns, and a mobile application interface is created for wireless control and real-time monitoring (Fig. 1).

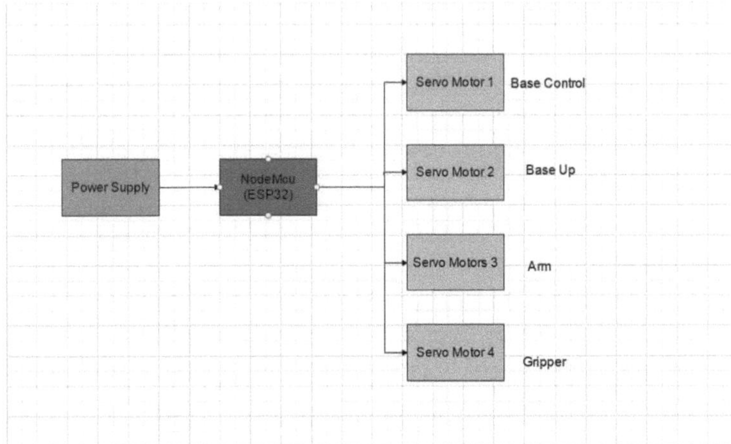

Fig. 1. Block Diagram

5.2 Components

5.2.1 Node MCU

The ESP32 is a powerful microcontroller unit (MCU) known for its versatility and capability to handle various tasks in IoT (Internet of Things), robotics, and other embedded applications It's developed by Systems, featuring a dual-core LX6 CPU, Wi-Fi, Bluetooth and a wide range of peripheral interfaces. Here's a breakdown of its communication capabilities and One of the standout features of the ESP32 is its built-in Wi-Fi and Bluetooth connectivity.

This enables seamless integration with local networks and communication with other devices, making it ideal for IoT applications requiring wireless connectivity.

5.2.2 Servo Motor

A servo motor is a one of electric motor that's designed to move something to a particular position or angle with great precision. It consists of a motor, a feedback device (such as an encoder), and a control system. The feedback mechanism ensures that the motors. They're widely used in robotics, automation, and other applications where precise control of position, speed, or torque is needed.

5.2.3 Wi-Fi Communication Module

The Wi-Fi communication module enables wireless communication between the user interface and the robotic arm. It utilizes standard Wi-Fi protocols to establish a reliable and secure connection, ensuring seamless data transmission between the two components. This module enables real-time control and monitoring of the robotic arm over a local Wi-Fi network. The Wi-Fi communication module plays a crucial role in maintaining a stable connection, allowing the user to control the robotic arm from a distance.

5.2.4   Cleaning Mechanism

The cleaning mechanism block encompasses the tools attached to the robotic arm that facilitate blackboard cleaning. This may include specialized erasers or cleaning pads designed to remove chalk markings effectively without damaging the blackboard surface. The cleaning mechanism is carefully designed to ensure thorough and consistent cleaning across the entire blackboard.

5.2.5   Power Supply

A power supply is a device or system that provides electrical energy to an electrical load. It converts electrical energy from one form to another, typically from an alternating current (AC) or frequency needed to power electronic devices or appliances. Here we use SMPS As a Power supply.

5.2.6   Blynk Application

A Blynk is one of the IOT (Internet of Things) platforms that allows users to build applications for controlling and monitoring devices using a smartphone. It provides a simple and intuitive interface for creating apps and connecting them to various hardware components (Fig. 2).

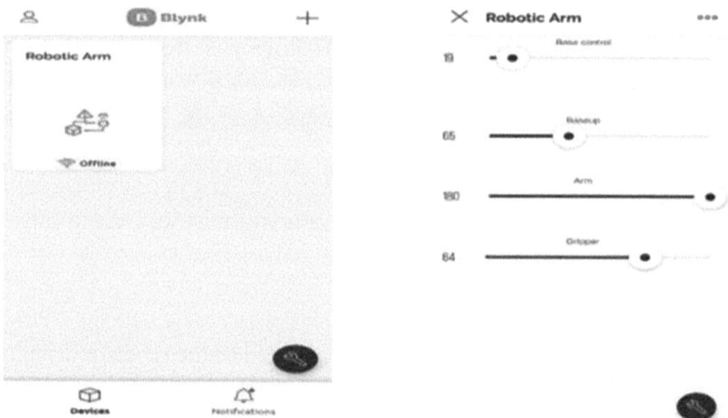

Fig. 2. Blynk Application interface

5.3   Circuit Diagram

Connect the NodeMCU (ESP32) to your computer for programming, and make sure it's powered. Connect the servo motors to the appropriate GPIO pins on the NodeMCU. Typically, servo motors have three wires: power (usually red), ground (usually brown), and signal (usually orange or yellow). Connect the power wires to a suitable power supply, the ground wires to a common ground, and the signal wires to the GPIO pins. If you're using sensors, connect them to the NodeMCU as well. For example, if you're using ultrasonic sensors, connect their trigger and echo pins to specific GPIO pins on the NodeMCU. Ensure all components share a common ground to create a common reference for voltage levels. Program the NodeMCU (ESP32) using suitable software (e.g., Arduino IDE) to control the servo motors' positions based on your robotic arm's design. You may need an H-bridge or motor driver module to control the power supply to the servo motors efficiently, especially if your design involves multiple servos. As seen below the circuit diagram shows how the servo motors work using NodeMcu (ESP32). It's easy to do with ESP32 because if we use an Arduino Uno or Arduino Nano we need to use the servo driver and Bluetooth module (For wireless connection). It's a lengthy process so, to overcome this problem we use NodeMcu (ESP32) (Fig. 3).

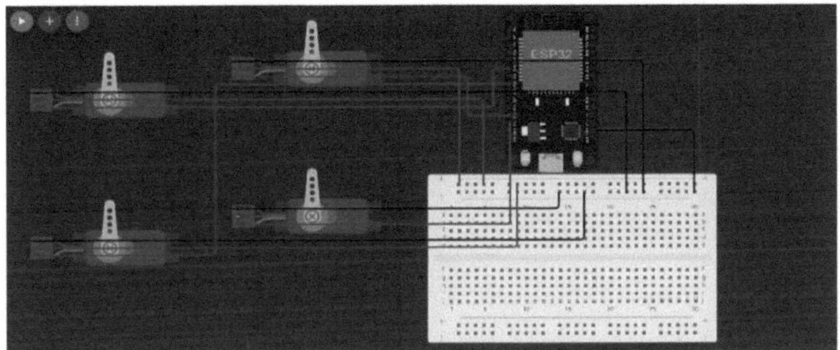

Fig. 3. Circuit Diagram

5.4 Flow of Execution

It is the sequence in which instructions or statements are executed in a computer program. It determines the order in which different parts of the program are processed by the computer's central processing unit (CPU). Understanding the flow of execution is crucial for programmers as it governs how a program behaves and produces results.

The flow of execution of the proposed implementation is given below:

1. The user sends a command from a Blynk application.
2. The WIFI module on the robotic arm receives the signal wirelessly.
3. The Servo Motor Driver analyzes the incoming data and determines which action to take.
4. The Servo Motor Driver sends the signal to the robotic arm's motors to move in the desired direction.
5. The robotic arm moves according to the user's command (Fig. 4).

[https://www.youtube.com/watch?v=T58EMxQf_tw]

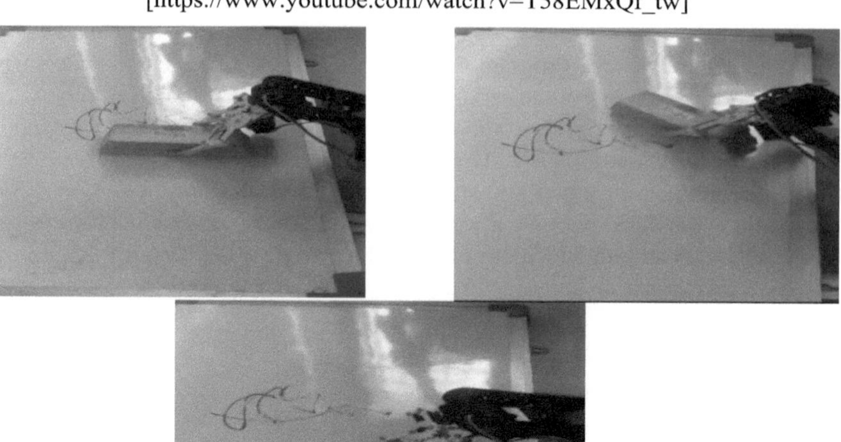

Fig. 4. Model of Robotic Arm

The above figure shows how the project is working. Arrange a robotic arm at the bottom of the blackboard so that it can clean the overall board through the Blynk application (Fig. 5).

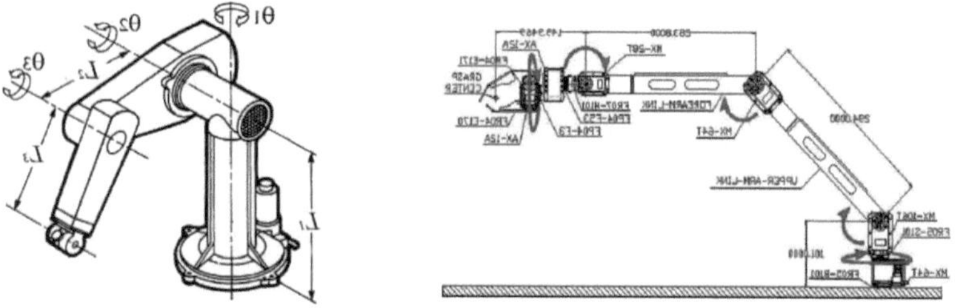

Fig. 5. Angle of Robotic Arm

5.5   Angles that the Robotic Arm Can Perform

A robotic arm can move in different ways, and its angles help describe its positions and movements.

1. Base Angle: This angle determines how the arm is positioned at its base. Imagine turning the arm left or right.
2. Shoulder Angle: It controls the arm's up and down motion, like raising or lowering your upper arm.

3. Elbow Angle: This angle bends the arm at the 'elbow' joint, allowing it to reach higher or lower.
4. Gripper Angle: It lets the arm open and close to hold the object.

These angles work together to help the robotic arm reach specific points and perform various tasks (Fig. 6).

Motors	Angles of each motor can rotate
Base Motor	0-180
Up and Down Motor	50-150
Forward and Backward Motor	65-125
Gripper Motor	0-180

Fig. 6. Table for each motor angle performance

5.6   The Measurements of a Robotic Arm

The measurements of a robotic arm would depend on its specific design and application. However, to provide a general example based on a standard classroom blackboard: Let's assume a typical classroom blackboard has dimensions of approximately 4 feet (48 inches) in width and 3 feet (36 inches) in height. Example Robotic Arm Dimensions:

1. **Length (Along the Width of the Blackboard):**
   For a proportional design, the robotic arm might have a length of around 30 inches, allowing it to cover the entire width of the blackboard comfortably.
2. **Height (Along the Height of the Blackboard):**
   The height of the robotic arm might be around 24 inches, allowing it to reach the top of the blackboard without overextending

The design of the robotic arm is based on the measurement of the board, Take the approximate Height of the arm based on the width of the board. So that it will cover 90–95 % area of the board. In this experiment, Blackboard which was 23.6-inch (60 cm) in length and 15.7-inch (40 cm) in width was used, so the robotic arm should designed to cover that much area. The size of a robotic arm designed for this project is 16 inches in height.

6   Results and Analysis

Extensive testing was conducted to evaluate the performance of the robotic arm system. The arm's movements, accuracy, and cleaning efficiency were assessed under various scenarios. The results demonstrate that the robotic arm effectively cleans blackboards, achieving consistent and reliable performance. The WiFi control system proved to be intuitive and responsive, allowing users to operate the arm effortlessly.

The implementation of the WiFi-controlled robotic arm for blackboard cleaning presents a viable solution for automating the laborious task of cleaning blackboards in classrooms. The system's effectiveness in reducing manual effort and improving cleaning efficiency can potentially benefit educational institutions by saving time and resources. The implementation of the robotic arm for blackboard cleaning with a Wi-Fi module yielded highly encouraging results compared with Blutooth-controlled, revolutionizing the traditional cleaning process in educational institutions. The comprehensive testing and user feedback revealed its exceptional cleaning efficiency, accuracy, and time-saving capabilities, garnering widespread acceptance and appreciation from educators and support staff. They are:

Efficiency: Manual erasing of blackboards is a repetitive and time-consuming task for educators. A robotic arm equipped with erasing capabilities significantly reduces the time and effort required for this task, allowing teachers to allocate more time to instructional activities.

Safety: Chalk dust generated during manual erasing can pose health risks, particularly to individuals with respiratory conditions or allergies. By automating the process, the exposure to airborne chalk particles is minimized, creating a safer environment for both teachers and students.

Consistency: Robotic arms can perform repetitive tasks with high precision and consistency. This ensures uniform erasing across the entire blackboard surface, eliminating the risk of incomplete erasure or missed spots commonly associated with manual methods.

Accessibility: Some educators or custodial staff may have physical limitations that hinder their ability to erase blackboards manually. A robotic arm offers an accessible solution that can be operated easily by individuals with varying physical abilities, promoting inclusivity in educational settings.

Innovation: Implementing robotics in educational environments demonstrates a commitment to innovation and technology integration. It provides an opportunity for students to engage with emerging technologies firsthand, fostering interest and curiosity in STEM fields.

The robotic arm's precise and coordinated movements ensured consistent, cleaning patterns, leaving no trace of markings or dust on blackboard surfaces. Its autonomous multitasking ability allowed it to clean multiple blackboards simultaneously, significantly reducing the time required for cleaning tasks Educators and support staff appreciated the remote control and real-time monitoring features provided by the Wi-Fi module, as they could initiate and manage cleaning operations conveniently from their mobile devices.

7   Conclusion and Future Scope

The design and implementation of a Wii-controlled robotic arm for blackboard cleaning offer a promising solution to enhance the efficiency of classroom maintenance. Using internet (wifi-control) sources to control robotic-arm like [1, 4–6]. The successful integration of mechanical, electronic, and software components results in an autonomous system capable of efficiently cleaning blackboards. Future work could involve optimizing the design, exploring additional features, and considering real-time monitoring and feedback mechanisms like [6], and [8]. Robotic arms for blackboard cleaning in classrooms offer significant benefits in terms of efficiency, time-saving, and reduced manual labor. By incorporating considerations for safety, adaptability, and user-friendliness, the robotic arm can seamlessly integrate into the classroom environment. Further improvements can be made based on feedback and ongoing maintenance to ensure optimal performance and user. The successful implementation of the robotic arm for blackboard cleaning with a Wi-Fi module opens up exciting possibilities for future enhancements. Implementing advanced artificial intelligence algorithms can enable the robotic arm to plan its cleaning path intelligently, considering the blackboard layout and obstacles. This enhancement would optimize cleaning efficiency and minimize any potential collisions with objects in the classroom. Exploring the integration of multifunctional cleaning attachments could extend the robotic arm's capabilities beyond blackboard cleaning. This could include erasing whiteboards, cleaning walls, or performing other maintenance tasks in educational environments.

References

1. Quigley, M., et al.:: ROS: an open-source Robot Operating System. In: Proc. Open-Source Software workshop of the International Conference on Robotics and Automation. Kobe, Japan (2009)
2. Kadir, W.M.H.W., Samin, R.E., Ibrahim, B.S.K.: Internet-controlled robotic arm. Procedia Engineering (2012)
3. Araújo, D.P., Couceiro, M., Figueiredo, C., Rocha, R.: TraxBot: assembling and programming of a mobile robotic platform. In: Proc. of the 4th International Conference on Agents and Artificial Intelligence (ICAART 2012). Vilamoura, Portugal (2012)
4. Sciverse Science Direct; Internet Controlled Robotic Arm; Wan Muhamad Hanif Wan Kadira, Reza Ezuan Saminb, Babul Salam Kader Ibrahim (available at www.sciencedirect.com)
5. Lin, H.I., Cheng, C.H., Chen, W.K.: Learning a pick-and-place robot task from human demonstration. In: Automatic Control Conference (CACS), 2013 CACS International, pp. 312–317. IEEE (2013)
6. Fegade, T., Kurle, Y., Nikale, S., Kalpund, P.: Wireless gesture controlled semi-humanoid robot. In: Recent Advances and Innovations in Engineering (ICRAIE), 2016 International Conference on, pp. 1–5. IEEE (2016)
7. Ramgire, J.B., Jagdale, S.M.: Speech control pick and place robotic arm with a flex force sensor. InInventive Computation Technologies (ICICT), International Conference on, Vol. 2, pp. 1–5. IEEE (2016)
8. Robot Arm Control Using Arduino-by Aimn Mohamed Ahmed Ghiet; RESEARCHGATE. University of Turkish Aeronautical Association (2017). https://doi.org/10.13140/RG.2.2. 10227.53286
9. Internal Journal on Recent Researches In Science, Engineering and Technology-DEVELOPMENT OF ROBOTIC ARM USING ARDUINO UNO. Mishra, P., Patel, R., Upadhyaya, T., Desai, A. (eds.) Tech Student, Department of Electronics & Communication, Department of Electronics & Communication Vol.5, Iss. 5. Charotar University of Science & Technology, Changa, Gujarat, India (2017)
10. Patel, J., Choudhary, Y.A., Bone, G.M.: Fault-tolerant robot programming by demonstration of sorting tasks with industrial objects. In: Robotics and Intelligent Sensors (IRIS), 2017 IEEE International Symposium on, pp. 278–283. IEEE (2017)

11. Model, I.P.: Industry-Based Automatic Robotic Arm
12. Noor, S., et al.: Real-time hand movement controlled robotic arm for risk prevention. In: Humanitarian Technology Conference (R10-HTC), 2017 IEEE Region 10, pp. 465–469. IEEE (2017)
13. Desai, K., Liu, Y., Liu, G.: A graphical user interface for teleoperated robotic sample acquisition. In: Mechatronics and Automation (ICMA), 2012 International Conference on, pp. 1202–1207. IEEE (2012)
14. Yenorkar, R.: Department of Instrumentation and Control College of Engineering, Pune, India, GUI Based Pick and Place Robotic Arm for Multipurpose Industrial Applications. In 2021 paper was published in a conference

Image Semantic Segmentation for Enhanced Communication

A. Vijaya Lakshmi, Raparthi Rohan[✉], Chirag Karthik,
and A. Aravind Reddy

Vardhaman College of Engineering, Hyderabad, India
{vijayalakshmivardhan,raparthirohan20ece,chiragkarthik20ece,
bandaruaravindreddy20ece}@vardhaman.org

Abstract. Semantic segmentation, a prominent deep-learning technique in computer vision, involves the assignment of specific labels or categories to each pixel within an image. This advanced approach goes beyond traditional image classification by dividing the image into multiple segments and offering precise labeling for individual pixels. This pixel-level categorization facilitates a comprehensive understanding of the image's content, thereby enabling precise object localization. Semantic segmentation finds wide-ranging applications across various domains, including autonomous driving, medical imaging, and satellite imagery analysis. It stands as a fundamental component in the quest to enable machines to perceive and interpret visual data in a manner analogous to human perception. The ability to categorize pixels at such a granular level empowers computer vision systems to attain a high level of scene comprehension, enabling them to discern between different objects and their boundaries. This enhanced understanding of the visual world supports sophisticated tasks such as object detection, instance segmentation, and scene parsing.

Keywords: Augmented Reality · Pixel-level Categorization · Scene Comprehension · Computer Vision · semantic segmentation

1 Introduction

Semantic segmentation represents a groundbreaking advancement in computer vision, allowing for the precise labeling of individual pixels in an image, thereby facilitating accurate object localization and comprehensive scene comprehension. Its impact extends to various domains, including urban planning, disaster management, and augmented reality, and it significantly contributes to the development of self-driving technology in autonomous vehicles [1].

The continuous evolution of deep learning has propelled the growth of semantic segmentation, with the effectiveness of models like FCNs, U-Net, and DeepLab. Overcoming challenges such as class imbalance and limited data, techniques such as semi-supervised and active learning have been employed. Additionally, domain adaptation ensures the robust performance of semantic segmentation models in diverse environmental conditions [2].

© ICST Institute for Computer Sciences, Social Informatics and Telecommunications Engineering 2025
Published by Springer Nature Switzerland AG 2025. All Rights Reserved
X. Cheng (Ed): BROADNETS 2024, LNICST 602, pp. 15–27, 2025.
https://doi.org/10.1007/978-3-031-81171-5_2

Reliable AI-driven decision-making relies on the estimation of uncertainty. Integrating semantic segmentation with LiDAR, GPS, and 3D data enhances spatial understanding, leading to more informed decisions. In conclusion, semantic segmentation is a transformative technology that pushes the boundaries of accuracy and efficiency in computer vision. Its potential transcends topological imagery, promising innovative applications across a wide range of industries [3]. As technology continues to advance, and interdisciplinary collaboration flourishes, semantic segmentation is set to revolutionize how we interpret and leverage visual data in our dynamic world.

Semantic segmentation, a groundbreaking technique within computer vision, possesses the capacity to fundamentally reshape our comprehension and interpretation of visual data. Through the precise assignment of class labels to each pixel in an image, it transcends conventional image classification, offering a detailed analysis crucial in various real-world applications. Recent advancements in deep learning and neural network architectures have significantly elevated the accuracy and efficiency of semantic segmentation models, opening up possibilities for transformative applications across multiple domains [4].

The motivation to explore and advance state-of-the-art semantic segmentation techniques arises from the escalating demand for precise and meticulous analysis of topological images, notably aerial photographs and satellite imagery. These images contain vital information about Earth's surface and find application in urban planning, environmental monitoring, disaster response, and infrastructure development. Semantic segmentation equips decision-makers with granular insights, facilitating informed decisions concerning sustainable urban growth, efficient resource management, and disaster readiness.

Additionally, semantic segmentation's potential extends beyond topological images. In fields like augmented reality (AR) and virtual reality (VR), it plays a pivotal role in overlaying virtual objects onto real-world scenes, enhancing user experiences and communication. In the automotive industry, semantic segmentation contributes to the development of safe autonomous vehicles, where precise scene understanding is vital for navigation and hazard detection.

The rationale for exploring advanced deep learning architectures, including fully convolutional networks (FCNs), U-Net, and DeepLab, lies in their proven track record across various computer vision tasks, including semantic segmentation. These architectures harness the power of convolutional neural networks to efficiently process spatial information and extract meaningful features, resulting in accurate and precise segmentation [5]. By adapting and fine-tuning these architectures specifically for topological image analysis, we aim to unlock their full potential in this critical domain.

In the digital age, communication has evolved beyond traditional text and voice interactions. Visual content has become an integral part of how we convey information, ideas, and emotions. However, to enable effective communication, it is crucial that the visual content is understood and interpreted accurately [6]. This understanding often depends on the ability to discern objects, regions, and context within images. Image Semantic Segmentation is a fundamental computer vision task that addresses this need by partitioning an image into semantically meaningful segments, allowing for enhanced communication through visual content [7].

Furthermore, this research will meticulously compare the performance of advanced deep learning architectures, including but not limited to fully convolutional networks (FCNs), U-Net, and DeepLab. The objective is to identify the most efficient and accurate models capable of effectively handling the intricacies presented by vast geospatial datasets and the ever-changing environmental conditions. Addressing the challenges inherent to topological image segmentation is another critical aspect of this research. These challenges encompass class imbalances, limited annotated data availability, and shifts in the data distribution. Innovative strategies such as semi-supervised learning, active learning, and domain adaptation will be explored to bolster the robustness and generalization capabilities of the segmentation models in real-world scenarios [8,9]. To enhance the practicality of these models, uncertainty estimation methods will be integrated to quantify and communicate prediction confidence. Additionally, adversarial defense mechanisms will be implemented to fortify the models against deceptive attacks, especially crucial in applications where data integrity is paramount [10,11].

This project will also delve into the fusion of semantic segmentation with other geospatial data sources like LiDAR point clouds and GPS data, facilitating a more holistic understanding of the spatial environment. Rigorous performance evaluations using metrics such as Intersection over Union (IoU), Mean Average Precision (mAP), and pixel-wise accuracy will be conducted to gauge the models' deployability in real-world geospatial analysis scenarios. Collaboration with domain-specific experts in cartography, geospatial analysis, and remote sensing will ensure the relevance and applicability of the developed semantic segmentation models. Ethical considerations and responsible AI practices will be at the forefront to mitigate potential biases and unforeseen consequences, particularly in domains impacting human lives and the environment [12,13].

2   Related Work

In this section we detail about previous methods, models used for unsupervised person re-id. We also present the limitations of these related works. It gives a brief about previous papers related to this project.

In [1] addresses the emerging field of semantic communication for image data, aiming to transmit essential information efficiently. Unlike previous work in natural language processing, it focuses on images, which are rich in semantics and bandwidth-sensitive. The authors introduce a novel approach called RL-ASC (Reinforcement Learning-based Adaptive Semantic Coding) that goes beyond pixel-level encoding. They define semantic concepts for images, propose a semantic encoder, and develop an image reconstruction criterion based on semantic similarity. They also create an RL-based bit allocation model to preserve task-related information effectively. Their Generative Adversarial Nets (GANs)-based semantic decoder produces visually pleasing and semantically consistent images even under low bit rate conditions, demonstrating noise robustness.

In [2] Semantic communication goes beyond Shannon's paradigm by prioritizing the transmission of meaningful information from the source, rather than focusing solely on the accuracy of individual symbols or bits. This approach utilizes deep learning to develop theoretical frameworks and system designs, introducing novel performance metrics distinct from traditional error rates. The article concludes by highlighting unresolved questions in the field.

In [3] Indoor RGB-D semantic segmentation faces challenges due to complex environments. This paper introduces a novel approach, the NAM model, which leverages pre-segmentation labels and RGB-D features for improved accuracy. Extensive experiments demonstrate superior performance compared to existing methods on popular neural network architectures.

In [4] the authors introduce an innovative approach to address the challenge of adapting pretrained semantic segmentation models to significantly different target domains in remote sensing data. They propose an unsupervised adversarial domain adaptation network that transforms deep features into 2-D feature curves. These curves are used to minimize the dissimilarity between the source and target domain data, employing conditional generative adversarial networks (cGANs). The method proves effective in enhancing semantic labeling accuracy when applying a pretrained model to the target domain, as demonstrated on the ISPRS 2-D Semantic Labeling dataset. Notably, it performs well even across diverse cities and sensors, outperforming existing domain adaptation techniques in cross-domain semantic segmentation.

In [5] introduces CF-Net, a novel network designed for efficient multiscale semantic information extraction, especially for small-scale objects in images, like aerial photos. CF-Net enhances accuracy through a channel attention refinement block for informative feature selection and a cross fusion block to expand the receptive field of low-level feature maps.

In [6] the realm of remote sensing semantic segmentation, the cost of annotation has been a challenge. To address this, recent research highlights the effectiveness of consistency training in semi-supervised learning. However, existing methods lack consideration for model uncertainty, which leads to semantic ambiguity in outputs. To tackle this, the proposed Certainty-Aware Consistency Training (CACT) strategy comprises two novel components: Certainty-Aware Consistency Correction (CACC) and Class-Balanced-Adaptive Threshold (CBAT). CACC enhances prediction quality by focusing on reliable predictions based on certainty maps. CBAT employs dynamic thresholds to filter out unreliable predictions. Experiments on multiple datasets, including DLRSD, WHDLD, and Potsdam, affirm the superior performance of this framework in semi-supervised remote sensing semantic segmentation.

In [7] UNet++ addresses limitations in medical image segmentation models like U-Net and FCN by using an ensemble of U-Nets of varying depths and redesigning skip connections for flexible feature fusion. It outperforms baseline models consistently across different datasets and enhances segmentation of varying-size objects. Additionally, Mask RCNN++ based on UNet++ design improves instance segmentation, and pruned UNet++ models achieve faster inference with modest performance trade-offs.

In [8] discusses the challenges of automating tree segmentation in forests using satellite and aerial images, focusing on spectral variations, data scarcity, and occlusions. The study conducts extensive experiments with deep learning models, exploring the integration of hand-crafted spectral vegetation indices like NDVI, concluding that combining these indices in a three-channel input alongside advanced semantic segmentation architectures can enhance tree segmentation accuracy compared to high-resolution visible or near-infrared inputs, without added computational complexity.

In [9] the realm of deep learning-based semantic segmentation, the conventional process of feature extraction, often involving subsampling, poses a challenge by sacrificing intricate image details, leading to the loss of small-scale objects and blurry segmentation boundaries. This paper presents a novel approach to address this issue: a semantic edge optimization model. It leverages an end-to-end semantic edge detection network to acquire semantic edge features from the image and subsequently integrates these features with the semantic segmentation ones. This fusion process enhances the preservation of critical edge information within the final segmented image. On benchmark datasets like CamVid and Cityscape, this optimization model demonstrates notable improvements, surpassing the original semantic segmentation model by 1.4% and 1.5% in mean IoU performance.

In [10] the realm of remote sensing, addressing the challenge of ultra-high resolution images, which contain intricate spatial details, required innovative approaches. The study employed fully convolutional deep learning networks for semantic segmentation of such images. A novel segmentation strategy was devised to simplify training without compromising dataset integrity. Experiments conducted on the Potsdam ultra-high resolution remote sensing dataset showcased promising results, with a remarkable 93.7% Mean Intersection over Union (MIoU) and 97.39% Pixel Accuracy (PA) achieved on the training set. This approach offers a robust solution for effectively segmenting ultra-high resolution remote sensing images.

3   Image Semantic Segmentation

In this project, we collect and preprocess a diverse topological image dataset, including aerial imagery and street-level photographs. We implement UNet for semantic segmentation and utilize ResNet for weight initialization to enhance training. The UNet model is trained on the dataset, and we explore model ensemble techniques for improved segmentation performance. Additionally, we employ R-CNN for object masking, using ResNet as the backbone for feature extraction and bounding box regression. Model evaluation is conducted using metrics like IoU, mAP, and pixel-wise accuracy to assess segmentation quality. Finally, we consider the feasibility of real-world deployment for the models, taking into account their computational requirements and potential practical applications.

The proposed methodology combines various advanced techniques to enhance topological image segmentation for imagery. It begins with curating a diverse dataset and applying data augmentation to increase its size and diversity. Core segmentation models, including UNet, ResNet, and R-CNN, are used, with UNet for pixel-level segmentation, ResNet for weight initialization, and R-CNN for object masking. Ensemble learning is explored to improve segmentation accuracy and robustness by combining multiple model predictions. Additionally, semi-supervised and self-supervised learning methods are investigated to leverage unlabeled data for improved generalization. Uncertainty estimation techniques help measure model confidence, critical in safety-critical applications. Robustness is assessed by evaluating models against adversarial attacks, and defenses are developed accordingly. Domain adaptation techniques are used to ensure models can generalize across different aerial image sources. Performance 26 evaluation includes metrics like IoU, mAP, and pixel-wise accuracy, considering computational efficiency and memory requirements for real-world deployment. Overall, this comprehensive methodology aims to advance topological image segmentation for aerial imagery and contribute to dynamic cartography and GIS applications.

3.1 Block Diagram

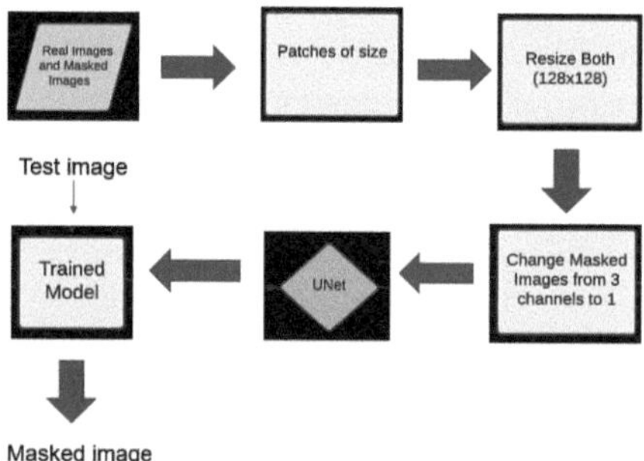

Fig. 1. Block diagram of Image Semantic Segmentation

The Fig. 1 details about block diagram which is divided into distinct stages represented by different blocks, each serving a specific purpose. The process begins with "Real images," which are unaltered images from sources like cameras, and "Masked images," where specific regions are segmented out using binary or alpha masks. The technique of "Patchifying" is introduced to efficiently process large images in semantic segmentation by dividing them into smaller overlapping patches. These patches are then "Resized" to match model requirements, ensuring memory and computational efficiency. Subsequently, the concept of "Change masked images" is discussed, involving the conversion of RGB masked images to grayscale to represent masks in a single channel. The central architecture, "UNet," is highlighted, characterized by its encoder, bottleneck, decoder, and skip connections, enabling effective semantic segmentation. Finally, the interconnections among the blocks illustrate the flow of information from input to output, with potential feedback loops for refining the system's operation.

3.2   Unet

The Fig. 2 is UNet architecture which is characterized by its unique U-shaped structure, comprising two key components: the contracting path (encoder) and the expansive path (decoder). The contracting path, inspired by traditional convolutional neural networks (CNNs), is designed to extract high-level features from input images through convolutional and pooling layers. While this reduces spatial resolution, it increases channel depth, enabling abstract feature learning. UNet primarily addresses semantic segmentation, classifying each pixel in an image into distinct classes, notably in medical imaging. Its U-shaped design and skip connections make it ideal for limited labeled datasets, widely adopted in medical imaging and other segmentation tasks. The expansive path, with upsampling and skip connections, recovers spatial information and generates segmentation masks, capturing fine details and context for precise segmentations. UNet's versatility and real-time capabilities contribute significantly to various computer vision applications requiring accurate image analysis.

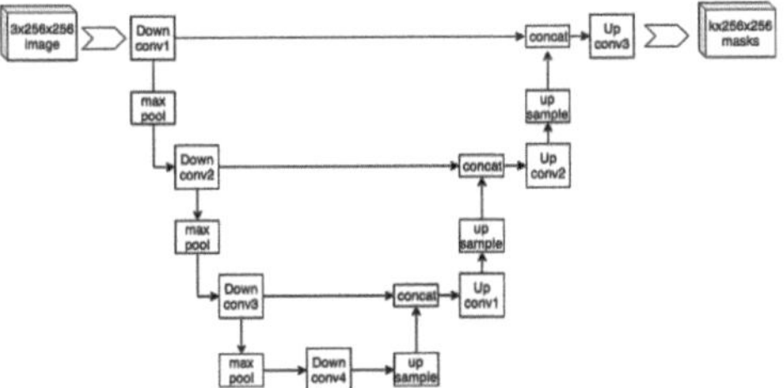

Fig. 2. Unet

3.3   Resnet and Maxpooling

The Fig. 3 is ResNet, or Residual Network, which is a pivotal component in the realm of semantic segmentation and topological image analysis. Its significance lies in weight initialization, mitigating the challenge of vanishing gradients in deep neural networks. ResNet shines as a potent pre-trained backbone for diverse tasks. Leveraging models like ResNet-50 or ResNet-101, pre-trained on vast datasets like ImageNet, equips subsequent tasks, including semantic segmentation, with a wealth of foundational knowledge in low-level image features, textures, and patterns. In topological image segmentation, ResNet kickstarts the UNet architecture or other custom models, with fine-tuning focusing on task-specific layers. The deeper ResNet layers retain their pre-learned image features, accelerating training and enhancing performance in advanced deep learning applications, such as semantic segmentation in cartography.

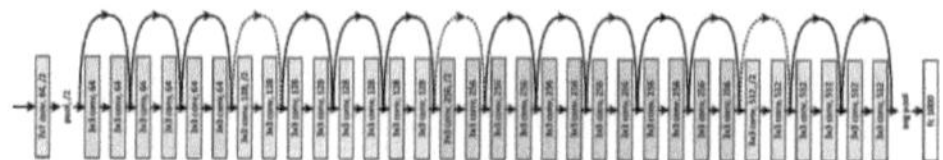

Fig. 3. Resnet

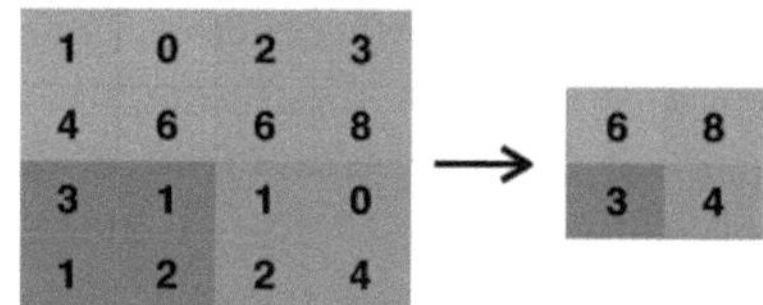

Fig. 4. Max Polling

The above Fig. 4 is max pooling example. It operates by dividing the input image into smaller regions and selecting the maximum pixel value from each region. This process effectively reduces the spatial dimensions of the image while retaining essential features. Max pooling helps in capturing important patterns, edges, and textures, making it easier for the neural network to recognize and segment objects within the image. It aids in downsampling the image, reducing computational complexity, and enhancing the model's ability to generalize. Max pooling is a non-linear operation that aids in extracting salient information for accurate image segmentation in deep learning-based projects.

4   Results and Discussion

4.1   Results

The below figures shows the predicted results by the trained model. The model is trained with aerial images captured by the drone. In an image semantic segmentation project, the primary objective is to assign precise semantic labels to individual pixels within an input image, essentially dividing it into distinct regions based on content. Specifically, in the context of using drone imagery, the outcome is a segmentation map where each pixel is color-coded to signify its corresponding class, such as buildings, roads, trees, or water bodies. The segmentation model's success is measured by its ability to accurately delineate object boundaries, identify regions of interest, offer fine-grained segmentation within classes, ensure label consistency across the image, maintain the original spatial resolution, and perform efficiently in real-time. Additionally, the model should exhibit robustness in handling variable lighting, weather, and environmental conditions, facilitating effective analysis and decision-making for diverse drone-based applications (Figs. 5 and 6).

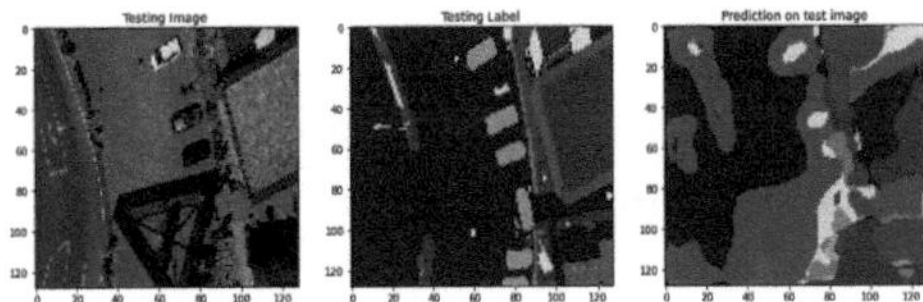

Fig. 5. Predicted Result-1

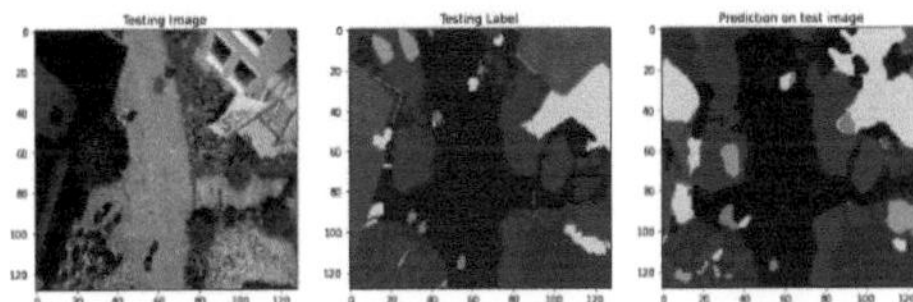

Fig. 6. Predicted Result-2

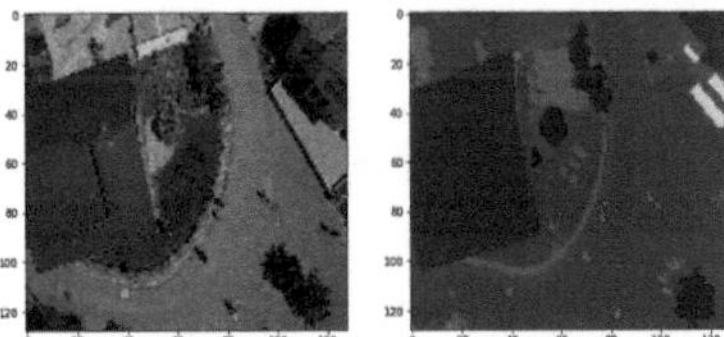

Fig. 7. Masked Image-1

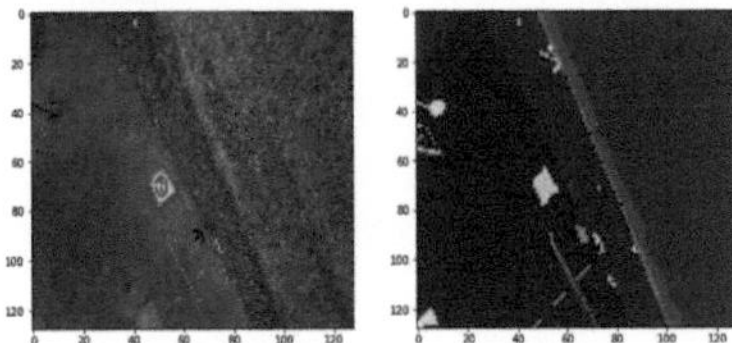

Fig. 8. Masked Image-2

The above Figs. 7 and 8 are the masked images of image semantic segmentation, the primary objective is to assign semantic labels to individual pixels within an input image, effectively partitioning the image into distinct categories.

This process generates a visually informative output where each pixel is color-coded based on its semantic classification, offering a clear delineation of elements within the aerial image. These categories typically encompass buildings, roads, vegetation, water bodies, and vehicles, each represented by a unique color for easy identification. Depending on the dataset and model capabilities, additional objects like pedestrians and streetlights may also be categorized. The resulting segmented image serves as a map-like depiction, invaluable for applications spanning urban planning, land cover analysis, environmental monitoring, and drone autonomous navigation.

4.2   Training and Validation Accuracy

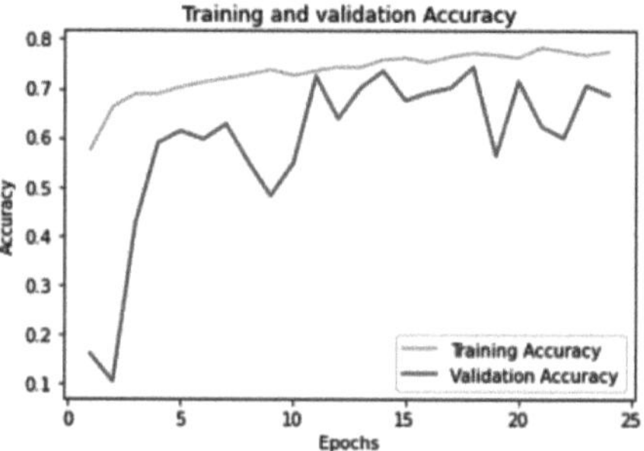

Fig. 9. Accuracy and Validation plot

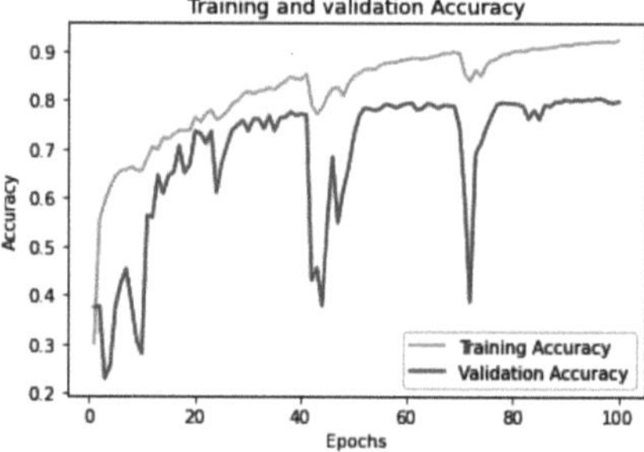

Fig. 10. Accuracy and Validation plot

The above Figure is graph of Accuracy vs Number of Epochs. In an image semantic segmentation project, monitoring training and validation graphs is crucial for assessing model performance. By the 100th epoch, the training loss should have reached a low, stable point, indicating model convergence. Sudden loss spikes later on may suggest overfitting. While not ideal, accuracy can still show improvement over epochs. In validation, loss trends should mirror training, demonstrating good generalization. Additionally, validation IoU/mIoU (Intersection over Union/mean Intersection over Union) should steadily rise, surpassing values from earlier epochs, indicating improved performance on unseen data. These metrics help ensure the model is effectively learning and generalizing semantic segmentation tasks (Figs. 9 and 10).

5   Conclusions and Future Scope

Semantic segmentation of aerial imagery is a groundbreaking field with immense potential across various domains, including urban planning, environmental monitoring, disaster response, and infrastructure development. By harnessing advanced deep learning techniques and powerful tools such as UNet, ResNet, and R-CNN, researchers and practitioners can achieve precise pixel-level image analysis, enabling a profound understanding of intricate landscapes and objects. The utilization of UNet, ResNet, and R-CNN in topological image segmentation yields promising results. UNet's U-shaped architecture and skip connections enable accurate and detailed segmentations, while ResNet's weight initialization enhances training efficiency and performance. R-CNN excels in object masking, further refining the segmentation process.

The future of this field holds exciting opportunities, including merging artistic vision with AI advancements to create visually stunning maps that resonate emotionally with users. Real-time dynamic maps, multi-modal data fusion, interactive user-driven maps, and ethical considerations for inclusive mapping are areas for further enrichment. Integrating semantic segmentation with aerial imagery in tools like Spyder and Visual Studio Code streamlines workflows, enhances efficiency, and promotes collaboration. These versatile IDEs, with Python support, Jupyter Notebook integration, Git capabilities, and interactive consoles, empower researchers to tackle complex tasks iteratively for optimal results.

In the realm of image semantic segmentation, a promising future unfolds as artistic creativity merges with cutting-edge AI. By infusing artistic styles into AI-generated segmentations, visually captivating maps that retain geographical precision while evoking emotions can be crafted. This fusion promises maps that engage and resonate deeply across domains like tourism, education, and heritage preservation. Dynamic maps that adapt in real-time using AI-driven segmentation and data from sensors and social media stand to provide instant updates on traffic, weather, and events. Further evolution lies in multi-modal data integration, combining aerial imagery, LiDAR, and street-level photos for more accurate results. Interactive user-driven maps, tailored through AI-powered segmentation and user feedback, offer customization and usability. Yet, ethical dimensions remain crucial, demanding unbiased, inclusive models that mitigate inequalities. The future holds transformative potential at the crossroads of artistic vision and AI progress, revolutionizing image segmentation's impact on our evolving world.

References

1. Huang, D., Gao, F., Tao, X., Du, Q., Lu, J.: Toward semantic communications: deep learning-based image semantic coding. IEEE J. Sel. Areas Commun. **41**(1), 55–71 (2023). https://doi.org/10.1109/JSAC.2022.3221999
2. Lokumarambage, M.U., Gowrisetty, V.S.S., Rezaei, H., Sivalingam, T., Rajatheva, N., Fernando, A.: Wireless end-to-end image transmission system using semantic communications. IEEE Access **11**, 37149–37163 (2023). https://doi.org/10.1109/ACCESS.2023.3266656
3. Zheng, Y., Yuan, X., Qiu, S., Li, W., Zhong, G., Sarem, M.: A novel semantic segmentation algorithm for RGBD images based on non-symmetry and anti-packing pattern representation model. IEEE Access **11**, 36290–36299 (2023). https://doi.org/10.1109/ACCESS.2023.3266251
4. Liu, W., Su, F.: Unsupervised adversarial domain adaptation network for semantic segmentation. IEEE Geosci. Remote Sens. Lett. **17**(11), 1978–1982 (2020). https://doi.org/10.1109/LGRS.2019.2956490
5. Peng, C., Zhang, K., Ma, Y., Ma, J.: Cross fusion net: a fast semantic segmentation network for small-scale semantic information capturing in aerial scenes. IEEE Trans. Geosci. Remote Sens. **60**, 1–13 (2022). https://doi.org/10.1109/TGRS.2021.3053062
6. Guo, Y., Wang, F., Xiang, Y., You, H.: Semisupervised semantic segmentation with certainty-aware consistency training for remote sensing imagery. IEEE J. Sel. Top. Appl. Earth Obs. Remote Sens. **16**, 2900–2914 (2023). https://doi.org/10.1109/JSTARS.2023.3255553
7. Zhou, Z., Siddiquee, M.M.R., Tajbakhsh, N., Liang, J.: UNet++: redesigning skip connections to exploit multiscale features in image segmentation. IEEE Trans. Med. Imaging **39**(6), 1856–1867 (2020). https://doi.org/10.1109/TMI.2019.2959609
8. Zhang, Y., Zhang, Y., Zhang, Q.: Semantic segmentation of traffic scene based on DeepLabv3+ and attention mechanism. In: 2023 3rd International Conference on Neural Networks, Information and Communication Engineering (NNICE), pp. 542–547 (2023). https://doi.org/10.1109/NNICE58320.2023.10105805
9. Hu, H., Cai, H., Ma, Z., Wang, W.: Semantic segmentation based on semantic edge optimization. In: 2021 International Conference on Electronic Information Engineering and Computer Science (EIECS), pp. 612–615 (2021). https://doi.org/10.1109/EIECS53707.2021.9587939
10. Zhang, H., Jiang, Z., Xu, J., Yao, X.: Semantic segmentation of ultra-high resolution remote sensing images based on fully convolutional neural networks. In: 2023 4th International Conference on Computer Vision, Image and Deep Learning (CVIDL), pp. 159–165 (2023). https://doi.org/10.1109/CVIDL58838.2023.10164846
11. Xie, X., Xu, Z., Tao, J., Yuan, J.Y., Wu, S.D.: Semantic segmentation algorithm for night traffic scene based on visible and infrared images. In: 2022 3rd Asia Conference on Computers and Communications (ACCC), pp. 103–108 (2022). https://doi.org/10.1109/ACCC58361.2022.00024
12. Tran, T., Kwon, O.-H., Kwon, K.-R., Lee, S.-H., Kang, K.-W.: Blood cell images segmentation using deep learning semantic segmentation. In: 2018 IEEE International Conference on Electronics and Communication Engineering (ICECE), pp. 13–16 (2018). https://doi.org/10.1109/ICECOME.2018.8644754

13. Chen, H., Yang, S., Lyu, T.: Multitask semantic segmentation network using adaptive multiscale feature fusion. In: 2022 International Conference on Computing, Communication, Perception and Quantum Technology (CCPQT), pp. 64–69 (2022). https://doi.org/10.1109/CCPQT56151.2022.00018
14. Deng, C., Liang, L., Su, Y., He, C., Cheng, J.: Semantic segmentation for high-resolution remote sensing images by light-weight network. In: 2021 IEEE International Geoscience and Remote Sensing Symposium IGARSS, pp. 3456–3459 (2021). https://doi.org/10.1109/IGARSS47720.2021.9554244

Performance Analysis of Dadda Multiplier Using Kogge Stone Adder

B. Srikanth$^{(\boxtimes)}$ ⓘ, Dodda Sai Pranathi, Padmaraju Sai Kumar Raju, and Vemula Sarika

Department of ECE, Vardhaman College of Engineering, Rangareddy, Telangana, India
srikanth.vlsi.2011@gmail.com

Abstract. In many computer systems, the need for effective and high-performance multiplication processes has been increasing quickly. This work gives a thorough performance analysis of a Kogge-Stone adder-based 16-bit Dadda Multiplier. The goal is to assess the multiplier designs computational effectiveness and speed while taking things like power usage and space utilization into account. The performance analysis findings show that the 16-bit Dadda Multiplier, which uses the Kogge-Stone adder architecture, is superior to other multiplier designs. The experimental results show important improvements in multiplication speed due to a reduction in the critical path delay. This work is done with 90 nm technology. By utilizing the parallelism provided by the Kogge-Stone adder, the suggested architecture also demonstrates considerable improvements in power efficiency. A more compact solution is also suggested by the area utilization study, allowing for easier integration into integrated circuits. The findings of this study aid in the selection and optimization of multiplier designs in various computing applications as well as the body of information on effective multiplication methods. The results provided in this paper demonstrate the benefits of combining the 16-bit Dadda Multiplier with the Kogge-Stone adder and show how it can improve computing performance while taking power and space limits into account. In this the total power of the system reduced by 4.8% and the total area also reduced by 8.3%.

Keywords: Dadda Multiplication (DM) · Kogge-Stone Adder (KSA) · Power-Area constraints · Computational performance

1 Introduction

A crucial component of digital systems such arithmetic and logic units, digital signal processors, etc. are multipliers. Indicators of system performance like power, latency, and space utilization are frequently triggered by them [1]. Due to this rising demand, the multipliers performance needs to be enhanced. Three stages make up the multiplier: partial product development, partial product reduction, and adding at the end. More time and energy are used in the multiplier second stage. Different methods to reduce multiplier critical stages were proposed. The compressor is most frequently used during the reduction step of partial product. A simple adder circuit serves as the compressor. It adds a number of bits that are all equally weighted and then generates some sum signals.

X. Cheng (Ed): BROADNETS 2024, LNICST 602, pp. 28–41, 2025.
https://doi.org/10.1007/978-3-031-81171-5_3

A multipliers performance is often assessed using parameters like speed, power consumption, and area utilization. Using a Kogge-Stone adder, addition is completed at its conclusion. The 16×16 multipliers structure is depicted in Fig. 1. In comparison to multipliers with compressors employing various adders, such as parallel adders, simulation results demonstrate that the approximate multiplier with Kogge Stone Adder provides great performance [2]. The sections below provide more detail on this essay. In next section, designs for a roughly 16×16 Dadda Multiplier are described. The objective is to assess the multiplier design computational effectiveness and speed while taking things like power usage and space utilization into account. The outcomes of this research will offer insightful information on the efficiency of the suggested multiplier design and its potential to improve computing performance.

2 Dadda Multiplier

Dadda Multiplier is efficient hardware-based multiplication algorithm used in digital circuits and computer architecture to perform binary multiplication operations [3]. It is particularly well-suited for applications where high-speed multiplication is crucial, such as in modern microprocessors, digital signal processors (DSPs), and other computational devices. The Dadda Multiplier is known for its ability to minimize both the number of partial products generated during multiplication and the number of adder stages required to obtain the final product. This reduction in partial products and adder stages leads to significant improvements in both speed and power efficiency, making it an attractive choice for hardware designers aiming to optimize the performance of their digital systems.

The Dadda Multiplier is a powerful and efficient multiplication algorithm used in digital circuits to accelerate binary multiplication operations [4]. Its ability to minimize partial products and adder stages makes it a valuable tool for enhancing the speed and power efficiency of various computational devices, from microprocessors to specialized hardware accelerators. The Dadda Multiplier is known for its ability to minimize both the number of partial products generated during multiplication and the number of adder stages required to obtain the final product [5]. This reduction in partial products and adder stages leads to significant improvements in both speed and power efficiency, making it an attractive choice for hardware designers aiming to optimize the performance of their digital systems.

At its core, the Dadda Multiplier employs a tree-based structure to perform multiplication. The algorithm takes advantage of the fact that each bit in the binary representation of a number can be thought of as a coefficient in a polynomial. By using a clever grouping and addition strategy, the Dadda Multiplier [6] efficiently calculates the product of two binary numbers by minimizing the number of additions required.

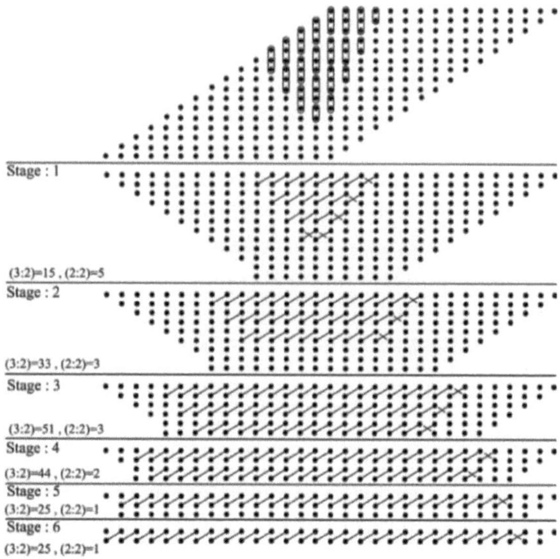

Fig. 1. Structure of 16 × 16 Dadda Multiplier

3 Kogge Stone Adder

The Kogge-Stone Adder, often referred to as the Kogge- Stone Parallel Prefix Adder, is a high-speed and highly parallelized hardware circuit used for binary addition operations in digital systems [7]. It named after its inventors, Peter Kogge and Harold Stone, who introduced the concept in the early 1970s. This adder architecture is known for its efficient and scalable design, making it popular in applications where fast arithmetic operations are essential, such as in microprocessors, digital signal processors (DSPs), and custom integrated circuits (ICs). The key features and principles behind the Kogge-Stone Adder are Parallel Prefix Structure, Tree-Based Architecture, Scalability, Efficient Carry Propagation, Trade-Offs.

The Kogge-Stone Adder employs a parallel prefix structure, which means that it breaks down the addition process into multiple stages that can be performed simultaneously [8]. This parallelism is achieved by computing intermediate carry values at each stage in parallel, significantly reducing the propagation delay and improving overall speed. The adder structure resembles a binary tree, where each node in the tree represents a stage of the addition process. At each node, partial carry values are calculated based on the input bits and the carry from the previous stage. The carry propagation occurs simultaneously at multiple levels of the tree. One of the notable advantages of the Kogge-Stone Adder is its scalability [9]. You can easily expand the size of the adder to accommodate larger binary numbers by adding more stages to the tree structure. This scalability allows for efficient implementation of multi-bit adders with minimal increase in delay.

In traditional ripple-carry adders, carry bits ripple through each bit position, leading to a linear delay. The Kogge-Stone Adder, on the other hand, significantly reduces the carry propagation delay by allowing carry values to propagate in parallel through multiple paths in the tree structure. While the Kogge-Stone Adder is known for its speed and parallelism, it may require more hardware resources compared to simpler adder designs like the ripple-carry adder. Therefore, designers often choose it when optimizing for speed and are willing to allocate additional hardware resources.

Essentially, it is a parallel prefix adder. Based on design time, this type of adder excels at providing the quickest addition [10]. It is renowned for its unique addition, which is the fastest in terms of design time. In Figs. 2 and 3 (from base paper), the functional block diagram and RTL view of a 4-bit Kogge-Stone Adder is shown. The propagate signal "Pi" and the generate signal "Gi" are calculated using the ith bit of the supplied input. Similar to how they generate signals, they also produce and carry signals [11]. Therefore, Prefix Adders are primarily divided into three kinds by minimizing the computation delay.

1.1. Pre- processing
1.2. Generation of Carry
1.3. Final processing

3.1 Pre-processing

This is the first stage; in this two signals are generated. They are generate signal and propagate signals. The expressions for generate signal and propagate signals are 1 and 2.

$$P_i = A_i \oplus B_i \tag{1}$$

$$G_i = A_i . B_i \tag{2}$$

3.2 Generation of Carry

This is the second stage. Carriers are now calculated using the appropriate bits, and this process is carried out in parallel. As intermediate signals, carry propagation and generation are employed. Carry, propagate, and generate signals have the expressions 3 and 4.

$$G_i = \left(P_i . G_{i\,prev}\right) + G_i \tag{3}$$

$$P_i = \left(P_i . P_{i\,prev}\right) \tag{4}$$

3.3 Final Processing

These is the final processing stage, in this the sum and carry outputs bits are calculated based on the input bits that are provided, and the logic equation for the last processing step is provided by 5 and 6.

$$C_i = G_i \tag{5}$$

$$S_i = P_i \oplus C_{i-1} \tag{6}$$

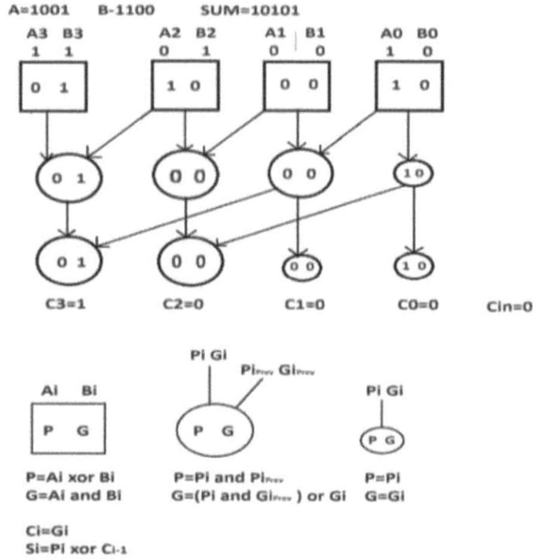

Fig. 2. Block diagram of Kogge Stone Adder

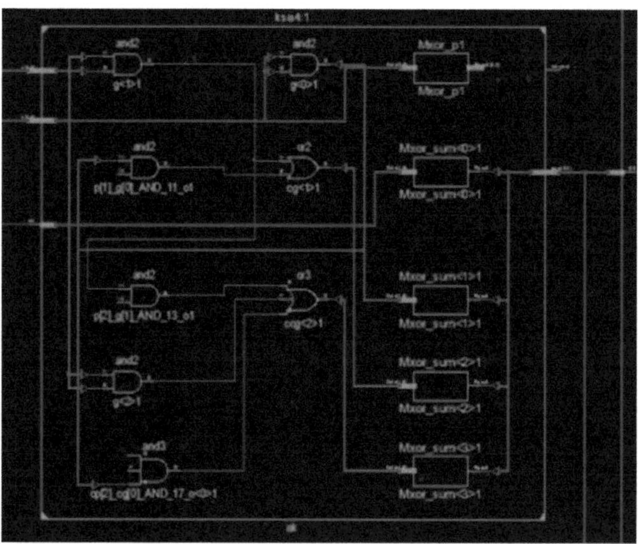

Fig. 3. RTL view of Kogge-Stone Adder

4 Proposed Work

The working of a Dadda Multiplier using Kogge Stone Adders can be summarized as follows:

The operands are represented as binary numbers. The partial products are generated by multiplying the corresponding bits of the operands. The partial products are added together using Kogge Stone Adders. The final product is generated by adding together the outputs of the Kogge Stone Adders. The speed of a Dadda Multiplier using Kogge

Stone Adders is determined by the number of gates required and the type of adder used. Kogge Stone Adders are typically faster than other types of adders, such as carry-save adders, because they can perform addition in a single clock cycle. As a result, Dadda Multipliers using Kogge Stone Adders are typically faster than other types of multipliers [12]. The area of a Dadda Multiplier using Kogge Stone Adders is determined by the number of gates required and the size of the adders.

Kogge Stone Adders are typically larger than other types of adders, but they can be implemented in a variety of ways to reduce area. As a result, the area of a Dadda Multiplier using Kogge Stone Adders can be comparable to or even smaller than the area of other types of multipliers. The power consumption of a Dadda Multiplier using Kogge Stone Adders is determined by the number of gates required and the type of adder used. Kogge Stone Adders are typically more power-efficient than other types of adders, such as carry-save adders, because they do not require as many gates. As a result, Dadda Multipliers using Kogge Stone Adders are typically more power efficient than other types of multipliers.

In general, Dadda Multipliers using Kogge Stone Adders offer a good trade-off between speed, area, and power consumption. They are typically faster than other types of multipliers, but they can also be implemented in a variety of ways to reduce area and power consumption. Some additional considerations for the working of Dadda Multipliers using Kogge Stone Adders are the size of the operands, implementation of the multiplier, the size of the operands affects the number of gates required and the speed of the multiplier. Larger operands require more gates and are slower than smaller operands. There are different types of Kogge Stone Adders, and the type of adder used can affect the speed, area, and power consumption of the multiplier. The multiplier can be implemented in a variety of ways, and the implementation can affect the speed, area, and power consumption of the multiplier [13]. Overall, the working of a Dadda Multiplier using Kogge Stone Adders can be optimized by considering the size of the operands, the type of Kogge Stone Adder, and the implementation of the multiplier (Fig. 4).

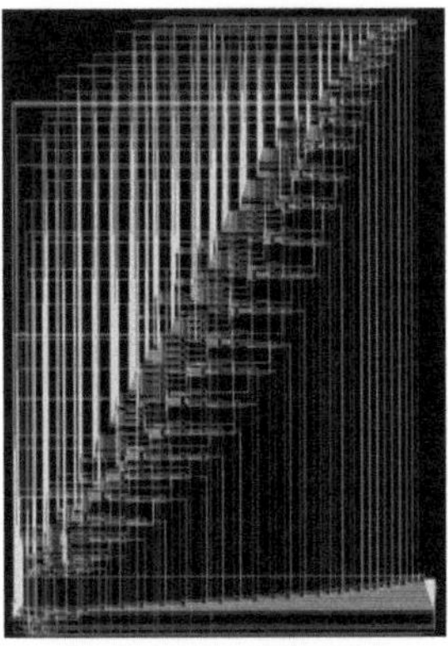

Fig. 4. Schematic View of Dadda Multiplier using Kogge Stone Adder

5   Result Analysis

While both Full Adders and Kogge-Stone adders serve the purpose of adding binary numbers, their design, speed, efficiency, and applications differ significantly. Full Adders are simple and suitable for small-scale applications, whereas Kogge-Stone adders are complex but excel in high-speed, large-scale addition operations. A Full Adder and a Kogge-Stone adder are both digital circuits used in digital logic design and computer architecture for performing addition operations. However, they differ in terms of their structure, performance characteristics, and applications. The choice between them depends on the specific requirements of the digital system being designed. They are Structure, Speed and Efficiency, Area and Complexity, Scalability, A Full Adder is a basic building block for addition operations. It takes three input bits: A, B, and a carry input (Cin), and produces two outputs, Sum (S) and carry output (Cout). The Full Adder can be used to add two binary numbers bit by bit. The Kogge-Stone Adder is a more complex structure compared to the Full Adder. It is a parallel prefix adder that uses a tree-like structure to compute the sum of binary numbers more efficiently. It consists of multiple Full Adders interconnected in a specific way.

Full Adders are used for small-scale addition operations, and they are relatively slower compared to parallel adders like the Kogge-Stone adder. For large binary numbers, multiple Full Adders need to be cascaded, which can result in slower operation. The Kogge-Stone Adder is designed for high- speed addition of large binary numbers. It takes advantage of parallelism by computing multiple bits of the sum simultaneously, making it much faster for large inputs compared to cascaded Full Adders [14]. Full Adders have a relatively simple and compact structure, making them suitable for low-complexity applications. Kogge-Stone Adders are more complex and require more hardware resources due to their parallel nature. They are typically used in high-performance computing applications where speed is a priority. Full Adders can be easily cascaded to create multi-bit adders, but this approach becomes less efficient as the number of bits increases. Kogge-Stone Adders are designed for efficient scalability, making them well-suited for adding large binary numbers.

Full Adders are commonly used in small-scale applications, such as arithmetic units of microcontrollers and simple digital systems. Kogge-Stone Adders are used in high-performance computing systems, such as CPUs and GPUs, where the speed of addition operations is crucial for overall system performance. The four instances of Full Adder are replaced with a single Kogge Stone Adder instance. In this process the area is reduced

Table 1. Power analysis of Full-Adder Vs Kogge Stone Adder

Instances	Leakage Power (uW)	Dynamic Power (uW)	Total Power (uW)	Percentage improvement
Full Adder	1.180	112.069	113.249	-
Kogge Stone Adder	0.753	82.889	82.959	26.74%

by 24.6% and the total power is reduced by 26.74% when compared between Full Adder and Kogge Stone Adder (Figs. 5 and 6 and Tables 1 and 2).

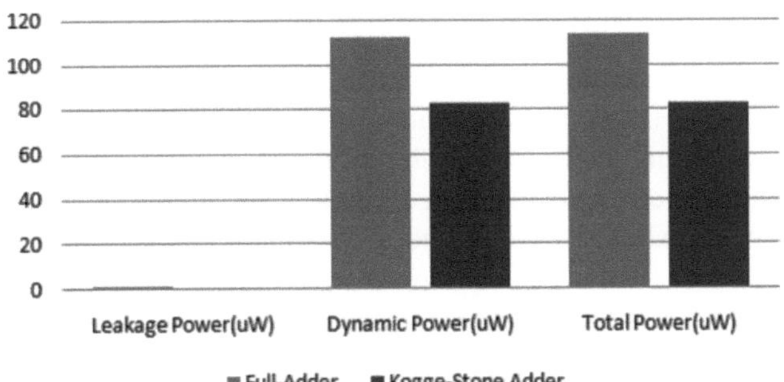

Fig. 5. Power dissipation analysis of Kogge Stone Adder Vs Full Adder

Table 2. Area analysis of Full-Adder Vs Kogge Stone Adder

Instances	Cell Area	Total Area	Percentage improvement
Full Adder	205.876	205.876	-
Kogge Stone Adder	155.165	155.165	24.6%

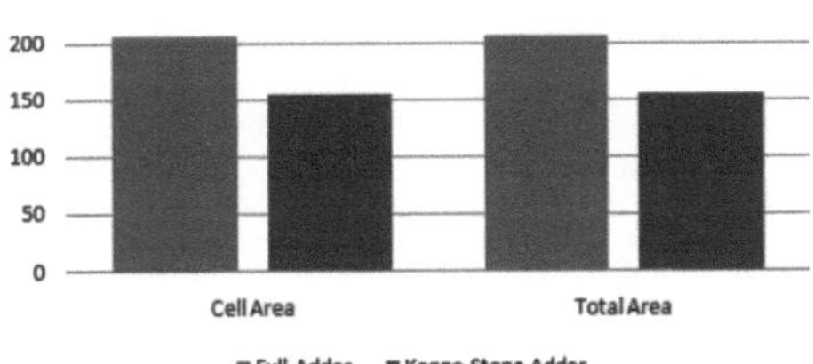

Fig. 6. Area analysis of Kogge Stone Adder Vs Full Adder

The different reports generated are the timing report, power report, area report. The tool used to generate all these timing report, area report, power report is the Genus Tool.

Genus is a popular RTL synthesis tool used in digital circuit design to convert RTL (Register Transfer Level) code into gate-level net-lists. When you run the synthesis process using Genus, it generates a timing report that provides essential information about the performance of the synthesized design. The timing report helps you understand the timing characteristics of our design and identify potential issues. The key components of a timing report in Genus:

In terms of critical path, the timing report highlights the critical path in your design. The critical path is the longest path through the combinational logic that determines the maximum delay for the design. The timing analyzer in Genus identifies the gates and signals involved in this critical path, and their cumulative delay is reported as the critical path delay. In terms of critical path slack, Slack represents the timing margin available on the critical path. It is calculated as the difference between the required time (usually based on the target clock frequency) and the actual time taken by the critical path. When there is positive slack, the design complies with timing specifications; when there is negative slack, there is a timing infraction.

In terms of setup and hold time violations, the timing report also indicates any setup and hold time violations. Hold time is the minimum amount of time that data must remain stable after the clock edge, and setup time is the minimum amount of time that data must remain stable before the clock edge. Violations of these constraints can lead to data integrity issues. In terms of clock frequency, the timing report provides information about the achieved clock frequency after synthesis. This frequency is based on the critical path delay and can give you an idea of the design performance in terms of speed. In terms of timing paths with violations, it will highlight the specific reasons for the violation, such as excessive delay or setup/hold violations. In terms of input and output delay, the timing report may include information about the input and output delays for various cells and interfaces in the design. Input delay is the time taken for the input signal to propagate through the logic to the output, while output delay is the time taken for the output signal to stabilize after changes in inputs.

In terms of Constraint Information, the timing report may also include details about the timing constraints applied during synthesis, such as clock frequency targets, setup/hold constraints, and input/output delays (Fig. 7 and Table 3).

Table 3. Timing Report of Dadda Multiplier without Kogge-Stone Adder Vs Dadda Multiplier with Kogge-Stone Adder

Instances	Required Time (ps)	Input Delay (ps)	Data Path (ps)	Slack (ps)
DM without KSA	1200	800	134	266
DM with KSA	1805	800	937	68

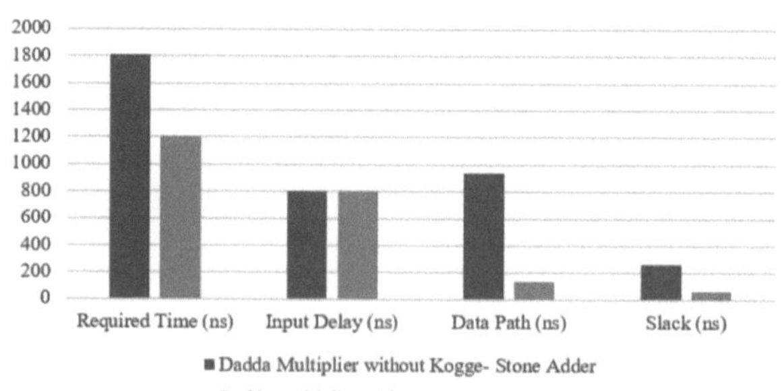

Fig. 7. Timing analysis of DM without KSA Vs DM with KSA

In Genus, the power report provides essential information about the power consumption of the synthesized digital circuit. Power analysis is crucial in modern integrated circuits design as power consumption impacts the overall performance, battery life (in case of portable devices), and heat dissipation of the chip. The power report generated by Genus helps designers understand the power characteristics of the design and identify areas where power optimization may be needed. The key components typically found in a power report from Genus:

Using power report, the total power can be calculated. The power report provides the total power consumption of the design in watts or milli watts. This is the sum of all the power consumed by the various components in the chip, including combinational logic, registers, memories, and other elements.

The power report, the dynamic power is calculated. Dynamic power is the power dissipated due to the charging and discharging of capacitive loads as a result of switching activities in the circuit. It is the dominant component of power consumption in most digital designs. The power report shows the dynamic power along with a breakdown of its components, such as switching power and short- circuits power. The power report provides the leakage power. Leakage power is the power consumed by a transistor even when it is not actively switching. As transistor sizes decrease and leakage currents become more significant, leakage power becomes a significant portion of total power consumption. The power report provides the leakage power along with a breakdown of its components.

Using the power report the internal power can be calculated. Internal power represents the power consumed within the core logic of the chip, excluding the I/O pads and interfaces. It includes power consumption in registers, combinational logic, and other internal elements (Fig. 8 and Table 4).

Table 4. Power Report of DM without KSA Vs DM with KSA

Instances	Leakage Power (uW)	Dynamic Power (uW)	Total Power (uW)	Percentage improvement
DM without KSA	75.224	8791.656	8866.88	-
DM with KSA	68.904	8364.326	8433.23	4.8%

In Genus, the area report provides information about the physical size or area of the synthesized digital circuit. Area analysis is crucial in integrated circuit design as it directly impacts the chip manufacturing cost, performance, and overall feasibility. The area report generated by Genus helps designers understand the physical characteristics of the design and identify areas where area optimization may be needed.

The key components typically found in an area report from Genus:

The area report provides the total area of the design in terms of square micrometers or square millimeters (mm^2). This is the cumulative size of all the components in the chip, including standard cells, memories, I/O pads, and other elements. The area report may provide a breakdown of the total area into different categories, such as core area, I/O area, and any other user-defined areas. The core area typically refers to the area

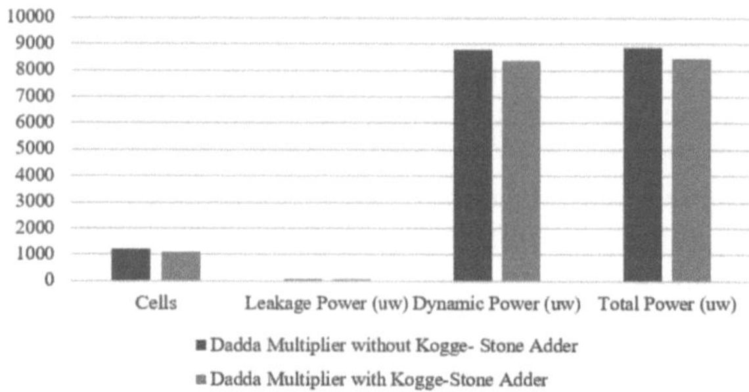

Fig. 8. Power Dissipation analysis of DM without KSA Vs DM with KSA

occupied by the main functional logic of the chip, while the I/O area includes the space taken by input/output pads and interfaces. The area report provides the overall cell area. Genus can provide details about the individual area of each standard cell used in the design. This information helps designers identify cells with large footprints and focus on optimizing them.

Using the area report, the hierarchical area analysis is performed. Genus can perform hierarchical area analysis, breaking down the area consumption into different blocks or modules in the design. This breakdown helps identify area- intensive blocks and facilitates area optimization at the block level. Using the area report, the utilization is generated. The area report may include utilization metrics, such as the percentage of core area used and the percentage of unused or "white space" in the chip. Low utilization may indicate inefficient use of resources, while high utilization could lead to potential congestion issues. The aspect ratio can also be calculated using the area report. The aspect ratio is the ratio of the chip height to its width. A balanced aspect ratio is often desirable to ensure efficient chip manufacturing and layout.

By analyzing the area report, designers can gain insights into the physical size of the design, identify potential area bottlenecks, and implement area optimization strategies to reduce the chip footprint and manufacturing costs. Properly optimizing area and power requirements is crucial for designing efficient and cost-effective integrated circuits (Fig. 9 and Table 5).

Table 5. Area Report of DM without KSA Vs DM with KSA

Instances	Cell Count	Cell Area	Total Area	Percentage improvement
DM without KSA	1104	14247.885	1424.885	-
DM with KSA	1193	13052.740	1305.740	8.3%

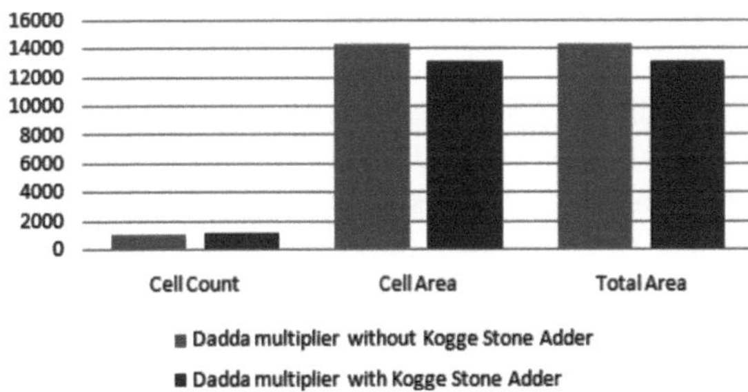

Fig. 9. Area Analysis of DM without KSA Vs DM with KSA

6 Simulation Results

In this output of the Dadda Multiplier we get the clock latency. For one particular test case we get the 10 clock latency. So, due to this clock latency the output is delayed for 10 clock cycles of the CLK input.

Clock latency, also known as clock cycle time or clock period, refers to the time duration between successive rising edges or falling edges of a clock signal in a digital system. It is a crucial parameter in digital electronics and computer architecture, as it directly affects the performance and speed of the system. In synchronous digital systems, such as CPUs, GPUs, and other digital logic circuits, operations are synchronized and controlled by a clock signal.

The clock signal is used to regulate the timing of various operations and to synchronize the transfer of data between different components within the system. The clock latency is determined by the inverse of the clock frequency. If the clock frequency is denoted as f (measured in Hertz, Hz). A lower clock latency means that the clock signal rising edges occur more frequently, allowing the digital system to perform operations faster. However, decreasing the clock latency often requires sophisticated and more expensive circuitry, as it poses challenges related to signal integrity, power consumption, and thermal management (Fig. 10).

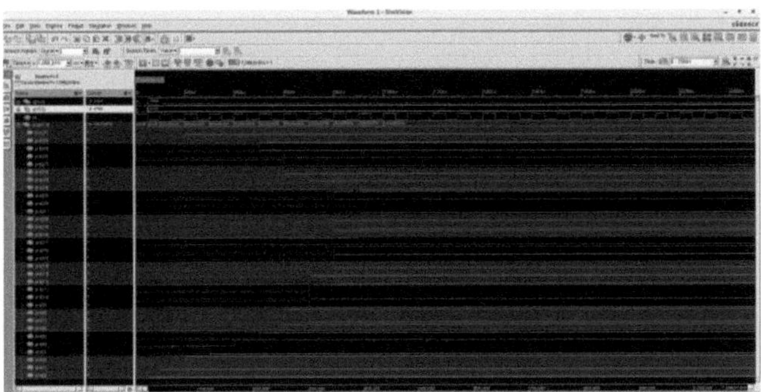

Fig. 10. Simulation Result

7 Conclusion

The efficiency of a Dadda Multiplier using Kogge Stone Adders can be analyzed in terms of speed, area, and power usage. Dadda Multipliers using Kogge Stone Adders are typically faster than Dadda Multipliers without using Kogge Stone Adder. The area of a Dadda Multiplier using Kogge Stone Adders is even smaller. Dadda Multipliers using Kogge Stone Adders are typically more power- efficient. In this work the clear view of the comparisons between Full Adder and the Kogge Stone Adder is demonstrated in terms of their usage in Dadda Multiplier.

Based on the results, the area is reduced by 24.6% and the power is less by 26.74%. The type of Kogge Stone Adder used can also affect the performance of the multiplier. Overall, the performance of a Dadda Multiplier using Kogge Stone Adders can be optimized in terms of area by 8.3% and in terms of power by 4.8%.

References

1. Pathak, K.C., Darji, A.D., Sarvaiya, J.N.: Low power Dadda Multiplier using approximate almost full adder and Majority logic based adder compressors. IEEE Region 10 Symposium 2022 (TENSYMP), pp. 1–6. Mumbai, India (2022). https://doi.org/10.1109/TENSYMP54 529.2022.9864428
2. Naresh, K., Sai, Y.P., Majumdar, S.: Design of 8-bit Dadda multiplier using gate level approximate 4:2 compressor. 35th International Conference on VLSI Design and 2022 21st International Conference on Embedded Systems (VLSID), pp. 269–274. Bangalore, India (2022). https://doi.org/10.1109/VLSID2022.2022.00059
3. Chanda, S., et al.: An energy efficient 32 bit approximate dadda multiplier. IEEE Calcutta Conference (CALCON), pp. 162–165. Kolkata, India (2020). https://doi.org/10.1109/CAL CON49167.2020.9106548
4. Sundhar, A., Deva Tharshini, S., Priyanka, G., Ragul, S., Saranya, C.: Performance analysis of wallace tree multiplier with kogge stone adder using 15–4 compressor. International Conference on Communication and Signal Processing (ICCSP), pp. 0903–0907 (2019). https://doi.org/10.1109/ICCSP.2019.8697981
5. Riaz, M.H., Ahmed, S.A., Javaid, Q., Kamal, T: Low power 4×4 bit multiplier design using Dadda algorithm and optimized Full Adder. 15th International Bhurban Conference on Applied Sciences and Technology (IBCAST), pp. 392–396 (2018). https://doi.org/10.1109/IBCAST.2018.8312254
6. Ye, J.-H., Shieh, M.-D.: High-performance NTT architecture for large integer multiplication. 2018 International Symposium on VLSI Design, Automation and Test (VLSI-DAT), IEEE
7. Sinthura, S.S., Begum, A., Amala, B., Vimala, A., Vidhya Aparna, V.: Implementation and analysis of different 32-bit multipliers of aspects of power. Speed and Area. 2nd International Conference on Trends in Electronics and Informatics (ICOEI), pp. 312–317 (2018). https://doi.org/10.1109/ICOEI.2018.8553859
8. Madhavi, S., Rasagna, K., Kavya, N., Sindhu, M., Kaveri, V.: Implementation of programmable FIR filter using dadda multiplier and parallel prefix adder. IEEE 2018 International Conference on Inventive Research in Computing Applications (ICIRCA). https://doi.org/10.1109/ICIRCA.2018.8597249
9. James, R.M., Ravindran, A.: Review of full adder performance analysis using kogge stone adder and magnetic tunnel junction. 4th International Conference on Devices, Circuits and Systems (ICDCS), pp. 84–90. Coimbatore, India (2018). https://doi.org/10.1109/ICDCSyst.2018.8605064

10. Sebastian, A., Jose, F., Gopakumar, K., Thiyagarajan, P.: Design and implementation of an efficient dadda multiplier using novel compressors and fast adder. IEEE 2020 International Symposium on Devices, Circuits and Systems (ISDCS). https://doi.org/10.1109/ISDCS49393.2020.9263014
11. Penchalaiah, U., Vg, S.K.: Design of high-speed and energy-efficient parallel prefix kogge stone adder. IEEE International Conference on System, Computation, Automation and Networking (ICSCA), pp. 1–7. Pondicherry, India (2018). https://doi.org/10.1109/ICSCAN.2018.8541143
12. Raju, A., Sa, S.K.: Design and performance analysis of multipliers using Kogge Stone Adder. 3rd International Conference on Applied and Theoretical Computing and Communication Technology (iCATccT), pp. 94–99. Tumkur, India (2017). https://doi.org/10.1109/ICATCCT.2017.8389113
13. Ganesh, K., Pushpalatha, P.: Implementation of a high-speed pipelined FFT processor using dadda multipliers to process two independent data streams. IEEE 2017 6th International Conference on Reliability, Infocom Technologies and Optimization. https://doi.org/10.1109/ICRITO.2017.8342479
14. Abraham, S., Kaur, S., Singh, S.: Study of various high-speed multipliers. International Conference on Computer Communication and Informatics (ICCCI), pp. 1–5. Coimbatore, India (2015). https://doi.org/10.1109/ICCCI.2015.7218139

Design and Implementation of Unsigned Serial Divider Using TG Logic

G. Kavya[1]($\boxtimes$), K. Shreshta Reddy[1], D. Vishnu Prasad[1], J. V. R. Ravindra[1],
and Himanshu Rajeshbhai Dodiya[2]

[1] Center for Advanced Computing Research Laboratory (C-ACRL), Department of Electronics
and Communication Engineering, Vardhaman College of Engineering Hyderabad, Hyderabad,
India
kavyag39147@gmail.com, jayanthi@ieee.org
[2] RK University, Rajkot, Gujrat, India

Abstract. The paper details the design and implementation of a 4-bit unsigned binary serial divider using 90 nm CMOS technology. It utilizes Transmission Gate (TG) logic for the division process and offers a comparison with an alternative CMOS logic approach featuring a Kogge Stone adder. The TG Logic implementation boasts a lower transistor count (402) but exhibits higher propagation delay (379.6 femtoseconds) and power consumption (18.42 micro-Watts). In contrast, the CMOS Logic with Kogge Stone adder employs more transistors (792) but results in a shorter propagation delay (494.9 femtoseconds) and lower power consumption (5.987 micro-Watts). The choice between these two methods should be based on the specific application's needs and priorities.

Keywords: power consumption · high-speed · TG logic · CMOS

1 Introduction

In the realm of digital systems, division stands as a fundamental operation. Binary dividers can be categorized into two types: serial and parallel dividers. The process of serial division involves repetitive subtraction. Consider the scenario where we aim to divide 18 by 3. We iteratively subtract 3 from 18. After six such subtractions, the remainder reaches zero, indicating that it's now smaller than the divisor. As a result, the further subtraction process ceases. Consequently, the quotient is six, and the remainder is zero. To mitigate area and power usage, various techniques such as CMOS, TG, and PT logic are employed [1]. While these techniques have aimed to reduce area and power consumption, they've encountered limitations such as low logic levels and increased circuit complexity.

2 The Proposed Algorithm – Motivation

The advancement of digital technology has made mathematical operations more efficient, but there's a noticeable focus on improving methods for addition and multiplication, rather than division [2]. This bias exists because creating efficient division logic is more

© ICST Institute for Computer Sciences, Social Informatics and Telecommunications Engineering 2025
Published by Springer Nature Switzerland AG 2025. All Rights Reserved
X. Cheng (Ed): BROADNETS 2024, LNICST 602, pp. 42–50, 2025.
https://doi.org/10.1007/978-3-031-81171-5_4

complex. In terms of speed, addition and multiplication usually require only a few clock cycles, while division takes much longer, spanning many cycles. Neglecting to improve division for modern computer applications can lead to a decline in overall computer performance.

2.1   One's Complement Binary Subtraction Algorithm

Assuming that Y and X are both nonzero values and X is greater than Y, we initially observe a high carry output from the adder. This is because we are adding X with the two's complement of Y (Fig. 1).

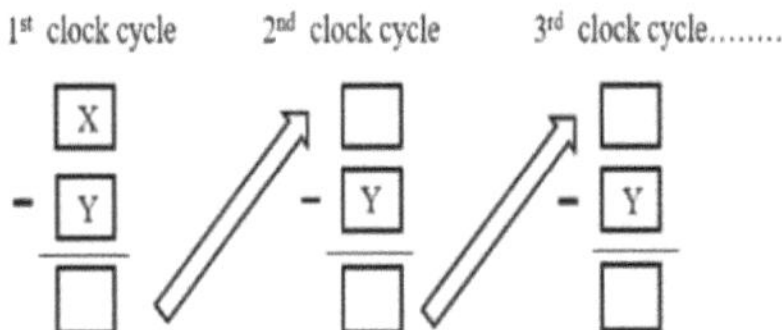

Fig. 1. Execution flow of the algorithm

Upon examining the adder's output after the first clock cycle, we find the result of X - Y, which is then stored within the data register. Meanwhile, the counter's output is incremented to 0001. Subsequently, in the following cycle, if the condition (X - Y) is still greater than Y, we proceed to subtract Y from X. This action leads to an increment in the counter's output, now reflecting the value 0010. This process of subtraction continues iteratively until the output of the adder becomes high [4]. This occurrence marks the point where the subtraction process stops.

2.2   Execution Flow of Algorithm with Example Sum

The One's complement method of subtraction is used to divide binary values 1010 (decimal 10) 0010 (decimal 2). In the serial divider circuit, this action is repeated. When the difference is positive, the ultimate carry is 1, which is added to the actual difference. When the difference is negative, the carry is zero, and the real result is one's complement of the sum output (Fig. 2).

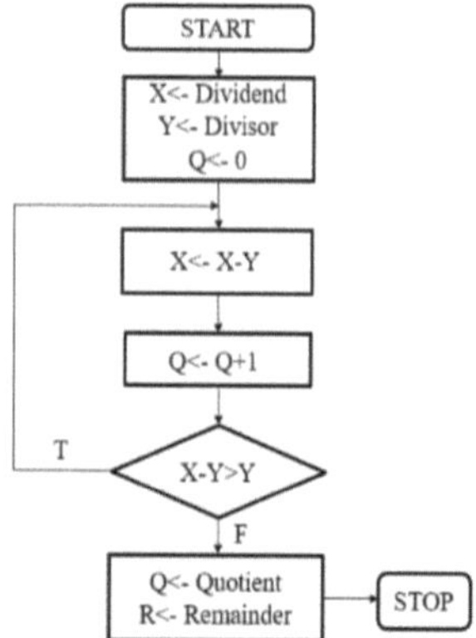

Fig. 2. Flow Chart of 1's Complement Binary Subtraction algorithm

3 Design of Unsigned Serial Divider

Serial hardware architecture employs a sequential approach to implement the various components of an algorithm [5]. This type of architecture finds its utility primarily in general-purpose applications, whether in central processing units (CPUs) or field-programmable gate arrays (FPGAs).

3.1 Design Approach

This section outlines the strategy for constructing a 4-bit unsigned binary serial divider via the technique of iterative subtraction involving two 4-bit unsigned binary numbers. The divisor, denoted as Y3 Y2 Y1 Y0, is subtracted from the dividend X3 X2 X1 X0 using the one's complement subtraction method. The fundamental building blocks employed in this design are as follows:

Adder: This component handles the addition of two 4-bit binary numbers.

2:1 Multiplexers (MUX): A group of four of these multiplexers is utilized.

D Flip-Flops: A set of four D flip-flops.

4-bit Binary Synchronous Up Counter: Used to count synchronously (Fig. 3).

3.2 Design of the 4-bit Adder

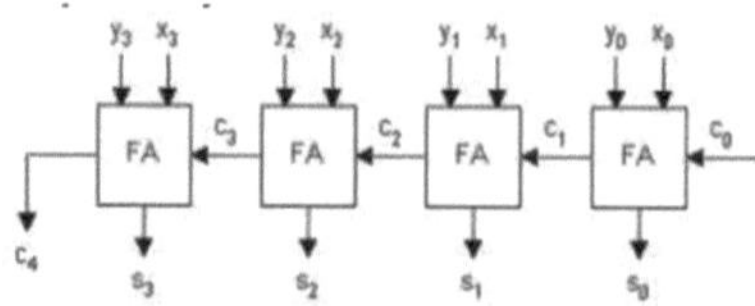

Fig. 3. 4-bit Ripple Carry Adder

The design incorporates a ripple carry adder, which is constructed by utilizing multiple full adders [10]. A depiction of the straightforward implementation of the 4-bit ripple carry adder is provided in Fig. 4. In this setup, C0 signifies the input carry, while X0 through X3 and Y0 through Y3 represent the two 4-bit input binary numbers.

3.3 Design of 2:1 Multiplexer

The divider's multiplexer, composed of two transmission gates and an inverter, switches between inputs A and B according to control signal S. This mechanism allows controlled and flexible data selection, making it a vital component in digital circuit operations.

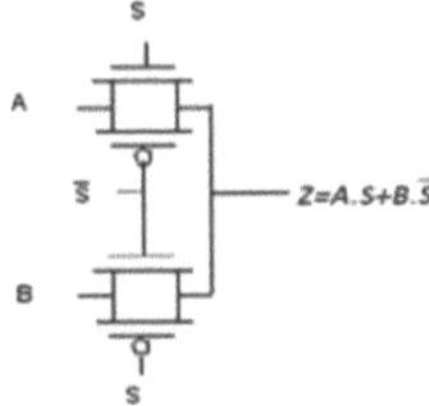

Fig. 4. Transmission gate 2:1 MUX

3.4 Kogge Stone Adder Design

The Kogge Stone Adder is fundamentally a parallel prefix adder, recognized for its remarkable speed in addition operations based on design considerations [7]. This design approach stands out for its exceptional speed during the design phase. It operates by calculating propagate signals denoted as 'Pi' and generate signals denoted as 'Gi' using the ith bit of the provided input [9] (Fig. 5).

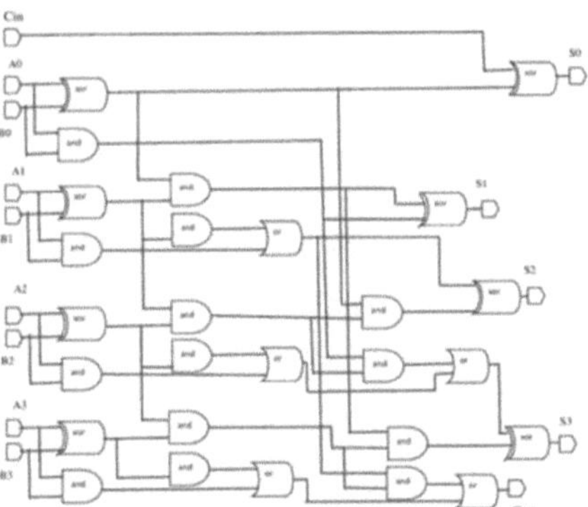

Fig. 5. 4-bit Kogge Stone Adder

3.5 Design of D Flip-Flop

The negative edge-triggered master-slave D flip-flop utilizes D latches with an enable input to synchronize changes with a clock signal's falling edge. During the high clock phase, it stores the D input in the master latch, while the slave latch remains unchanged. As the clock transitions from high to low in the low clock phase, the master latch's output transfers to the slave latch, allowing the flip-flop's output to change [11]. This design ensures that the output can only change during the clock's high-to-low transition. The master latch tracks the D input when the clock is high, and the inactive slave latch maintains the output. This flip-flop is crucial for precise timing in digital circuits [15]. Incorporating the clear (clr) and enable (CE) inputs enhances the flip-flop's functionality:

– When the clear input is activated (high), regardless of the D input and enable signal, the output is forced low.
– When the enable input is deactivated (low), regardless of the D input and clear signal, the output maintains its previous state (Fig. 6).

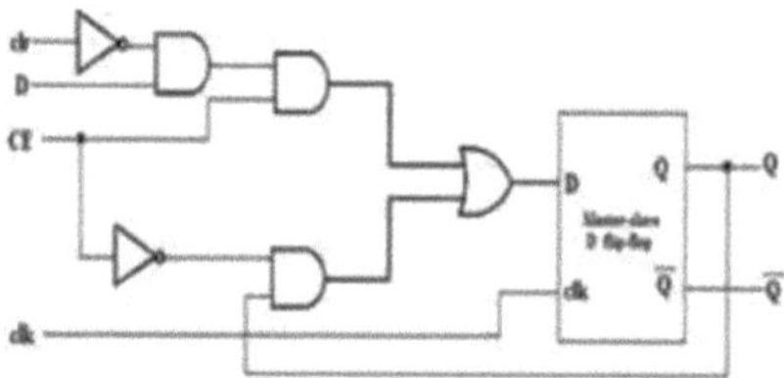

Fig. 6. D-Flip Flop with clear and CE inputs

3.6 Design of 4-bit Synchronous up Counter

The synchronous 4-bit up counter is composed of three AND gates, four XOR gates, and four master-slave D flip-flops. Each flip-flop receives the same clock pulse, leading to synchronized operation. Here's how it functions:

– The counter is designed as an up counter, commencing from the value 0000.
– With every clock pulse, the counter increments by one step. This means it progresses from 0001, 0010, 0011, 0100, and so on, until it reaches 1111.
– After reaching 1111, it resets back to 0000, thus completing one full counting cycle (Fig. 7).

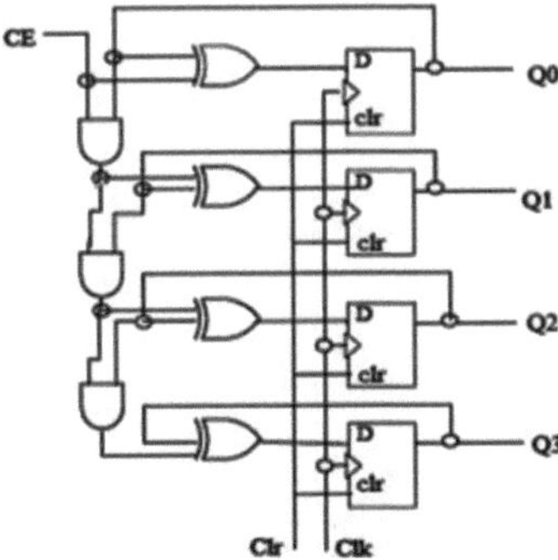

Fig. 7. 4-bit Synchronous up counter

4   Simulation Results

Using the Cadence EDA tool, the design of the final divider circuit is simulated and the transient responses are examined.

4.1   Schematic Diagrams and Simulations

Figures 8, 9, 10 and 11.

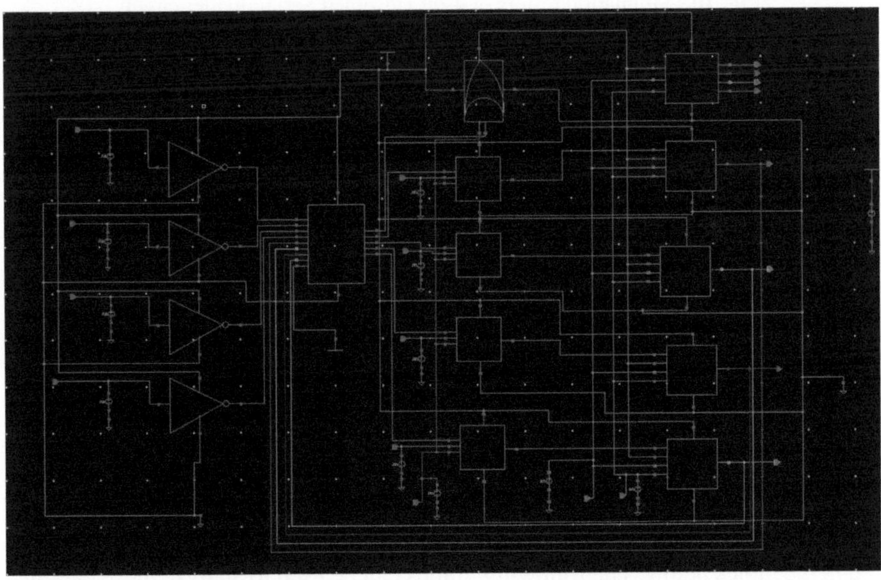

Fig. 8. Schematic of 4-bit Unsigned Serial divider circuit

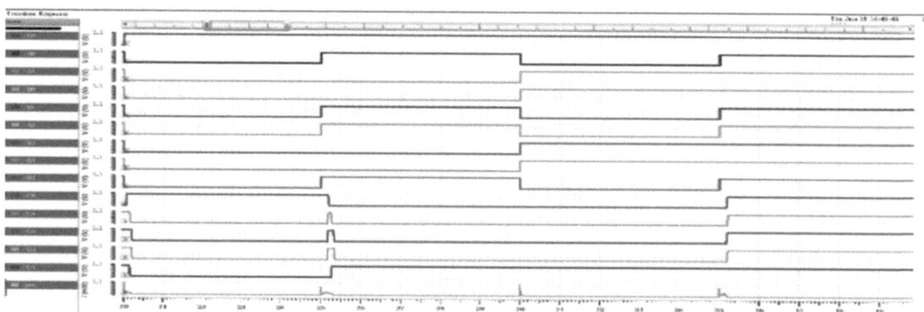

Fig. 9. Simulation results of Kogge Stone Adder circuit

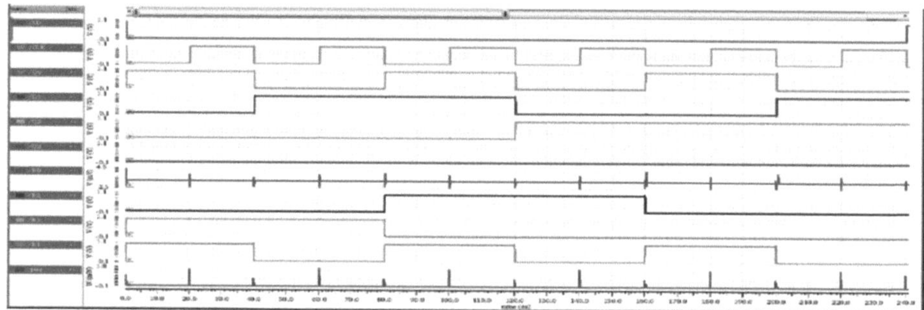

Fig. 10. Simulation results of 4-bit Unsigned Serial divider circuit

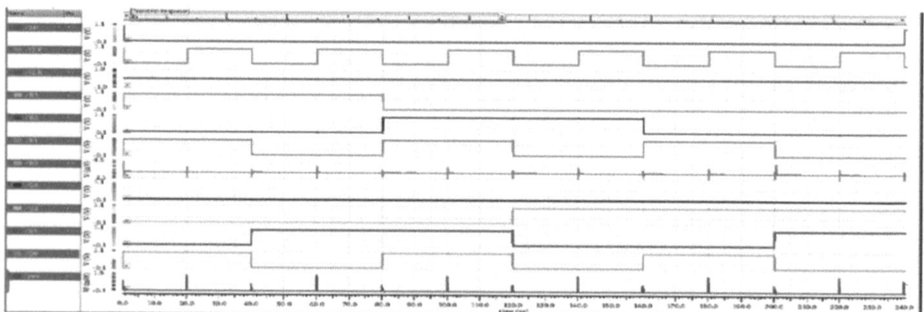

Fig. 11. Simulation results of Divider with Kogge Stone adder circuit

4.2 Performance Analysis

The transistor count, power, and delay of each individual block in the serial divider are listed in the tables below. The following graphs can be used to analyze these parameters (Fig. 12 and Tables 1 and 2):

Table 1. Power and Delay Analysis of CMOS and TG based serial divider

Conventional CMOS				TG Logic		
Circuits	Transistor Count	Power	Delay	Transistor Count	Power	Delay
Full Adder	28	1.036 μW	37.31 ps	20	0.497 μW	20 ps
RCA	112	6.31 μW	298.5 ps	80	1.94 μW	20.08 ps
2:1 MUX	20	41.76 μW	277.6 ps	6	0.097 μW	16.71 ps
Master Slave D Flip Flop	62	106.9 μW	71.31 ns	46	500.8 μW	498.5 fs
Counter	210	2.049 μW	211.4 ns	114	1.72 μW	499.6 fs
Serial Divider	664	5.7 μW	85.68 ps	402	18.42 mW	379.6 fs
Full Adder	28	1.036 μW	37.31 ps	20	0.497 μW	20 ps

Table 2. Power and Delay Analysis of serial divider with Kogge Stone Adder

Circuits	Transistor Count	Power	Delay
Kogge Stone Adder	240	8.314 μW	500 fs
Serial Divider	792	5.987 μW	494.9 fs

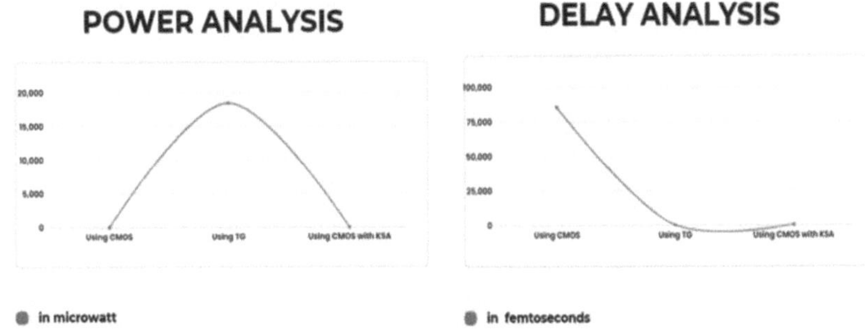

Fig. 12. Power and Delay graphs

5 Conclusion

Division, a fundamental arithmetic operation, has posed implementation challenges. Focus on improving its efficiency spans digital circuits, computers, and embedded systems, aiming to optimize area, hardware, and latency. Efforts have introduced novel algorithms with simplified logic for diverse applications, but sequential implementation offers simplicity at the expense of latency and conversion time. In specific results, a TG Logic divider showcased 402 transistors, 379.6 fs delay, 18.42 μW consumption, while a CMOS/Kogge Stone approach yielded 792 transistors, 5.987 μW, 494.9 fs delay. Balancing efficiency factors drives division implementation strategies.

References

1. Soheil Hashemi, R.I.B., Reda, S.: A low-power dynamic divider for approximate applications. IEEE Design Automation Conference (DAC), pp. 1–6 (2016)
2. Liu, W., Tao, X., Li, J., Wang, C., Montuschi, P., Lombardi, F.: Design of unsigned approximate hybrid dividers based on restoring array and logarithmic dividers. IEEE Trans. Emerg. Top. Comput. **10**(1), 339–350 (2022)
3. Santhosh Reddy, G., Sai Vandana, K., Subramanya Sai, S.V.R., Ravindra, J.V.R.: Efficient Design of MISTO CDL Adder Cell for High Throughput and Power-Efficient Array Divider. Soft Computing and Signal Processing 3rd ICSCSP 2020, Volume 1, pp. 595–605 (2020)
4. Parhami, B.: Computer Arithmetic: Algorithms and Hardware Designs. Oxford series in electrical and computer engineering. Oxford University Press (2010). ISBN: 9780195328486
5. Patankar, U.S., Koel, A.: Review of basic classes of dividers based on division algorithm. IEEE Access, 23035–23069 (2021)
6. Purohit, S., Laddha, P., Parekh, R.: Implementation and Physical Design of 8/4-Bit Signed Divider. 8th International Conference on Signal Processing and Integrated Networks (SPIN), pp. 829–834 (2021)
7. Kommineni, R., Arunsai, G., Ravindra, J.V.R.: Low Power, Noise-Immune High Performance Arithmetic Adder Circuit Design Using Modified Parallel Prefix Adders. Inventive Communication and Computational Technologies (2023)
8. Deepak, S., Ganesan SaiKrishnan, D.R., Ravindra, J.V.R.: Seek-method based 2's complement circuit for low power circuit and high-speed operation. AIP Conference Proceedings, vol. 2407. AIP Publishing (2021)
9. San, A.M., Yakunin, A.N.: Reducing the hardware complexity of a parallel prefix adder. IEEE Conference of Russian Young Researchers in Electrical and Electronic Engineering (EIConRus), pp. 1348–1351 (2018)
10. Koyada, B., Meghana, N., Jaleel, O., Jeripotula, P.R.: A comparative study on adders. International Conference on Wireless Communications, Signal Processing and Networking (WiSPNET), pp. 2226–2230 (2017)
11. Panda, S., Sharma, S., Asati, A.R.: Clock gating analysis of TG based d flip-flop for different technology nodes. IEEE 7th Uttar Pradesh Section International Conference on Electrical, Electronics and Computer Engineering (UPCON), pp. 1–6 (2020)
12. Robertson, J.E.: A new class of digital division methods. IRE Transactions on Electronic Computers EC-7.3, pp. 218–222 (1958)
13. Mitchell, J.N.: Computer multiplication and division using binary logarithms. IRE Transactions on Electronic Computers EC-11.4, pp. 512–517 (1962)
14. Aoki, T., Nakazawa, K., Higuchi, T.: High-radix parallel VLSI dividers without using quotient digit selection tables. Proceedings 30th IEEE International Symposium on Multiple-Valued Logic, pp. 345–352 (2000)
15. Sharma, M., Noor, A., Tiwari, S.C., Singh, K.: An area and power efficient design of single edge triggered DFlip flop. International Conference on Advances in Recent Technologies in Communication and Computing, pp. 478–481 (2009)

Speed Control of BLDC Motor Using Bi-directional Converter

B. Raja Gopal Reddy[1], N. Karuppiah[1], Patil Mounica[1(⊠)], Jaydeep Kumar[2], and Keval Jitendrabhai Dasadiya[2]

[1] Vardhaman College of Engineering, Hyderabad, India
{b.rajagopalreddy,mounica.p}@vardhaman.org
[2] RK University, Rajkot, India
Jaydeep.parmar@rku.a.c.in

Abstract. The environmental pollution is enlarging due to the existence of a greater number of gasoline vehicle. Electric vehicles are highly important to reduce pollution, and they are the best option when compared to conventional automobiles. Since they offer higher power densities, superior speed-torque characteristics, maximum efficiency, wide speed ranges, and require less maintenance, brushless DC motors are a viable option for electric cars.This paper uses a bidirectional DC-DC converter to regulate the speed of the BLDC motor.Bidirectional DC-DC converters are frequently used for battery charging and discharge. The buck boost mode of bidirectional converter is an option. The battery's energy reserves give the Brushless DC motor its full power, whilst the same bidirectional buck as well as boost converter returns energy to the source during regenerative braking.

Keywords: BLDC Motor · Buck-Boost converter · PID controller

1 Introduction

Electric vehicles (EV), commercial use, manufacturing turbines, and especially aerospace industries are a few common uses for brushless DC (BLDC) motors [1]. Because of their quick response times, high power factors, silent operation, compact size, reliability, high efficiency, and cheap maintenance costs, brushless DC motors are used extensively. Since they are electronically commutated, BLDC motors do not require brushes for commutation. This motor generates a quasi-rectangular square waves with a trapezoidal back EMF. A permanent-magnetic synchronous motor with a trapezoidal emf waveform is frequently referred to as a "BLDC motor." As its name suggests, BLDC motors do not employ brushes for transmission; instead, they use electronics [2–4].

BLDC motors have such a variety of benefits over brushed DC motors. Because of electromechanical commutator is just no longer required, they require less maintenance, and they are perfect for applications requiring a high torque-to-weight proportion because to their high power density. Compared to the induction machines, they also have less

© ICST Institute for Computer Sciences, Social Informatics and Telecommunications Engineering 2025
Published by Springer Nature Switzerland AG 2025. All Rights Reserved
X. Cheng (Ed): BROADNETS 2024, LNICST 602, pp. 51–57, 2025.
https://doi.org/10.1007/978-3-031-81171-5_5

inertia, allowing for a quicker dynamic response to reference commands. They are also more efficient due to an electromagnets, which virtually completely eliminate rotor losses [5–8].

The buck boost converter supplied with PI controller is another name for the bidirectional dc-dc converter. The bidirectional DC-DC converter offers two operational modes: Boost (increasing voltage from a low level to a higher level) and Buck (decreases the voltage from high level to low level) [9–13].

2 Bidirectional DC-DC Converter

The Bidirectional DC-DC Converter module illustrates a converter that is powered by a controller and signal generator to increases or decreases the DC voltage is applied from one converter side to the other. For instance, bidirectional converters can be used in electric automobiles to transition among energy storage and consumption (Fig. 1).

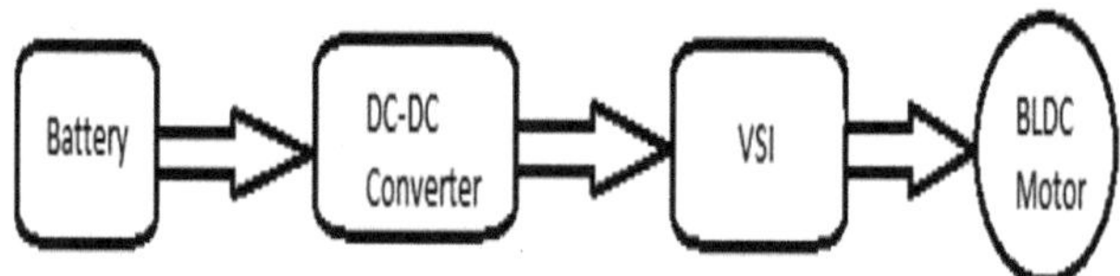

Fig. 1. Overall Block Diagram

The use of MOSFETs or IGBTs to change the current's state rather than all diodes is the key difference between a bidirectional DC - DC converter and also unidirectional DC-DC converter. The bi-directional DC DC converter may still function as a Buck converter by lowering the voltage from a higher level to a lower level as well as a Boost converter by raising the voltage from a lower level to a higher level, depending on the amount of current and voltage being generated along with the location of the energy storage items (Fig. 2).

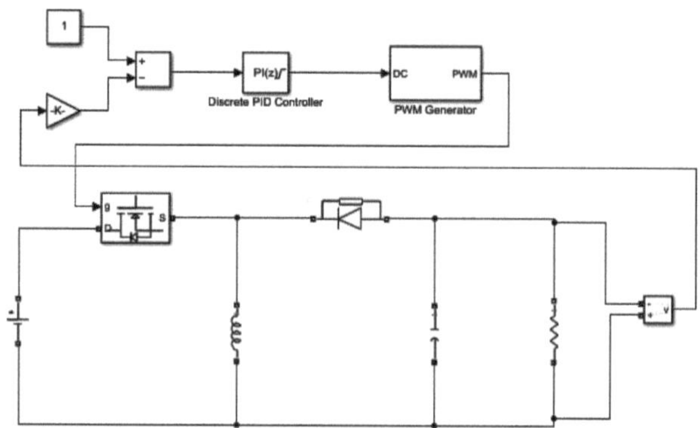

Fig. 2. Bidirectional DC-DC Converter

An example of a DC-DC converter is a "buck-boost converter", which has an output voltage magnitude that can be either more than or lower than the input voltage magnitude. It is utilized by "step up" incoming DC voltage, just like an AC transformer would.

3 Brushless DC Motor

An electronically commutated motor, often known as a brushless DC electric motor, is a synchronous motor that uses a direct current (DC) power supply. The motor windings, which are effectively made to rotate in space by switching DC currents to them, produce magnetic fields that the permanent magnet rotor follows. The controller alters the DC current pulses' phase and amplitude to control the motor's speed and torque. With this control system, the mechanical commutator present in many common electric motors can be swapped out. These motors can provide a lot of power over a wide range of speeds extremely effectively. Brushless motors utilise a fixed armature with permanent magnets, which takes care of the problem of feeding the armature with current. Transportation based on electronics gives a wide range of options and adaptability (Fig. 3).

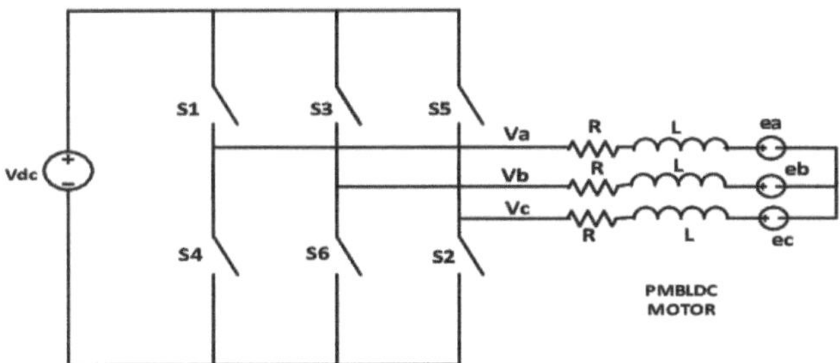

Fig. 3. Circuit of Brushless DC Motor

The use of brushless DC (BLDC) motors is widespread in a variety of industries, including automotive, computing, industrial, and aerospace. Compared to brushed DC motors, BLDC motors provide a number of benefits.They are ideal for applications needing very high torque-to-weight ratio because to their high power density also low maintenance requirements due to the absence of a mechanical commutator. They have less inertia than induction machines, which enables a quicker dynamic reaction to reference commands. Additionally, they have nearly no rotor loss because of the permanent magnets' increased efficiency.

3.1 Mathematical Model of Brushless DC Motor

The electrical as well as mechanical mathematical equations of the BLDC motor are:

$$V_p = Ri_p + L\frac{di_p}{dt} + e_p \tag{1}$$

$$V_q = Ri_q + L\frac{di_q}{dt} + e_q \tag{2}$$

$$V_r = Ri_r + L\frac{di_r}{dt} + e_r \tag{3}$$

where,

V_p, V_q, V_r = Terminal phase voltage
R = Armature resistance
I_p, I_q, I_r = Phase Currents
L = Phase Inductance
e_p, e_q, e_r = Phase Back EMF

We can plot this induced emf as a parameter of rotor position for a three-phase BLDC motor, and it is obvious that there is a 120° change in the phase angle of the in-phase back EMF

$$e_p = k_w \omega f(\theta_e) \tag{4}$$

$$e_q = k_w \omega f\left(\theta_e - \frac{2\pi}{3}\right) \tag{5}$$

$$e_r = k_w \omega f\left(\theta_e + \frac{2\pi}{3}\right) \tag{6}$$

where,

K_w = induced emf
θ_e = Torque angle
ω = Speed of the Rotor

The total of the torque outputs from each phase can be used to represent the overall torque. The following equation shows the overall torque output:

$$T_e = \frac{e_p i_p + e_q i_q + e_r i_r}{\omega} \tag{7}$$

4 Four Quadrant Operation

The motor has the ability to break and move forward as well as backward. Since a DC motor may run in both directions of revolution and generate both motoring and breaking, it is known as having four quadrant action (Fig. 4).

The machine transforms electrical power into mechanical power to sustain motion when it is in driving mode, acting as a motor. When the machine is braking, it functions as a generator, converting mechanical energy into electrical energy and creating an opposing force to motion. The motor has the ability to operate in both driving and braking actions, or perhaps both forward again and backward motion.

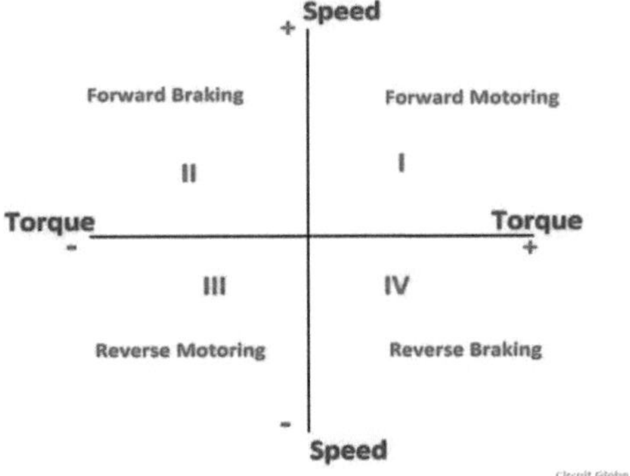

Fig. 4. Four Quadrant

5 Circuit Description and Simulation Results

Figure 5 shows the functional circuit of speed control of BLDC electric motor with the help of PID controller. The Simulink model is composed of an inner loop for current control as well as an outer speed feedback control. PI controller is used to implement the current control loop. PID controllers are used in the outer speed feedback loop.

Figure 5 shows speed control of Brushless DC electric motor, there are three main circuits named BLDC motor model block, Bidirectional DC-DC converter circuit which uses PI controller and Speed control circuit which uses PID controller.

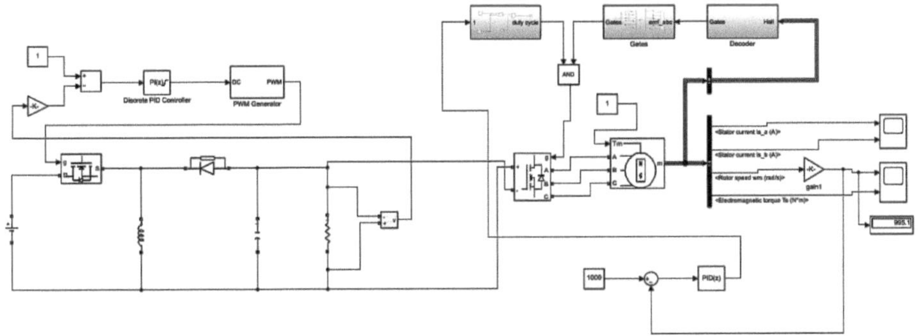

Fig. 5. Simulation figure of the proposed speed control of Brushless DC motor with the help use of Bidirectional converter

Figure 6 uses a PI controller to demonstrate the rotor speed and electromagnetic torque outputs of the Brushless DC motor.

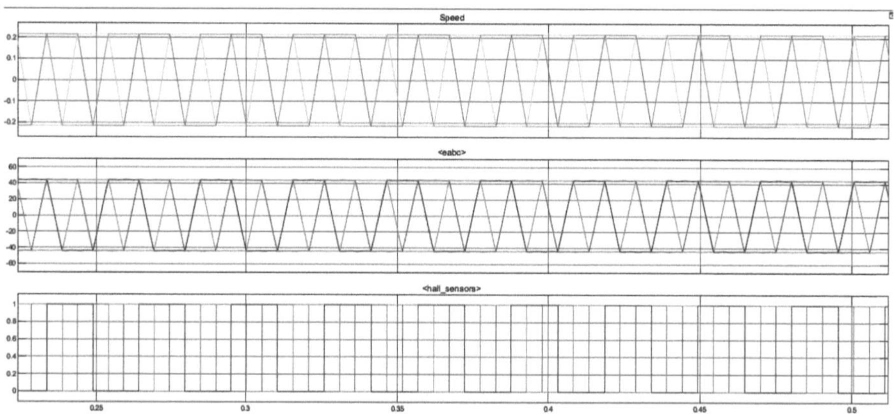

Fig. 6. Rotor speed and Torque

Figure 7 shows overall field winding current of a brushless DC motor.

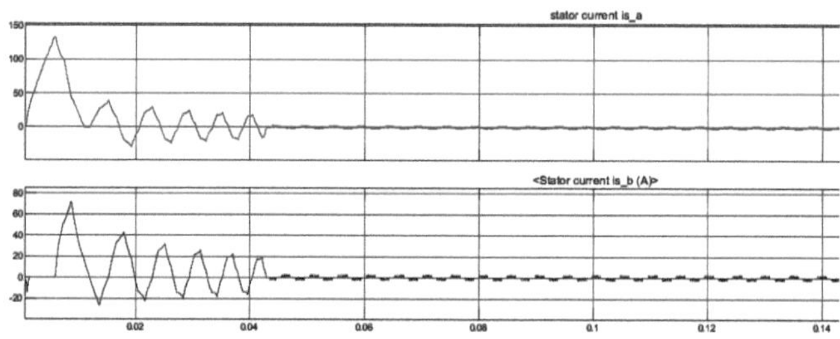

Fig. 7. Stator Currents

Figure 8 gives the speed of brushless DC motor which is 2000 rpm and matches with the actual rating of the motor.

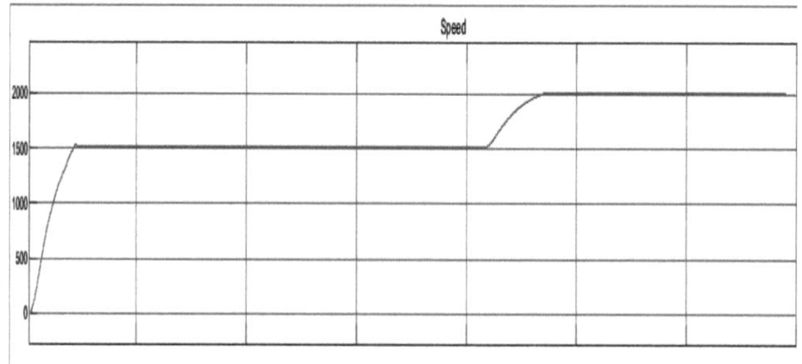

Fig. 8. Speed of Brushless DC motor

6 Conclusion

In this project, the functionality of the BLDC motor's controller is verified under various load conditions using simulation and a PI controller. Here, the motor speed is managed by the controlled voltage of a bidirectional dc-dc converter. Multiple trigger gate signals are produced under various circumstances. The dynamic characteristics, such like speeds, voltage, and also electromagnetic Torque, can be examined with the help of MATLAB/SIMULINK software. Simulation findings show enhanced performance whenever the suggested control is applied under various operating situations.

References

1. Ravivarman, S., Natarajan, K., Raja Gopal, R.B.: Non-isolated Modified Quadratic Boost Converter with Midpoint Output for Solar Photovoltaic Applications. E3S Web Conf. **87**, 01025 (2019)
2. Suganthi, P., Nagapavithra, S., Umamaheswari, S.: Modeling and Simulation of Closed Loop Speed Control for BLDC Motor. Proc. IEEE Conference on Emerging Devices and Smart Systems [4] Ramachandran R, Ganeshaperumal D, Subathra B "Closed-loop Control of BLDC Motor in Electric Vehicle Applications"
3. Ismail, M., Majumdar, S., Albadri, S.S., Jayaram, K.: Simulation and analysis of closed loop speed control of brushless DC motor. International Journal of Advanced Information Science and Technology (IJAIST) (2014)
4. Mukherjee, P., Sengupta, M.: Closed loop speed control of a laboratory fabricated Brush-less DC Motor drive prototype using position sensor. 2017 National Power Electronics Conference (NPEC)
5. College of Engineering Pune. India (2017)
6. Rajesh, G., Balaji, C.: Speed Control of BLDC Motor Using PID Controller. International Journal of Advanced Research in Electrical, Electronics and Instrumentation Engineering (An ISO 3297: Certified Organization) (2007)
7. Neethu, U., Jisha, V.R.: Speed control of brushless DC motor: a comparative study. 2012 IEEE International Conference on Power Electronics, Drives and Energy Systems (2012)
8. Ananthababu, B., Ganesh, C,, Pavithra, C.V.: Fuzzy based speed control of BLDC motor with bidirectional DC-DC converter. 2016 Online International Conference on Green Engineering and Technologies
9. Lin, C.-H., Liu, H.-W., Wang, C.-M.: Design and implementation of a bi-directional power converter for electric bike with charging feature. Industrial Electronics and Applications (ICIEA), 2010 the 5th IEEE Conference on. IEEE (2010)
10. Kumar, R., Singh, B.: Buck-boost converter fed BLDC motor drive for solar PV array based water pumping. IEEE International Conference on Power Electronics, Drives and Energy Systems (PEDES), pp. 1–6 (2014)
11. Li, Y., Ang, K.h., Chong, G.C.G.C.Y.: PID control system analysis and design. IEEE Control Systems Magazine **26**(1), 32–41 (2006)
12. Lee, W., Kim, J.H., Choi, W., Sarlioglu, B.: Torque ripple minimization control technique of high-speed single phase brushless DC motor for electric turbocharger. IEEE Transactions on Vehicular Technology **67**(11), 10 357–10 365 (2018)
13. Low, T., Chen, S., Gao, X.: Robust torque optimization for BLDC spindle motors. IEEE Transactions on Industrial Electronics **48**(3), 656–663 (2001)

Direct Torque Controller of SRM for EV Application Based on Neural Network

Anuradha Devi Tellapati[1](✉) [iD], Malligunta Kiran Kumar[2] [iD],
Natarajan Karuppaiah[1] [iD], S. Ravi Teja[2] [iD],
and Kambhampati Venkata Govardhan Rao[3] [iD]

[1] Department of Electrical and Electronics Engineering, Vardhman College of Engineering,
Shamshabad, Hyderabad, Telangana, India
anuradhadevi.eee@gmail.com
[2] Department of Electrical and Electronics Engineering, Koneru Lakshmaiah Education
Foundation, Vaddeswaram, Guntur, A.P., India
[3] Department of Electrical and Electronics Engineering, St. Martin's Engineering College,
Secunderabad, Hyderabad, Telangana, India

Abstract. This paper presents the machine learning based control of cascaded converter fed SRM drive of electric vehicle. The electric vehicle which is driven by a 6/4 Switched Reluctance Motor (SRM) powered by four battery banks is considered in this paper. The new topology of converter is proposed to drive SRM effectively for application of electric car. The direct torque controller is implemented with the help of neural network for effective speed controller with minimum ripples in electromagnetic torque. The required pulses are generated with space vector Pulse Width Modulation (PWM) technique. The electromagnetic torque generated by SRM needs to be maintained at ripples free for smooth operation of electric car. The mathematical validation is implemented to achieve the required power rating of SRM for Toyota Car. The proposed topology of converter has a facility of using four battery banks, hence the charging time of batteries will be minimized. The direct torque controller with model reference adaptive controller is implemented for establishing sensor less operation. The proposed system is implemented in MATLAB/Simulink. The extensive results are presented which validate the proposed system for steady state and transient state requirements of the drive.

Keywords: Electric Car · Direct Torque Control · SRM · SVPWM

1 Introduction

Global warming is creating many major problems in worldwide with the increasing consumption of fossil fuel. However, the use of fossil fuel is increasing day by day. The major share in consumption of fossil fuel is utilizing for transport and unfortunately fossil fuels are limited which leads to increasing price day by day. Hence, worldwide researchers are searching for an alternative solution and developing electric vehicles

X. Cheng (Ed): BROADNETS 2024, LNICST 602, pp. 58–69, 2025.
https://doi.org/10.1007/978-3-031-81171-5_6

which can reduce carbon emissions to protect nature from pollution [1, 2]. Generally, cars are using by many people and it is becoming and fascinate vehicle in our life. Moreover, utilization of cars is increasing day-by-day and diesel/petrol cars are becoming major sources of pollution. Therefore, electric cars need to be developed for fulfill our transportation needs. The design, manufacturing and usage of electric vehicles started long back throughout the world. SRM proved as a good companion for electric vehicle drive for it simple construction and torque capacity. However, it is the converter and controller that decides the robustness of drive.

A review of comparison between different power electronic converters for SRM drives such as asymmetric converter, H-bridge type converter, C-Dump type converter, R-Dump type converter, variable voltage at dc link and three phase bridge module converters were reported [3, 4]. The results show that the asymmetric converter produces better results for SRM. The detailed analysis SRM by using different types of converters were discussed. The asymmetric converter provides better results compared to the other type of converters and the converter has the bridge circuit at the input side which in turn increases the conduction losses [5–7]. A regeneration mode of SRM which was examined by using C-Dump converter and the energy recovery mechanism. The braking mode control was achieved by dynamically adjusting the excitation reference as a control variable [8]. A negative torque generation model of asymmetric converter which to reduce the torque ripple of by high magnetization & demagnetization voltage. But the cost is increased due to the boost capacitor & diodes in the input side [9, 10].

With these findings, a novel converter with novel control for SRM drive is presented in this paper. Rest of the paper is organized as follows. Section 2 presents description of the system, Sect. 3 presents sizing of components, Sect. 4 presents controller model, Sect. 6 presents results and discussion and finally conclusions are presented.

2 System Description

The schematic of the proposed cascaded converter based SRM drive for electric vehicle is shown in Fig. 1. The new topology of converter is implemented which provides reliable voltage waveform owing to its cascaded structure. Apart from many controllers, Direct Torque Controller (DTC) is having high priority to operate motor under fewer ripples in torque. Therefore, DTC is employed along with Space Vector Pulse Width Modulation (SVPWM) for effective control of SRM. To reduce ripples in torque and smooth operation of speed, the artificial neural network (ANN) is developed. The new topology of converter can have facility to divide all batteries in four battery banks. This can provide felicity to adjust battery banks at different places in car according to availability of space. An optimized ANN based direct torque control is employed for the EV drive. The direct torque control is selecte4d for the reasons of quick response and independent torque and speed control. An improved ANN networked was used to determine control parameters for DTC. Speed was estimated using model resonance adaption technique.

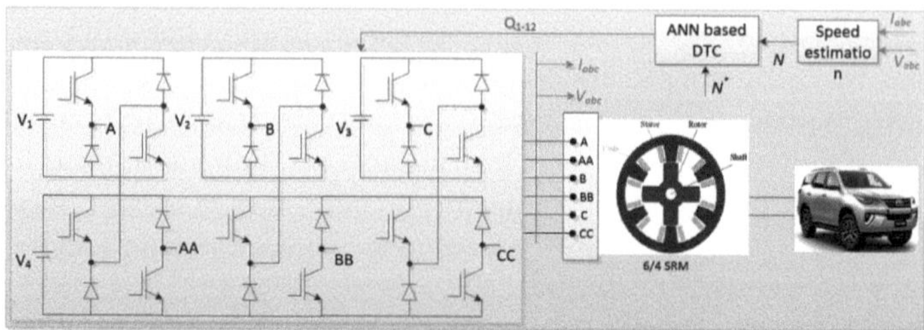

Fig. 1. Proposed System in Electric Vehicle with SRM

2.1 Modeling of the Battery

Battery energy storage is important part of the electric or hybrid electric vehicle. The proper controller with precious energy management system is needed for enhancing charge cycles which shall supervise for proper charge and discharge sequence. The battery bank used in EV usually consists of series connected battery to establish required rated voltage. Therefore, current flowing through all individual batteries is same during both charging and discharging. However, in order to achieve unique flow of current through all batteries, active balancing of the system is required which ensures equal charging or discharging among the cells in the battery pack.

The state of the charge (SOC) of the complete battery bank is measured and stored for the controlling purpose. A generic model of the battery bank is implemented from [11–13] in this paper. The parameter of temperature is also considered for more realistic in this implantation. The basic controlled voltage dependent source is described through following basic expressions.

$$E_m = E_{m0} - K_E(273 + \theta)(1 - SOC) \tag{7}$$

$$Q_e(t) = Q_{e\_init} + \int_0^t -I_m(\tau)d\tau \tag{8}$$

$$I_p = V_{PN}G_{P0}\exp\left(\frac{V_{PN}}{V_{P0}(\tau_p s + 1)} + A_P\left(1 - \frac{\theta}{\theta_f}\right)\right) \tag{9}$$

$$C(I, \theta) = \frac{K_c C_{0*} K_t}{1 + (K_c - 1)(I / I^*)^\delta}, \quad K_t = LUT(\theta) \tag{10}$$

where,

$$SOC = 1 - \frac{Q_e}{C(0, \theta)}, \quad DOC = 1 - \frac{Q_e}{C(I_{avg}, \theta)}, \quad \theta(t) = \theta_{init} + \int_0^t \frac{\left(Ps - \frac{(\theta - \theta_a)}{R_\theta}\right)}{C_\theta}d\tau$$

symbols are denoted as follows:

Q_e - extracted charge; Q_{e_init}- intial extracted charge; I_m – current deliverd; τ – time variable; I_P- parasitic current; V_{PN}- parasitic voltge (Figs. 2 and 3).

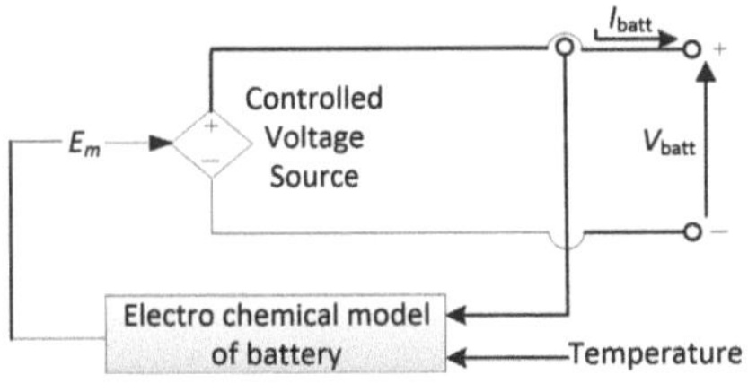

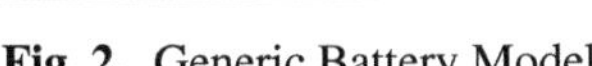

Fig. 2. Generic Battery Model

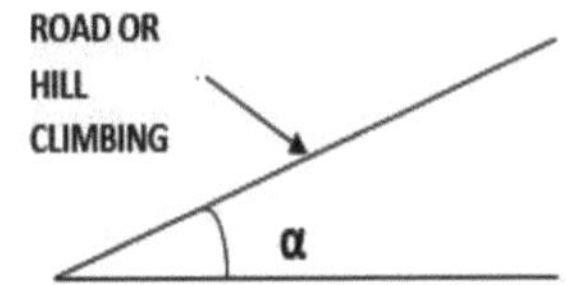

Fig. 3. Angle between the slope and the flat surface

3 Sizing of System Components

The Toyota EV [14] was considered for sizing the SRM drive. The technical details pertaining to weight [15], coefficients etc. was taken from [16, 17].

This section presents the sizing of following components of the drives:

- Power required by load [18, 19]
- Sizing of motor
- Sizing of battery

3.1 Load Power Sizing

The required tractive force is given as:

$$F_{total} = F_{rolling} + F_{gradient} + F_{aerodynamic} \tag{11}$$

where, F_{total} = Total force; $F_{rolling}$ = Rolling Resistance force; $F_{gradient}$ = Gradient Resistance force; $F_{aerodynamic}$ = Aerodynamic drag force.

A. **Tractive force for C_{rr}:** It is the resistance offered by the road due to the friction between tyres and road. To calculate the force offered by rolling resistance the following formula is used given in Eq. (12).

$$F_{rolling} = C_{rr} \times M \times g \tag{12}$$

where, C_{rr} = Rolling resistance coefficient; M = mass in kg; g = acceleration due to gravity = 9.81 m/s^2; For the application considered, Crr = 0.01; M = 3000 kg;

Therefore,

$$F_{rolling} = 294.30\,\text{N}$$

Required power to overcome the rolling resistance of 294.30 N is:

$$P_{rolling} = F_{rolling} \times \frac{V}{3600} = 6.20\,\text{kW}$$

B. **Tractive force for gradient:** Gradient resistance is the resistance offered by a slope surface while climbing a fly-over or hill. α is the angle between the slope and the flat surface as shown in Fig. 1.

62   A. D. Tellapati et al.

The gradient resistance can be calculated by using the formula given in Eq. (13):

$$F_{gradient} = \pm M \times g \times \sin \alpha \tag{13}$$

$$F_{gradient} \text{ at } 6° \text{ is } = 1538 \text{ N}.$$

$$P_{gradient} = F_{gradient} \times \frac{V}{360} = 10.2 \text{ kW}$$

C. **Tractive force for C_A:** It can be determined by the vehicle shape. The aerodynamic drag is calculated by using the formula given in Eq. (14):

$$F_{aerodynamic} = 0.5 \times C_A \times A_f \times \rho \times (V + V_0)^2 \tag{14}$$

One more force due to inertia also acts on the vehicle during acceleration and deceleration. In this work, the total power required to compensate all the resistive forces and drag is taken as 2.6 kW.

Thus, a 20-kW load power is calculated to meet all the above components of the load resistance and for required torque at nominal load of the vehicle.

3.2 Battery Pack Sizing

Section 2 presented the model for the battery which showed the significance of C-rate, initial charge, and chemistry for estimated power delivery and lifetime. Lead acid batteries vs Li-ion chemistry depends on economics of the drive [20, 21]. First one for low cost and second one for higher energy density. This section presents size of the batter pack required for meeting the 20-kW nominal load.

$$I_{Ah} = \frac{Power \times Time}{Voltage} = \frac{20000 \times 4.5 hr}{300} = 300 Ahr \tag{15}$$

3.3 SRM Sizing

SRM as stated in Sect. 1 provides high torque-to-ampere ration, superior control, and allows for smooth commutation. The immediate supplier to the load being 6/4 pole SRM, the power sizing of the SRM shall be 20 kW as nominal value. The A 400 V voltage limits the required current to around 20 A, thus could result in simple insulation requirement. However, the inertia of the motor shall be small to serve quick transient requirements [22–24]. Therefore, the windings with good aligned inductance and with less copper requirement shall make the inertia requirement possible. Also, the losses in the motor phase windings should be limited to 0.1 % of the total power rating. Thus, a lighter SRM with high torque capability is the resulting choice for motor.

The SRM parameters which are considered for drive provided in Table 1:

Table 1. SRM Parameters

S. No	Parameter	Value
1	Nominal Rated Power	20 KW
2	Nominal line to line Voltage	400 V
3	Stator Resistance (Rs)	0.7384
4	Stator Inductance (Lls)	0.003045
5	Inertia (J)	0.0343
6	Pole Pairs	6/4

4 Controller of SRM

The 6/4 pole 20 kW SRM is operated cascaded converter with the following control algorithm.

The objectives of Control are:

- Effective and accurate tracking for change in speed command
- Speed regulation for load change
- Quick transient interval for reverse command
- Zero steady state error for motor speed command

The control scheme includes the following salient aspects:

- The control does not require sensing of speed as this was achieved through model reference adaptive control for estimation of speed
- Machine learning for deriving torque command from speed error
- Space vector modulation for gating pulse generation

The stated objectives necessiate d-q model of the SRM for determining torque and flux commands which was stated in Eqs. (16) and (17).

$$[(1 - \sigma)T_s + T_r]\frac{d}{dt}\psi_{r\alpha} = \frac{L_m}{R_s}u_{s\alpha} - \psi_{r\alpha} - \omega T_r\psi_{r\beta} - \sigma L_m T_s\frac{d}{dt}i_{s\alpha} \qquad (16)$$

$$[(1 - \sigma)T_s + T_r]\frac{d}{dt}\psi_{r\beta} = \frac{L_m}{R_s}u_{s\beta} - \psi_{r\beta} + \omega T_r\psi_{r\alpha} - \sigma L_m T_s\frac{d}{dt}i_{s\beta} \qquad (17)$$

where:

L_s and L_r *are* stator and rotor self-inductance [in H] respectively

L_m = motor magnetizing inductance [in H]

R_r *and* R_s are denoted for rotor and stator Resistance [in Ohm] respectively

ω = Angular speed of the rotor[in rad.s-1]

The purpose of designing DTC is to control independently the direct-axis stator current i_{sd} and the quadrature-axis stator current i_{sq}. But unfortunately, the stator voltage components are in decoupled in nature. That means, the direct axis component u_{sd} and i_{sq} as well as quadrature axis component u_{sq} and i_{sd} are in coupled by depending on each other. Further, the i_{sd} and i_{sq} should be controlled independently (with decoupled control) if the stator voltage equations are decoupled and the stator current components i_{sd} and i_{sq} are indirectly controlled by controlling the terminal voltages of the motor.

The scheme for model reference adaptive control is shown in Fig. 4(a) and respective SRM motor speed estimation is depicted in Fig. 4(b). Usually sensing the speed by sensors are not preferable due to malfunctions of sensors, needs to provide extra protection and also costly. The block diagram for implementation of SMC for proposed system is shown in Fig. 5. The speed estimated through SMC based MRAC is compared to reference speed and the difference is provided as input to machine learning algorithm which is state in next section. The flux and torque commands generated by machine learning algorithm generates the voltage refence vector for subsequent sample. Then SVPWM technique generates appropriate pulses instantly based on sector. The scheme for identification of sectors, dwell time calculation and transforming in to gating pulses is depicted in Fig. 6. The generated pulses will go to respective switch of converter to produce required output accordingly load and reference speed of SRM.

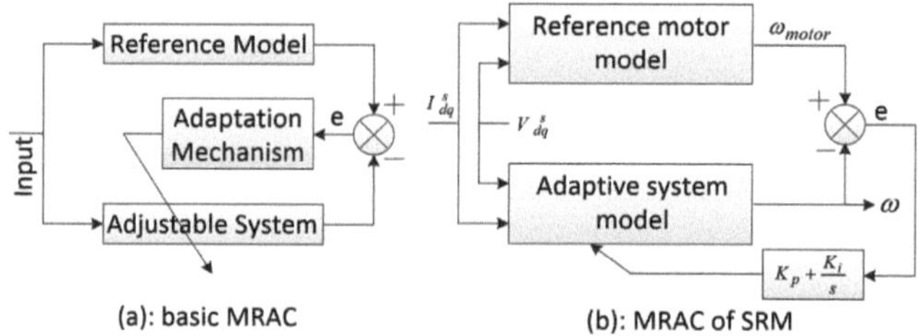

(a): basic MRAC   (b): MRAC of SRM

Fig. 4. Estimation of speed using MRAC model of SRM

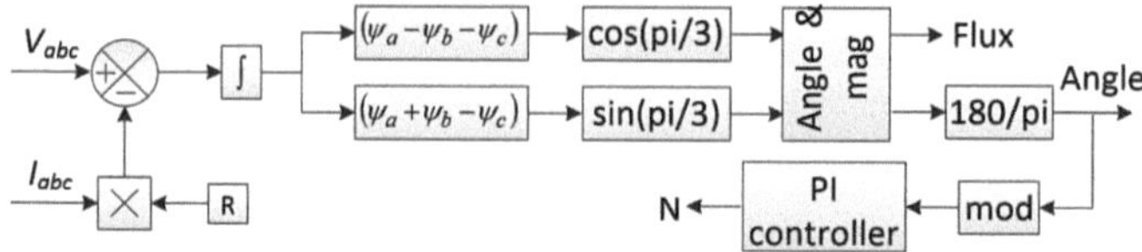

Fig. 5. Implementation of SMC of proposed system

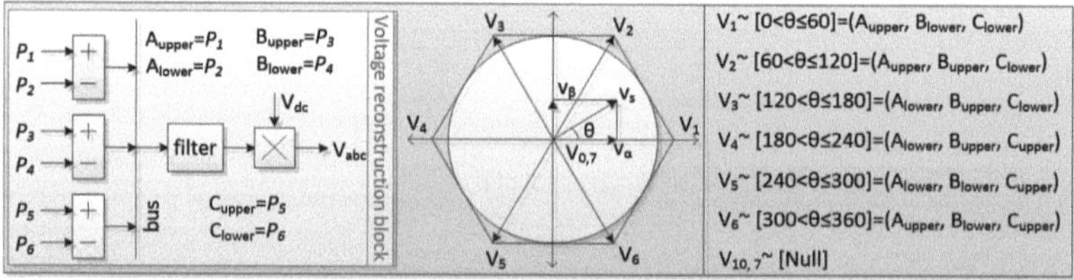

Fig. 6. Space Vector PWM strategy

4.1 Implementation of ANN

Generally artificial intelligent (AI) strategies are a simple computer-oriented programming applications to think and act brilliantly for taking decisions very sharply. To accomplish this objective, the machine learning through artificial neural network (ANN) was employed. The targeted output or results are always produced on the basis of adjusting weight factors accordingly neurons and its corresponding inputs neurons for every cycle in training structure of any neural network design model. The basic process of learning is depicted in Fig. 7 and the corresponding ANN implementation has been considered in this paper. The designed ANN can have ability to adjust their gains by learning process for any disturbance.

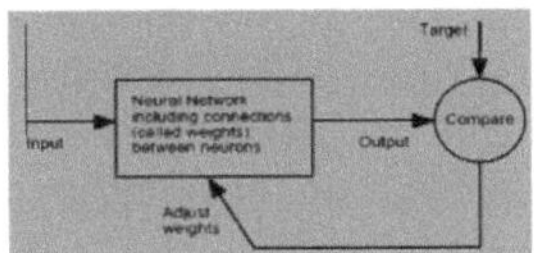

Fig. 7. ANN –Training Structure

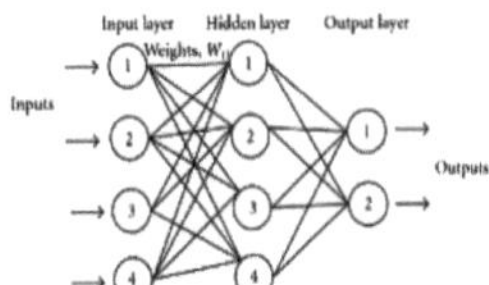

Fig. 8. Feed forward ANN

The basic learning process of the ANN system can be patterns subsequent based on response. Feed-forward ANNs are a very frontward- customary technique, The multilayer of ANN is depicted in Fig. 8. Moreover, due to existing of hidden layer, the controller can exhibit smooth controlling output during large variations in inputs.

Table 2. ANN Parameters

S. No	Parameter	Value
1	Activation Function	Sigmoid
2	Number of Hidden Layers	2
3	Input layers	1
4	Output variables	1
5	Error Bound	0.01
6	Pole Pairs	6/4

5 Results and Discussion

The proposed converter and control for SRM drive are tested in MATLAB/SIMULINK. This section presents the simulation results and observations. The parameters for motor presented in Table 1, ANN parameters presented in Table 2 are utilized for simulation. Other simulation parameters are provided in Table 3.

The simulation results are presented for three scenarios viz. Response of torque and speed for change in load on the vehicle, response pf torque and speed for change in

Table 3. Simulation Parameters

S. No	Parameter	Value
1	Battery Pack Voltage	100 V
2	Battery Packs capacity	P1, P2, P3: 50 AH, P4: 150 AH
3	Power Switches	IGBT: 600 V, 300 A
4	Power Diodes	600 V, 300 A
5	SRM Aligned Inductance	20 mH
6	SRM Unaligned Inductance	330 μH

speed command, response of torque and speed for speed reversal command. Following presents obtained results.

Case-1: Change in Load Torque: The load torque is changed to 50 N-m from zero load. Owing to this change in load, a quick settlement in motor developed torque is observed from Fig. 9. Also, at zero load and at changed load which is met by the motor torque, the steady state ripple in the motor torque is observed to be 2 N-m which accounts for reasonable torque ripple with SRM. The transient interval involved in tracking to new load is observed to be 0.1 s as depicted from Fig. 9. The response of the speed for change on load is depicted in Fig. 10. It is observed from Fig. 10 that the transient interval for the speed to settle back to reference speed is 0.5 s which proves the robustness of the proposed machine learning algorithm and direct torque control implementation. Also, there are only few oscillations at the transient which indicates the damping of the system. Power delivered from the battery pack for change in load is shown in Fig. 11. Battery pack c-rate is changed instantly following the change in load and thus supplying the power at increased current as depicted from Fig. 11.

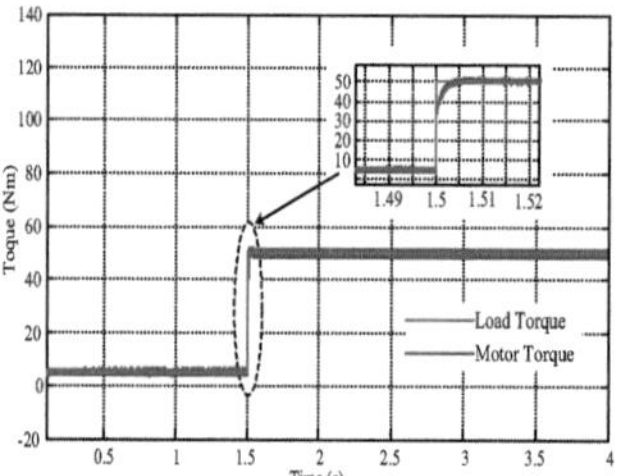
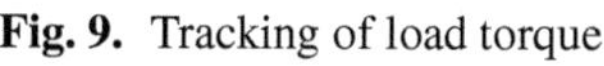

Fig. 9. Tracking of load torque

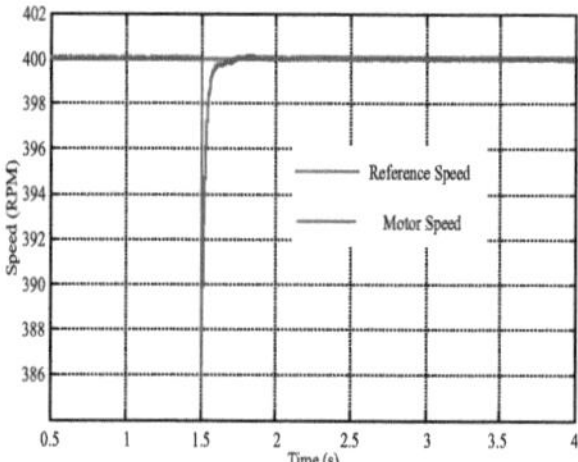

Fig. 10. Response of Speed under Increasing Load Torque

Case-2: Step change in speed command: EV loads demand for quickly changing speed requirements as per the throttle position for given load following various drive cycles. Therefore, the proposed control is tested for a step change in speed command with a magnitude of about 120 rpm. Following the change in speed command, a dip in dc link voltage is observed from Fig. 12 which settled back to reference value with in 05 s. Magnitude of dip pertains to the allowable maximum dip in voltage which

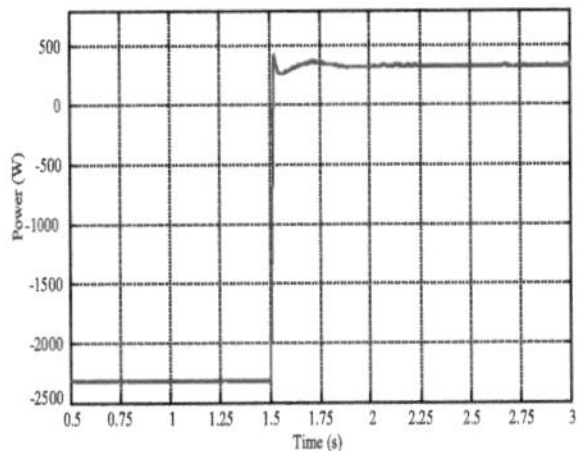

Fig. 11. Battery power dynamics

indicates the robustness of control algorithm. The tracking of speed command is shown in Fig. 13. The transient response presented in Fig. 14 shows the accurate tracking of speed command with zero steady state error and quick interval of 0.05 s. Also, the peak overshoot is marginal as 10 %. The change sis torque owing to speed change is depicted in Fig. 13. Pertaining to change in speed command the torque in transient period is held at maximum to achieve the quick acceleration to new speed and then the torque returns to meet the load which is observed from Fig. 13.

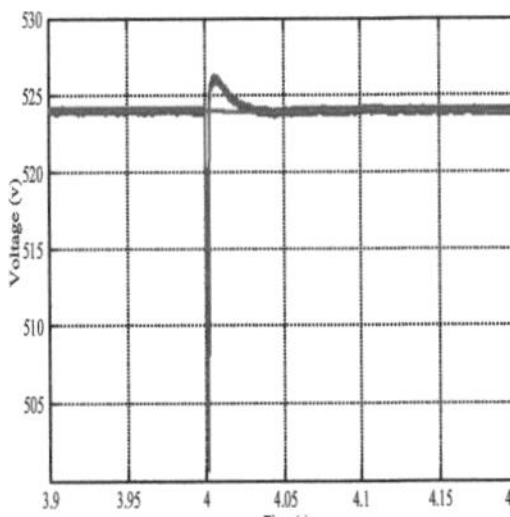

Fig. 12. DC link voltage

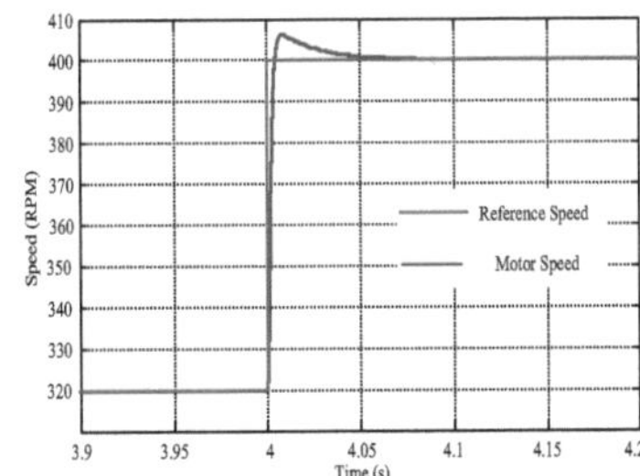

Fig. 13. Response of speed

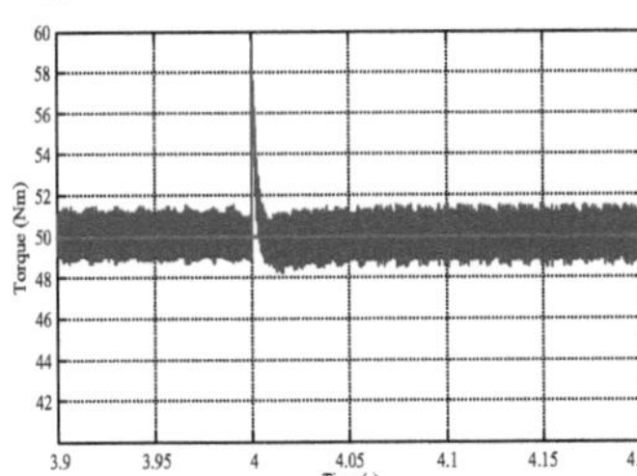

Fig. 14. Torque response for speed change command

Case-3: Reverse driving of the Vehicle: The condition of sudden reversal of speed is simulated. A step change in speed from +80 rpm to −80 rpm was demanded. The response of the speed and drive torque were analyzed. The response of speed as observed from Fig. 15 shows the accurate tracking of new speed with zero steady state error along with a quick transient time of 0.08 s. The dynamics of dc link voltage pertaining to speed reversal is shown in Fig. 16. A sudden dip owing to reversal command is observed and quick transient time of 0.05 s is observed for settling back to reference value. A sudden dip in drive torque was observed from Fig. 17 during change- over of drive speed to new value owing to the fact that the drive does not hold any load during transient speed reversal which was settled in quick interval of 0.01 s.

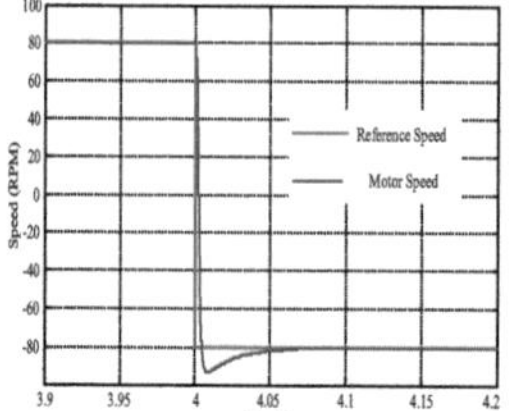

Fig. 15. Reference and motor speed in reverse direction

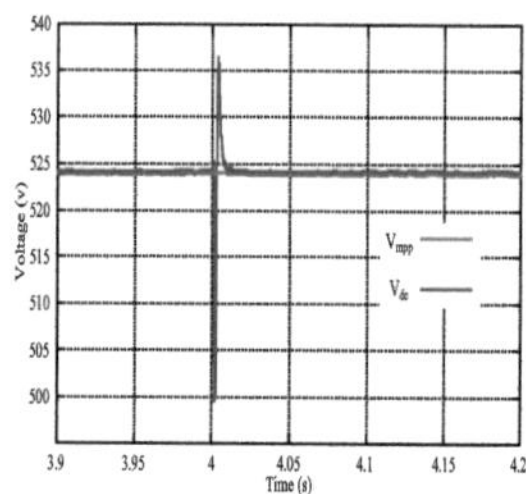

Fig. 16. dc link voltage under change in direction

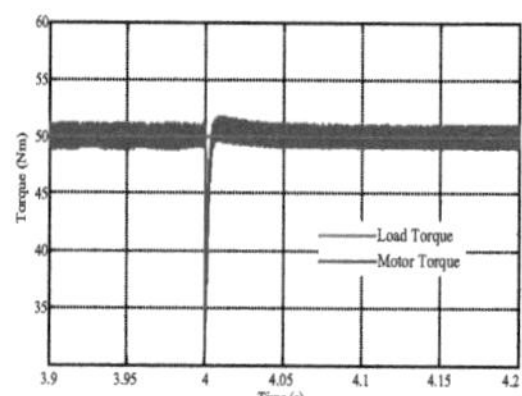

Fig. 17. Torque dynamics for speed change

From the simulation results presented, it is observed that the proposed cascaded converter structure is proved to be reliable with four battery packs supplying the load leading to an improved availability of source for failures in front or rare battery pack modules. The reliability index is increased to 66.67 % which is inly 50 % with conventional asymmetric converter based SRM drive. Then, the efficiency of the conversion is also increased as observed from quick transients of less than 0.5 s for speed and 0.05 s for torque.

6   Conclusion

A novel cascaded converter topology and machine learning based direct torque control of SRM drive for electric vehicle application is presented. The detailed models for load, battery, motor, and converter are discussed. Sizing of all these components was presented. Various stages of control algorithm were discussed which included speed estimation, torque reference generation through machine learning, and current control. The simulation results for steady state torque shown 2 N-m ripple at nominal load. The transients in torque and speed settle with in 0.5 s for any parameter change. The power requirements were met accurately and quickly by proposed battery structure. Thus, the proposed converter and control proved as a good solution for modular drives for SRM based EV drives with robust and efficient control.

References

1. Malla, S.G., et al.: Wind and photovoltaic based hybrid stand-alone power generation system. IEEE: International Conference on Energy, Communication, Data Analytics and Soft Computing (ICECDS 2017). Chennai, India (2017)
2. Malla, S.G., et al.: Solar-hydrogen energy based hybrid electric vehicle. IEEE: International Conference on Energy, Communication, Data Analytics and Soft Computing (ICECDS 2017). Chennai, India (2017)
3. Bose, B.K.: Power Electronics and Motor Drives. Academic Press, Imprint of Elsevier (2006)
4. Theraja, B.L., Theraja, A.K.: A Textbook of Electrical Technology, Vol. 2
5. Porselvi, T., et al.: Selection of power rating of an electric motor for electric vehicles. International Journal of Engineering Science and Computing (IJESC) 7(4) (2017)
6. https://en.wikipedia.org/wiki/Toyota_Fortuner
7. Reddy, N., et al.: Switched Quasi Impedance-Source DC-DC Network for Photovoltaic Systems. Int. J. Renew. Energy Res. 13(2), 681–698 (2023). https://www.ijrer.org/ijrer/index.php/ijrer/article/view/14097
8. http://www.letsrun.com/forum/flat_read.php?thread=3371381
9. https://comparativegeometrics.wordpress.com/2015/12/10/road-gradient-1-definition-and-vehicle-performance/
10. Venkata Govardhan Rao, K., et al.: Design of a bidirectional DC/DC converter for a hybrid electric drive system with dual-battery storing energy. Front. Energy Res. 10(November) (2022). https://doi.org/10.3389/fenrg.2022.972089
11. Rao, K.V.G., Kiran Kumar, M., Srikanth Goud, B.: An Independently Controlled Two Output Half Bridge Resonant LED Driver. Electr. Power Components Syst. 0(0), 1–21 (2023). https://doi.org/10.1080/15325008.2023.2238695
12. http://www.trunsunsolar.com
13. Malla, S.G., Bhende, C.N.: Enhanced operation of stand-alone "Photovoltaic-Diesel Generator-Battery" system. Electric Power Systems Research 107, 250–257 (2014)
14. Bhende, C.N., Malla, S.G.: Novel control of photovoltaic based water pumping system without energy storage. Int. J. Emerg. Electr. Power Sys. 13(5) (2012)
15. Malla, S.G., Bhende, C.N., Mishra, S.: Photovoltaic based water pumping system. International Conference on Energy, Automation, and Signal (ICEAS), 1–4 (2011)
16. Khare, A., Rangnekar, S.: Optimal Sizing an SPV/Diesel/Battery Hybrid System for a Remote Railway Station in India. Int. J. Renew. Ener. Res. 3(3) (2013)
17. Betka, A., Moussi, A.: Performance optimization of a photovoltaic induction motor pumping system. Renewable Energy 29, 2167–2181 (2004)
18. A Report on: Utilisation of Hybrid Energy Services in Island and Rural Communities: Indian and European Scenario. http://www.teriin.org/opet/reports/hybrid.pdf
19. http://www.energymatters.com.au/renewable-energy/solar-power/pumping/
20. Sera, R.T., Hantschel, J., Knoll, M.: Optimized maximum power point tracker for fast-changing environmental conditions. IEEE Trans. Indus. Electro. 55(7), 2629–2631 (2008)
21. Handbook of Secondary Storage Batteries and Charge Regulators in Photovoltaic Systems Final Report, prepared by Exide Management and Technology Company. West College Avenue, Yardley, Pennsylvania (1981). http://www.azsolarcenter.org/images/docs/tech-science/papers/batteries/start.pdf
22. Aneesha, K., Das, P.G.: A non isolated high step up DC to DC converter with continuous input current for PV system. Int. J. New Technol. Sci. Eng. (IJNTSE) 5(3), 1–11 (2018)
23. Nisha, C.K., Priya, S.: Bidirectional DC-DC converter for energy storage systems. Int. J. New Technol. Sci. Eng. (IJNTSE) 5(3), 12–21 (2018)
24. Kopylov, I.P.: Mathematical models of electric machines, translated from the russian by P.S. Ivanov, Revised from the Russian edition (1980)

Performance and Analysis of Cuk Converter for Electric Vehicle Battery Charger Along with Resonant Converter

Keval Dasadiya[1]([✉]), Jayraj Chanv[1], and N. Karupaiah[2]

[1] Electrical Engineering Department, School of Engineering, RK University, Rajkot, Gujarat, India
{keval.dasadiya,jayraj.chanv}@rku.ac.in
[2] Department of Electrical and Electronics Engineering, Vardhman College of Engineering, Hyderabad, Shamshabad, Telangana, India

Abstract. For electric vehicle (EV) battery chargers, this study suggests an HB-LLC resonant converter supplied by a cuk converter (EVBC). A typical home power supply, 230 V–50 Hz AC, is employed as the input in this investigation. A diode bridge rectifier, or DBR, changes the input voltage to DC. As DC-DC converters, a cuk converter and an LLC resonant converter are employed. The LLC resonant converter transforms the DC link voltage into the isolated DC voltage needed for the electric vehicle battery charger (EVBC), while the cuk converter functions in the primary inductor's continuous conductor mode (CCM). For quick charging of EV batteries, the Voltage fed LLC resonant converter provides an appropriate charge voltage. Here, MATLAB Simulink is used for simulation to analyze the parameters.

Keywords: Cuk Converter · HB – LLC Resonant Converter · Electrical Vehicle Battery Charger

1 Introduction

A DC-to-DC converter is an electrical device that converts electric power from one source of direct current (DC) to another. It uses high-frequency switching and capacitors, inductors, and transformers to smooth out switching noise. Batteries are the primary power source for portable electronics like laptops and cell phones. A resonant converter, made up of inductors and capacitors, filters harmonics to produce a sinusoidal wave. Electrical vehicles are introducing hybrid, hydrogen cell, and battery-powered options, with a wide range of technologies available. The selection process for batteries depends on the vehicle's weight, torque, speed, and motor type.

© ICST Institute for Computer Sciences, Social Informatics and Telecommunications Engineering 2025
Published by Springer Nature Switzerland AG 2025. All Rights Reserved
X. Cheng (Ed): BROADNETS 2024, LNICST 602, pp. 70–78, 2025.
https://doi.org/10.1007/978-3-031-81171-5_7

2 Literature Review

Tests of the suggested UPF converter's performance demonstrate its appropriateness for EV battery charging in CC-CV mode with improved power quality. Furthermore, cascade dual loop PI controllers have been adjusted for mainstream use with reduced THD and smooth charging characteristics. Because of the input and output side inductors, the suggested UPF converter topology provides the inherent benefit of decreased waveforms at the input and output sides [1].

A PQ correction feature is integrated into the design of a battery charger for electric vehicles (EVs) that has a non-inverting cuk converter. The additional inverse amplifier required to convert the inverting output voltage to a conventional cuk converter has been rendered unnecessary by the EV charger equipped with the suggested converter. As low as 2.8%, the primary current THD is observed, falling within the regulations' allowable range [2].

The suggested EV charger offers the combined benefits of enhanced charging, easy control, and isolation because of the single-phase converter's DCM operation and low stress on semiconductor devices. The charger's reliability is increased because the device voltage is lower than that of a typical isolated PFC converter-based charger and is clamped to the maximum input voltage. Furthermore, the charger's size and price have been decreased [3].

Low conduction losses with current conduction through a small number of components at single switching intervals are an advantage of the isolated BL converter. One more benefit of the suggested charger is that the normal input initiator is present for both half-cycles. Because the two PFC switches share the input investor, the size and cost of the charger are decreased [5].

This paper successfully investigates three types of buck converters: switched capacitor QZSC (SC-QZSC), QZS buck converter, and classical buck converter. Three DC-DC converters have had their load voltage ripple, load current waveform, and inductor current ripple computed for analysis and comparison. The findings suggest that, in comparison to the other two topologies, the suggested SC-QZSC has less ripple content in both the output and the inductor [7].

3 Proposed Topology

Figure 1 illustrates how the Cuk converter feeds the HB-LLC resonant converter. The front-end cock converter receives the AC input from the EVBC and uses the constant inductor mode (CICM) to maintain the sinusoidal input AC current while maintaining a regulated DC link voltage of Vd.

To isolate the low voltage Vo for the EVBC, the half bridge (HB) LLC builds the resonant converter second stage and disconnects the high voltage DC link Vb. Through the use of a two-loop structure and PWM control of the Cuk converter, the harmonic free input current is obtained. The internal current control loop is created by the input inductor current feedback, whereas the external loop is created by the DC link control.

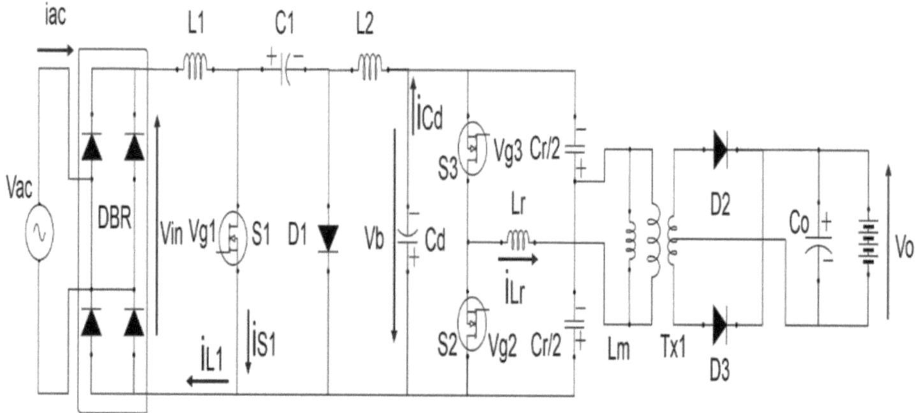

Fig. 1. Configuration of Cuk converter fed HB-LLC Resonant converter

3.1 Operation

Mode 1: Fig. 2 displays the cuk converter's operating modes. The input inductor stores energy during the switch S1 on period, and capacitor C1 releases its energy through S1 to the DC link capacitor Cd. In both inductors, the current grows linearly.

Mode 2: During the off period, both inductors discharge their energy through the Cd to the load, while C1 charges through the source voltage Vs.

Mode 3 and Mode 4: Fig. 3 illustrates the HB-LLC resonant converter's operating modes. The switching frequency of the LLC converter can be set to operate at, below, or above the resonant frequency. The maximum value of the magnetizing current is reached at the conclusion of each half-cycle of switching. When the power switch S3 flips off at the resonant frequency, the resonant circuit current decreases to this maximum magnetizing current and the power transfer to the output side is terminated. Following a dead-time delay, the converter reaches the primary ZVS condition and the power switch S2 activates with the same current.

The power transfer to the output side is halted when the converter operates below the resonant frequency, but the magnetizing current continues. This is because the resonant circuit current drops to the magnetizing current prior to the end of the power switch gate signal. ZVS is therefore still obtainable. Power switch conduction losses are decreased when the circulating current in the resonant circuit is smaller above the resonant frequency. Diodes on the secondary side commutate softly at and below the resonant frequency.

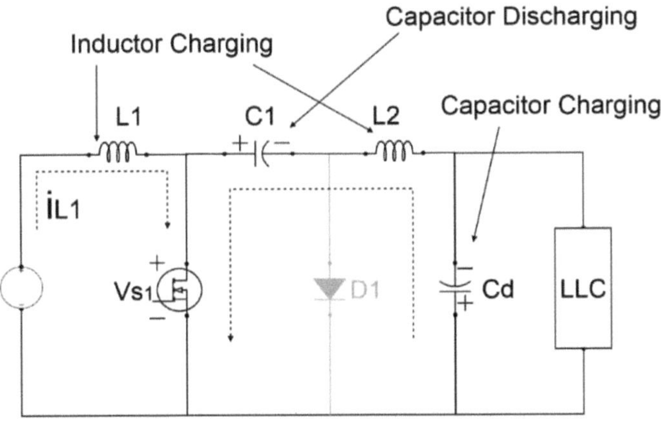

(a) Mode 1

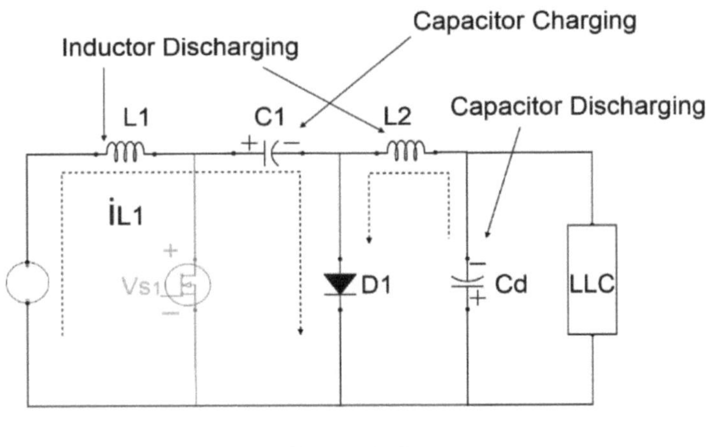

(b) Mode 2

Fig. 2. Operating modes of cuk converter

4 Simulation and Results

4.1 Simulation of Open Loop Cuk Converter

See (Fig. 4).

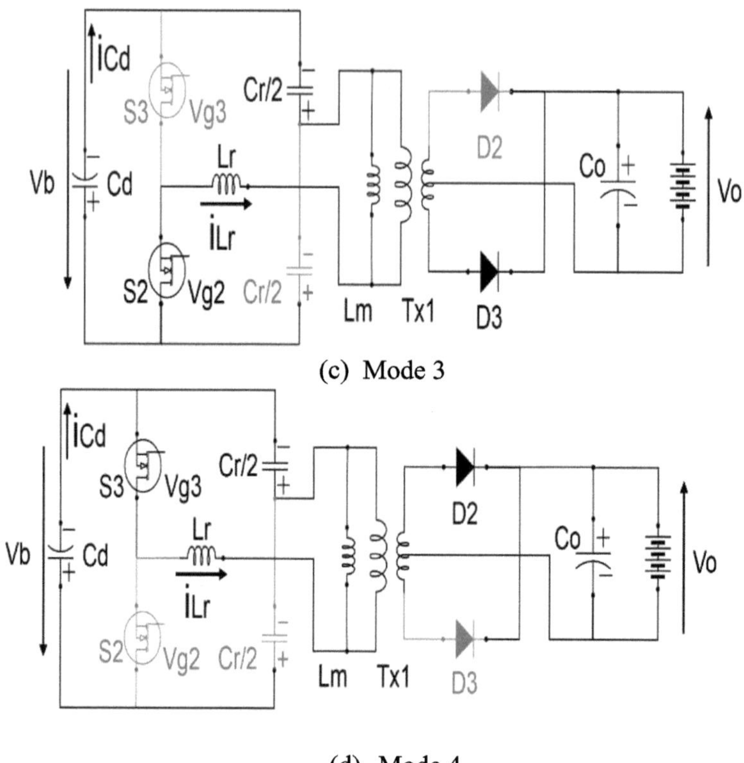

(c) Mode 3

(d) Mode 4

Fig. 3. Operating Modes of HB-LLC Resonant converter

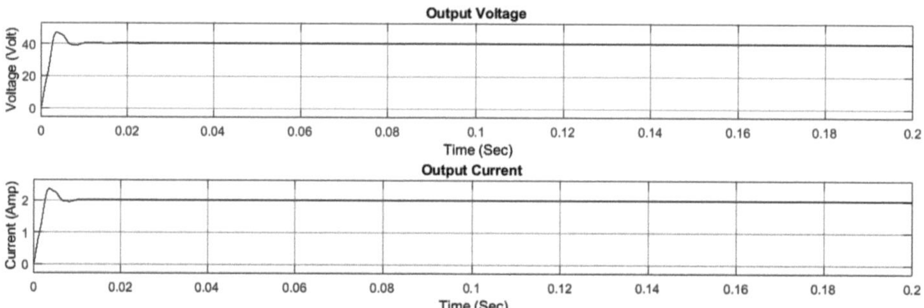

Fig. 4. Simulation results of open loop cuk converter output waveforms

4.2 Simulation of Closed Loop Cuk Converter

See Fig. 5.

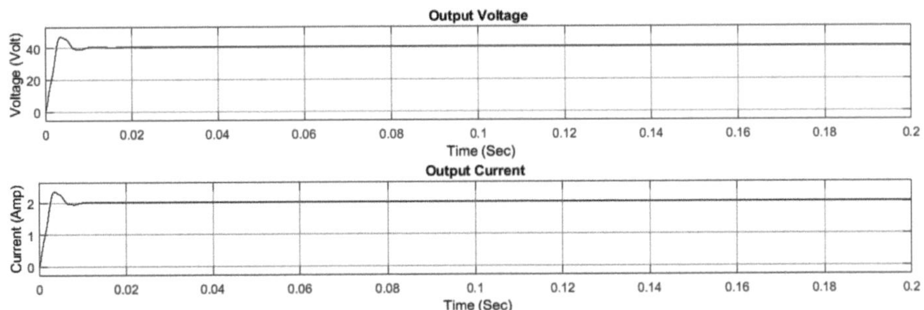

Fig. 5. Simulation results of closed loop cuk converter

4.3 Simulation of Cuk Converter Fed HB-LLC Resonant Converter with R Load in Open Loop

See Figs. 6 and 7.

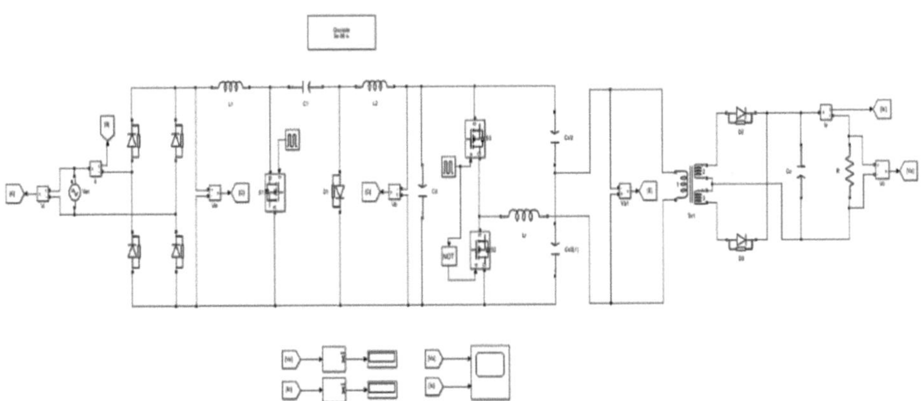

Fig. 6. Simulation of Cuk Converter Fed HB-LLC Resonant Converter with R Load in Open Loop

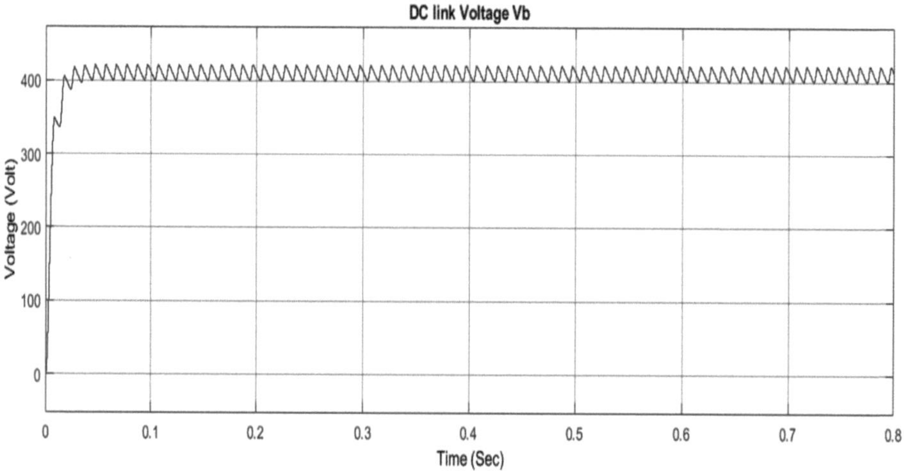

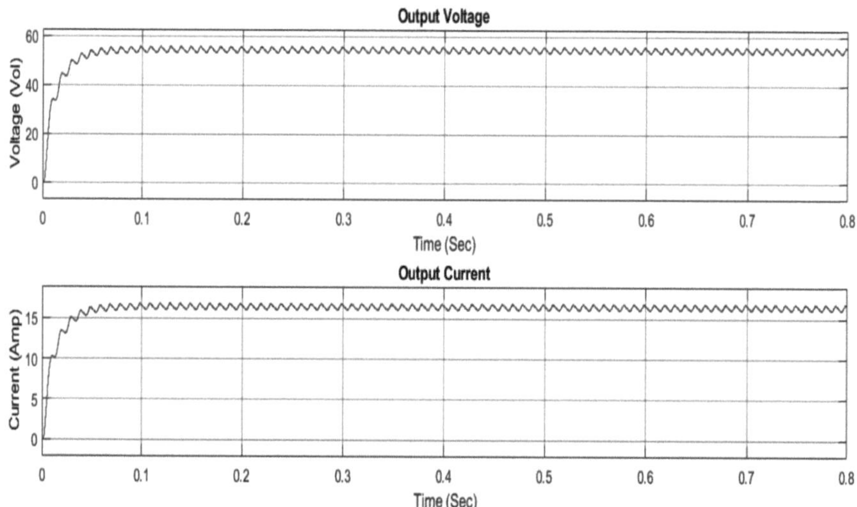

Fig. 7. Simulation result of Simulation of Cuk Converter Fed HB-LLC Resonant Converter with R Load in Open Loop

4.4 Simulation of Cuk Converter Fed HB-LLC Resonant Converter with R Load in Open Loop

See Figs. 8 and 9.

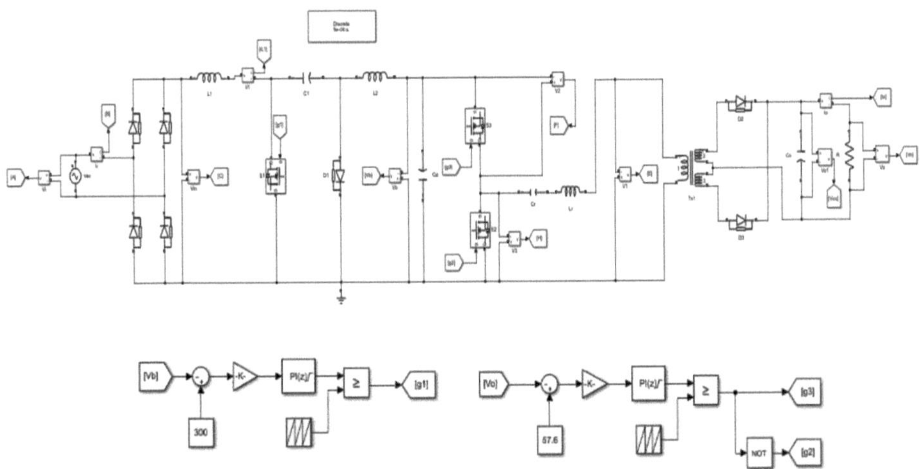

Fig. 8. Simulation of Cuk Converter Fed HB-LLC Resonant Converter with R Load in closed Loop

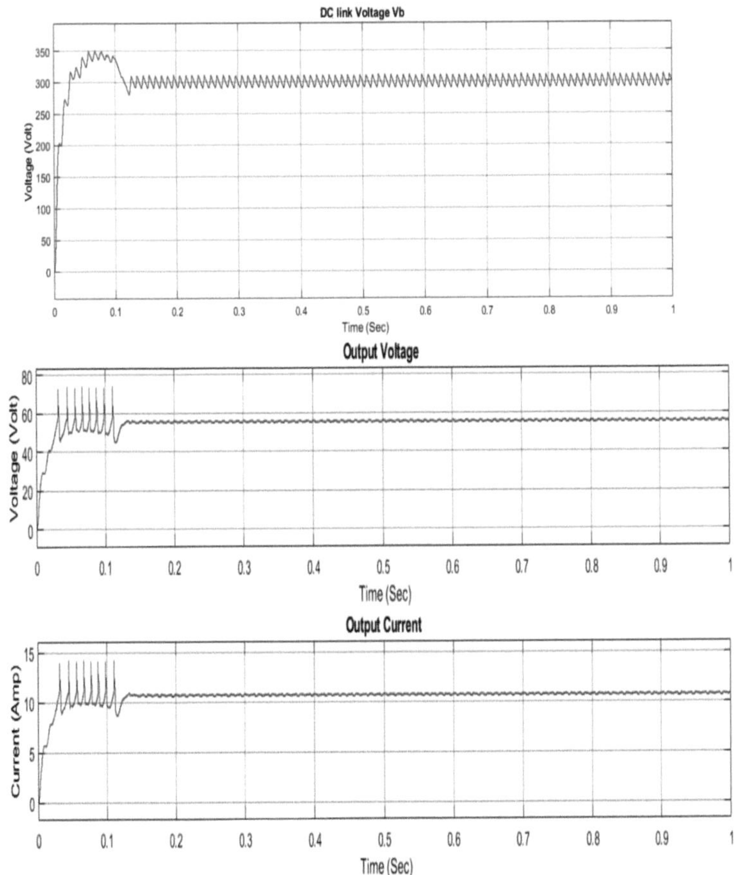

Fig. 9. Simulation results of Cuk Converter Fed HB-LLC Resonant Converter with R Load in closed Loop

5 Conclusion

For use with an electric vehicle battery charger (EVBC), a Cuk converter fed HB-LLC resonant converter has been developed. Results have been presented along with simulations of its performance and analysis. Through simulation, the suggested topology has been thoroughly examined in a steady state. There is minimal output voltage ripple as well. For battery charging applications, it is noted that the converter maintains a strictly regulated output voltage and exhibits good steady state response characteristics.

References

1. Radha, K., Singh, B.: A unity power factor converter with isolation for electric vehicle battery charger. In: 2018 IEEMA Engineer Infinite Conference (eTechNxT). IEEE (2018)
2. Bhim, S., Kushwaha, R.: EV battery charger with non-inverting output voltage-based bridgeless PFC Cuk converter. IET Power Electron. **12**(13), 3359–3368 (2019)
3. Radha, K., Singh, B.: A modified luo converter-based electric vehicle battery charger with power quality improvement. IEEE Trans. Transport. Electrification **5**(4), 1087–1096 (2019)
4. Bhim, S., Kushwaha, R.: A PFC based EV battery charger using a bridgeless isolated SEPIC converter. IEEE Trans. Ind. Appl. **56**(1), 477–487 (2019)
5. Khatab, A.M., Mostafa, I.M., Hadi, M.E.: An electric vehicle battery charger based on zeta converter fed from a PV array. In: 2018 IEEE International Conference on Environment and Electrical Engineering and 2018 IEEE Industrial and Commercial Power Systems Europe (EEEIC/I&CPS Europe). IEEE (2018)
6. Yildiran, N.: Design Methodology and Implementation of Half-Bridge LLC Resonant Converter. In: 2020 International Conference on Electrical, Communication, and Computer Engineering (ICECCE). IEEE (2020)
7. Harika, S., Seyezhai, R., Jawahar, A.: Investigation of DC Fast Charging Topologies for Electric Vehicle Charging Station (EVCS). TENCON 2019–2019 IEEE Region 10 Conference (TENCON). IEEE (2019)

Investigating the Effect of Compression on Face Recognition with OpenCV

Mallellu Sai Prashanth[1(✉)], Ramesh Karnati[1], Muni Sekhar Velpuru[2], H. Venkateshwara Reddy[1], and Charmi R. Jani[3]

[1] Department of Computer Science and Engineering, Vardhaman College of Engineering, Hyderabad, India
`saiprashanth08@ieee.org`
[2] Department of Information Technology, Vardhaman College of Engineering, Hyderabad, India
[3] RK University, Rajkot, Gujarat, India

Abstract. In the recent years have seen an increase in interest in computer vision. Recognition is now one of the more effective and successful uses of image analysis and algorithms, and it has evolved from a niche to a popular area of computer vision research. The system will develop an application that would grant user access to a specific machine based on a thorough analysis of a person's facial features due to widespread curiosity and interest in the subject. Python and OpenCV will be used in the development of this application. by using a face detection algorithm, which locates and acknowledges faces in images but does not identify them. I also like to extract the feature in an image that displays each face. In certain pipelines, face alignment has been shown to improve face recognition accuracy. An application that tracks and recognizes faces in cameras and videos and has multiple uses. The project aims to investigate face detection with an open CV in depth. Since OpenCV is C-based, it can be run on any device that supports C. It performs admirably under Linux, Mac OS X, and Windows. Compared to OpenCV, MATLAB is far more expensive. MATLAB is approximately \$2,150 while OpenCV is free. Due to its commercial, single-user license, even the basic version of Matlab is pricey. Furthermore, OpenCV is freely available due to its BSD license. Given that Java, which is derived from C, is the basis for MATLAB. As a result, when a script is run on MATLAB, the computer starts up by reading the code, translating it to Java, and then carrying out the script. Open CV, however, makes use of C/C++ library functions. Which aids in quicker execution by giving the computer the machine language code directly. When OpenCV is used, more time and resources are used for image processing and less for interpretation.

Keywords: Image · Face Detection · OpenCV · Computer Vision

1 Introduction

In the era of digital imagery, compression plays a vital role in reducing the storage requirements and transmission bandwidth of images. However, it is essential to understand the impact of compression on computer vision tasks to ensure reliable and accurate

X. Cheng (Ed): BROADNETS 2024, LNICST 602, pp. 79–88, 2025.
https://doi.org/10.1007/978-3-031-81171-5_8

results. One such critical task is face detection, which forms the basis for numerous applications like facial recognition, surveillance systems, and human-computer inter-action. This research paper aims to investigate the impact of compression on utilizing the open-source computer vision library OpenCV for face detection widely employed in academia and industry. The study delves into how different compression algorithms affect the accuracy and robustness of face detection algorithms and explores potential trade-offs between image compression and face detection performance [1].

The compression process, typically employed to reduce the file size of images, inherently involves the loss of certain image details. These lost details may include facial features crucial for face detection algorithms, thereby affecting their ability to detect and localize human faces accurately. Understanding the extent to which compression affects face detection performance is of paramount importance for real-world applications that heavily rely on this technology. To conduct this investigation, we employ OpenCV's face detection algorithms, which encompass various methodologies such as Haar cascades and deep learning-based techniques. These algorithms serve as a benchmark to evaluate the impact of compression on face detection accuracy. The study focuses on widely used compression algorithms such as JPEG, which offer adjustable compression levels that trade off image quality for reduced file size [2].

The experimental methodology involves systematically compressing a diverse set of facial images at different compression levels and subsequently subjecting them to face detection algorithms using OpenCV. The performance of the face detection algorithms on the compressed images is compared against that of the original, uncompressed images. Various evaluation metrics such as detection accuracy, speed, and robustness are analyzed to quantify the impact of compression on face detection. The findings of this research are expected to shed light on the relationship between image compression and face detection performance. By identifying the compression levels at which face detection algorithms start to exhibit degradation in accuracy and reliability, this study can provide valuable insights for optimizing compression settings in real-world applications. Additionally, the research aims to provide guidelines for practitioners and developers who utilize face detection in scenarios where image compression is a necessary consideration [3].

In conclusion, this research paper presents an investigation into the impact of com-pression on face detection using OpenCV. Through a systematic evaluation of various compression algorithms and their effect on face detection performance, this study aims to contribute to the understanding of the trade-offs and considerations when employ-ing image compression in face detection applications. The results and insights obtained from this research will pave the way for improved utilization of face detection algo-rithms in compressed image scenarios, enabling more efficient and reliable computer vision systems [4].

2   Related Work

Image compression algorithms, such as JPEG and JPEG2000, aim to reduce file sizes by exploiting redundancies in pixel data. JPEG, for instance, utilizes lossy compression that discards certain image details to achieve higher compression ratios. Familiarizing ourselves with different compression algorithms' characteristics is crucial to assess their impact on face detection [5].

Several studies have explored the influence of image compression on face detection accuracy. Research has shown that high compression ratios, particularly with lossy compression like JPEG, lead to increased false positives and reduced accuracy. It is important to understand how compression affects the performance of face detection algorithms [6].

Deep learning-based face detection algorithms have demonstrated remarkable accuracy and robustness. Research has examined the performance of these algorithms, such as SSD and YOLO, under different compression settings. The findings suggest that while deep learning-based methods generally outperform traditional approaches, they are still sensitive to high compression, resulting in degraded detection performance [6].

Transfer learning has emerged as a powerful technique in deep learning to address data scarcity. Some studies have explored the potential of training face detectors on compressed images and subsequently testing on uncompressed data. The research suggests that transfer learning from compressed images can mitigate the negative impact of compression on face detection performance. However, the effectiveness of this approach varies depending on the compression method and ratio [7].

To improve face detection accuracy on compressed images, researchers have proposed adaptation and enhancement techniques. Pre-processing methods, such as image enhancement and contrast normalization before applying face detection algorithms, have shown promising results. These techniques can help alleviate the impact of compression, although their effectiveness may depend on the specific compression method employed [8].

Understanding the impact of compression on face detection is crucial for real-world applications where images undergo compression during storage or transmission. Research has investigated the performance of face detection systems in surveillance scenarios where compressed video feeds are prevalent. The studies emphasize the need for robust face detection algorithms capable of handling the challenges posed by image compression in practical applications [9].

The literature survey reveals that image compression significantly affects the performance of face detection algorithms. Both traditional and deep learning-based approaches are impacted by compression, with deep learning methods showing better resilience to moderate compression levels. Transfer learning and adaptation techniques have shown promise in improving face detection accuracy on compressed images. However, further research is needed to address the complexities introduced by different compression methods and ratios [10].

3 Proposed Model

Architecture Diagram (Fig. 1):

The suggested setup is Using the MUHULANOBIC metric, faces existing in the complex background can be detected. Its foundation is the analysis of faces in two-dimensional photos of real-world scenes. It clearly utilizes the color segmentation procedure of the image being used as input. Thresholding the image in the hue color space is how the color is being segmented. This includes the effects of variations in the image's illumination on the uniqueness of the hue of human skin. After then, the image's results are combined for further analysis. The final step is to apply a restricted number of

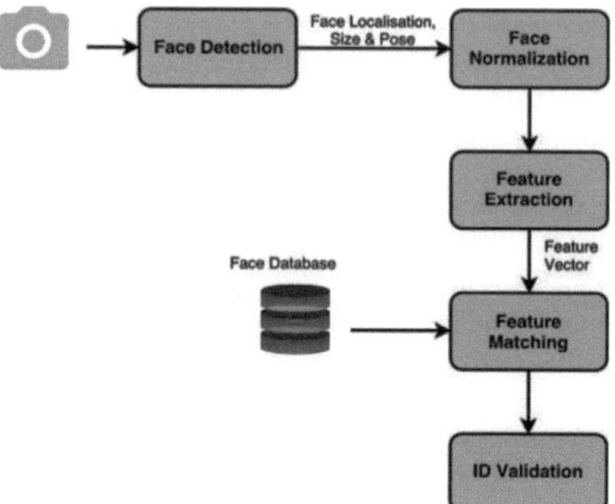

Fig. 1. Basic Architecture Diagram of proposed system

pixel accumulations to the median filter the resulting image. Ultimately, a multi-layer perceptron neural network is employed using the invariant moments as an input to distinguish between the faces and the remaining complicated backdrop. Three fundamental processes are involved in face recognition: face extraction, face recognition, and face detection. For any system to identify the position of the face, it must first encapsulate the image and then manage and record the essential elements. It records a number of variables, including skin tone and color, in order to identify the taken image. When an image from a camera or video is fed into face recognition software, the recognized image topic is produced as the output. Face cuts, structured and stylized angles, and different facial regions can all be considered facial features. Getting the features out of the camera is a face extraction process. Face detection involves removing the background and concentrating on the foreground, eliminating any other elements outside of the face region. Despite this, the system still has some limitations because it is unable to detect the head count, which could be caused by false positives for two faces with similar facial features or by overlapping faces. In a publication, Hussell Hardy suggests implementing face recognition using principal component analysis with four distance classifiers (Figs. 2 and 3).

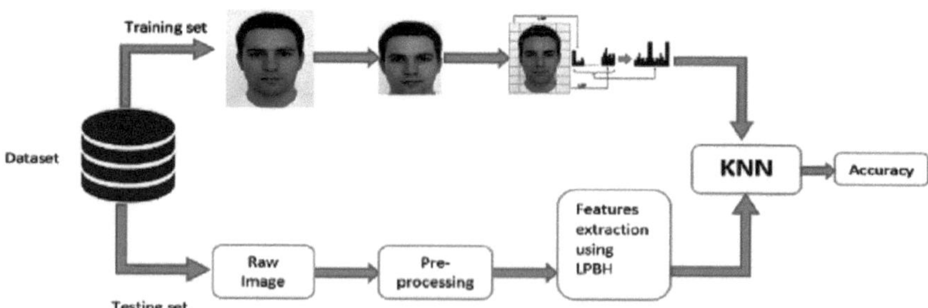

Fig. 2. Demonstrating Image JPEG Compression module

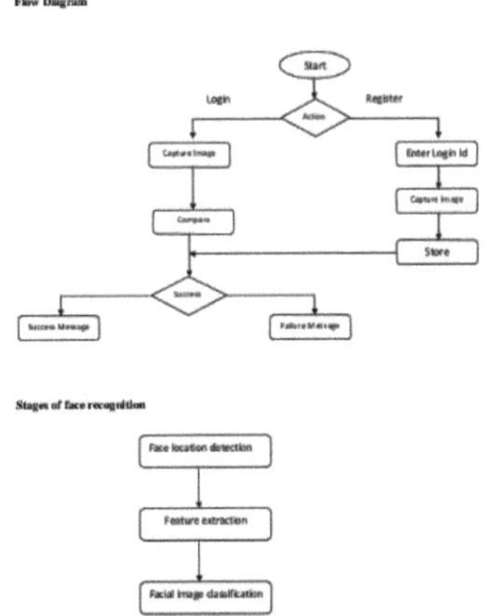

Fig. 3. Flow Chart Diagram of Image Detection using OpenCv

An image segementation, where users can perform for application, during registration process, we gather all the required information from users. To validate the users image, we are sending a verification token to the system, unless user verifies, he/she cannot login into web portal. After verification, users may login at any time. Portal consists of all the information like about our product, documentation and application to download.

Internal Images Concept

24 × 24 base window size, that would mean that this window would calculate over 180,000 features. Considering evaluating the difference in pixels for each feature. The Integral Image concept has been proposed as the solution for this computationally demanding process. Since the image is integral, all we need to know is the values of the four corners to find the total number of pixels under each rectangle. This means we do not need to add up each pixel by hand for us to calculate the sum of pixels in any feature window. All we have to do is use the four corner values to calculate the integral image. The following example will provide transparency for the process (Fig. 4).

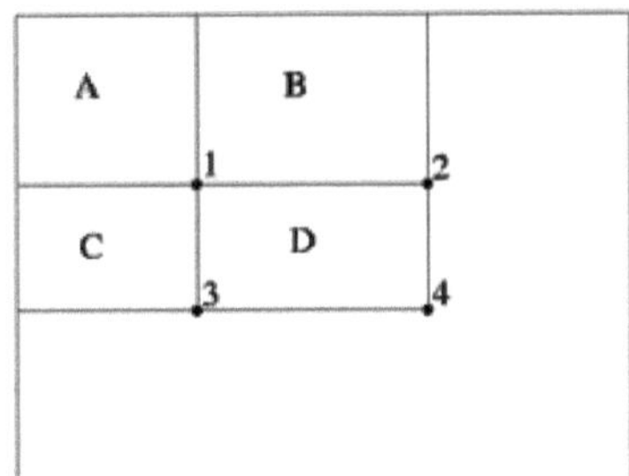

Fig. 4. Basic flow Diagram of Internal Image

We have developed application, compatible only for windows OS and implemented on different files varying from 1 mb to 30 mb of file size. Timing for image recognition as well as detection of such file are noted and compared with the respective recognition and detection timings of same files using Image Internals. As we are focusing only on security and not on timing as of now, we would like to work further on timing along with adding some more normalization techniques.

Explanation of Image Compression Functions
More than 13,000 face photos gathered from the internet are included in the Labelled Faces in the Wild Database set. Of these .jpg photos, 431 were arbitrarily chosen, and their average quality factor was 75. The majority of these pictures depict people's motivations during speeches or events. The images have varying resolutions, ranging from 233 × 409 to 410 × 450 pixels. There are multiple faces among the motives in this data set of images. This means that at high compression ratios, there's a good chance small faces won't be detected.

4 Results

See (Figs. 5, 6 and 7).

Fig. 5. No Image Detection for Preprocessing and No Normalization till 135 degress

Fig. 6. Multiple Image Detection

Fig. 7. Final Image Detection

4.1 Result Analysis

See (Figs. 8 and 9).

Existing Method	Proposed Method
Unknown faces cannot be classified with sufficient confidence	Unknown faces to the known classified with sufficient confidence
Compute 512-d face embeddings to quantify a face	Compute 128-d face embeddings to quantify a face
Automatic License Plate Recognition	Support Vector Machine for facial Recognization
Clustering, Representation and Classification	Clustering, Representation, Classification and Facial embedding
Facial landmarks	Facial landmarks with rotation and scaling
No Accuracy	Applied face alignment and cropping

Fig. 8. Comparision Analysis of Proposed Method & Existing Method

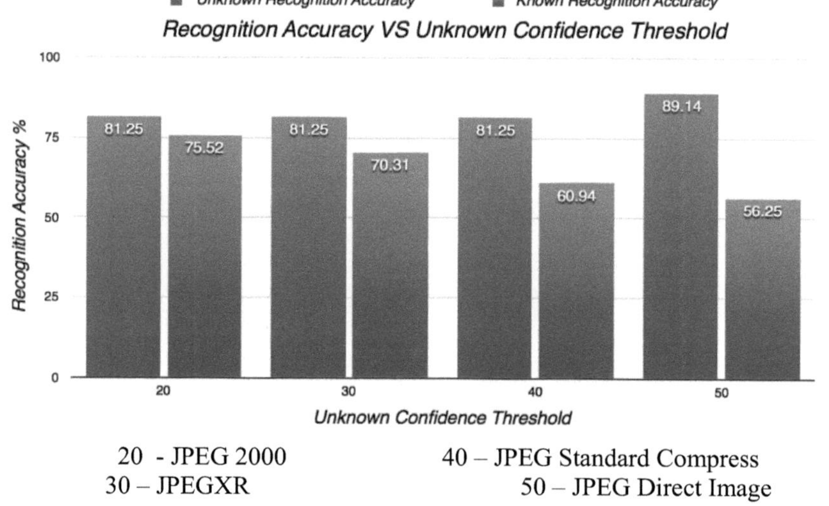

20 - JPEG 2000   40 – JPEG Standard Compress
30 – JPEGXR   50 – JPEG Direct Image

Fig. 9. Different Compression Standards

5 Conclusion

After studying different Image detection schemes, we get to know the pros and cons of each and possible attacks on each type. It turns out that, when comparing the similarity of the results obtained on pre-compressed and non-pre-compressed datasets, a small amount of JPEG precompression has no effect on the performance and ranking of the three compression methods. We have Made the Execution on the Open Cv Algorithm and produce the results at end. Prediction of the better Image Compression Performance using the Predicted values. Created a Python script to assist in collecting labeled faces. In the context of face detection using sets of Haar-like features, our experiment shows that JPEG XR and JPEG2000 outperform JPEG, particularly when the images are compressed at high ratios. JPEG XR is a good substitute for JPEG2000 in all circumstances because of the noticeably lower computational demand and marginally better face detection results. We present $\pm$ one standard deviation along with the mean values, confirming the first observation, in order to highlight the distinctions between JPEG XR and JPEG 2000. If we look at the relationship between PSNR and detection accuracy, we find that JPEG is correctly predicted by its PSNR values to be the worst algorithm; on the other hand, the small benefits of JPEG XR over JPEG 2000 are not correctly predicted by PSNR. Furthermore, when comparing the similarity of the results obtained on pre-compressed and non-pre-compressed datasets, it has been found that a small amount of JPEG precompression has no effect on the performance and ranking of the three compression algorithms.

Future Scope

The development of face detection technology is only getting started; there are a plethora of further uses for this technology. The different concepts are:It might be used in taxis operated by nighttime drivers. An algorithm can be set up so that if the driver blinks their eyes for longer than five seconds, the car's alarm system may sound, alerting everyone to the driver's drowsiness. Although it might not be able to completely eliminate the accident rates caused by this, it might be able to lower them. While adults who find themselves lost can return home, what about children who are lost, abducted to work as slaves, or even worse, where there are fears that the young females are being exploited as prostitution, Hundreds of lives could be spared from torture by producing a severe version of these faces and applying face identification algorithms. Regardless of the station—airport or metro—it can be utilized there. We may potentially lower the crime rate if face detection technology were installed at the entryway to every station and compared with the worldwide list of wanted individuals from every police agency.

References

1. Huang, G.B., Ramesh, M., Berg, T., Learned-Miller, E.: Labeled Faces in the Wild: A Database for Studying Face Recognition in Unconstrained Environments, pp. 07–49. University of Massachusetts, Amherst (2007)
2. Viola, P., Jones, M.: Rapid object detection using a boosted cascade of simple features. In: Proceedings of the 2001 IEEE Computer Society Conference on Computer Vision and Pattern Recognition. CVPR 2001, vol. 1, pp. I-511–I-518 (2001)
3. Wallace, G.K.: The JPEG still picture compression standard. IEEE Trans. Consum. Electron. **38**(1), 18–34 (1992)
4. Rakshit, S., Monro, D.M.: An evaluation of image sampling and compression for human iris recognition. IEEE Trans. Inf. Forensics Secur. **2**(3), 605–612 (2007)
5. Zhuang, S.-S., Lai, S.-H.: Face detection directly from h.264 compressed video with convolutional neural network. In: Proceedings of the IEEE International Conference on Image Processing, ICIP 2009, pp. 2485–2488 (2009)
6. Hämmerle-Uhl, J., Karnutsch, M., Uhl, A.: Evolutionary optimisation of JPEG2000 part 2 wavelet packet structures for polar iris image compression. In: Ruiz-Shulcloper, J., Sanniti di Baja, G. (eds.) CIARP 2013, Part I. LNCS, vol. 8258, pp. 391–398. Springer, Heidelberg (2013)

7. Goyal, K., Agarwal, K., Kumar, R.: Face detection and tracking: Using OpenCV. In: 2017 International conference of Electronics, Communication and Aerospace Technology (ICECA), Coimbatore, India, pp. 474-478 (2017). https://doi.org/10.1109/ICECA.2017.820 3730

8. Saini, N., Kaur, S., Singh, H.: A review: face detection methods and algorithms. Int. J. Eng. Res. Technol. **2**(6) (2013). www.ijert.org

9. Kirby, M., Sirovich, L.: Application of the Karhunen-Loeve procedure for the characterization of human faces. IEEE Trans. Pattern Anal. Machine Intell. **12**(1), 103–108 (1990)

10. Chen, D.-S., Liu, Z.-K.: Generalized haar-like features for fast face detection. In: Conference on Machine Learning and Cybernetics, 2007. Hong Kong, pp. 2131–2135 (2011)

Artificial Intelligence Research in Computer Network Technology

Jhansi Bharathi Madavarapu[1]($\boxtimes$) , Arnold Mashud Abukari[2], Shailaja Salagrama[1],
and Radha Krishna Yalamanchili[3]

[1] Department of Information Technology, University of the Cumberland's, Williamsburg,
KY 40769, USA
jhansimadavarapu@gmail.com
[2] Department of Computer Science, Tamale Technical University, Tamal, Ghana
amashud@tatu.edu.gh
[3] Department of Computer Science, Governor's State University, University Park , IL 60484,
USA

Abstract. The development of AI has witnessed significant advancements over the years; from rule-based systems to deep neural networks, AI has become more sophisticated in understanding and processing data. This progress has paved the way for various applications across different fields in the national economy. All the countries create new requirements simultaneously for developing high-tech technology due to the country's ongoing economic growth. The concept of "artificial intelligence" emerged in light of this social setting. Artificial Intelligence has improved our environment, changed our lives in ways never seen before, and made using computer networks more convenient. The demands of the general public are also continually evolving, and individuals are starting to look for a better quality of life. Computer network technology is a type of high-tech, novel technology that has slowly crept into our daily lives and evolved into a sophisticated industry in the modern period. It has also significantly impacted computer network technology, offering a fresh path for innovation and advancement. It discusses artificial Intelligence and analyzes its application in classification and identification services, network security, and computer network management for future research into the creation and use of AI in computer network technology. Artificial Intelligence can effectively address the issue and propose solutions following the relevant data issues, allowing for fast handling of all types of data information. This essay explores the use and importance of Artificial Intelligence in big data, focusing on how it is applied in computer networks.

Keywords: Security · Application of Artificial Intelligence · Computer Network System Management · network monitoring · network security · network optimization · predictive maintenance

© ICST Institute for Computer Sciences, Social Informatics and Telecommunications Engineering 2025
Published by Springer Nature Switzerland AG 2025. All Rights Reserved
X. Cheng (Ed): BROADNETS 2024, LNICST 602, pp. 89–95, 2025.
https://doi.org/10.1007/978-3-031-81171-5_9

1 Introduction

The Dartmouth Society's first proposal for the word "Artificial Intelligence (AI)" was in 1956. Artificial Intelligence mainly refers to the Intelligence exhibited by human-made robots that can observe, mimic, and evaluate human behavior [1]. AI is a field of computer science that seeks to comprehend the nature of Intelligence and build a machine with Intelligence that functions similarly to humans. Computers are currently a significant tool for researching the advancement of Artificial Intelligence.

AI's main problems are planning, learning, communication, tool use, and creating knowledge comparable to or even more significant than human understanding. As the economic status of every nation has improved, computer network technology has also become increasingly prevalent in daily life. Artificial Intelligence refers to the machine that academics think will be able to perform the complex and hazardous tasks that people perform with robots. This machine can both fast increase productivity and safeguard people's interests. The primary abilities of Artificial Intelligence are strong reasoning, language communication, operation, and recognition; these abilities are also continuously evolving in tandem with the advancement of technology.

Artificial Intelligence in computer network technology, a recent innovation in society, also improves people's quality of life. Its goal is to mimic human thought processes, behavior, and Intelligence to assist individuals in completing more laborious, repetitive tasks or more challenging, high-precision jobs [2].

Financial data computing, for instance, uses artificial intelligence technology to compute financial data correctly and efficiently. This helps financial staff by reducing their workload significantly. Artificial intelligence technology is becoming increasingly prevalent in computer networks, where it plays a critical role. It has garnered significant attention from people from all walks of life and is crucial in many facets of life by advancing social education.

Artificial Intelligence can effectively address this issue and propose solutions following the relevant data issues, allowing for fast handling of all types of data information. This essay explores the use and importance of Artificial Intelligence, focusing on how it is applied in computer networks [3].

Artificial Intelligence based on big data has made life much more accessible for people thanks to the in-depth development of computers. This technology not only speeds up the distribution of information in contemporary society but also offers crucial support for the steady growth of society. The foundation of artificial intelligence vision is information and communication technologies—the data processing method in the modern information age.

2 Concept of AI and Computer Network Technology

The terms "artificial" and "intelligence" can be used to separate the definition of artificial Intelligence. It is easier to understand "artificial" since it refers to an artificial system in the traditional sense. The term "intelligence" has many definitions, but "research human intelligent activities" is the more widely accepted definition in the field. This definition encompasses concepts like consciousness, the self, and thinking. Artificial Intelligence is a new technology for technical science research, simulation development, and extension of human intelligence theory, methods, and application systems. It is a subfield of computer science, sometimes called mechanical Intelligence. By enabling computers to mimic human audio-visual speech, specific thought processes, and intelligent behaviors, artificial Intelligence aims to Put it another way by incorporating knowledge about people's consciousness and thought processes into a machine; it is possible to imbue it with human wisdom and replace humans in high-risk, challenging, and complex tasks.

Almost all natural and social science fields, whose purview lies outside computer science, can be said to have this characteristic. Thinking science and artificial Intelligence are related as practice and theory are related. Thinking science applies technology, and Artificial Intelligence is a subset of that application. The advancement of artificial Intelligence is intimately related to Artificial Intelligence. It will immediately benefit from the route that computer network technology takes in its growth. Artificial Intelligence will also enable computers to move beyond basic digital processing to knowledge processing. It has been entirely changed by computer network technology. Networks run and maintain network security and optimization due to machine learning algorithms and data analytics developments.

This section will examine how AI changes computer networks and the range of applications it enables, including improved network security and intelligent routing algorithms. Artificial Intelligence (AI) has become a revolutionary idea within the quickly developing field of computer network technology [4, 10].

3 Applications of AI in CNT

Artificial Intelligence (AI) has transformed computer network system management like many other businesses. This part will examine the many AI applications for managing computer network systems.

3.1 Real-Time Network Traffic Monitoring

Anomaly detection and network performance analysis are all possible with AI-powered solutions. These technologies use Machine learning algorithms to identify trends and anticipate future problems before they arise. In order to spot trends and provide proactive recommendations for improving network performance, they can also study past data.

3.2 Security Management

Advanced security measures in computer networks are necessary due to the complexity of cyber threats. AI can significantly improve security management by identifying and thwarting prospective intrusions. AI systems can analyze network traffic.

3.3 Network Optimization

AI algorithms can improve load balancing, among other network characteristics. AI systems ensure the best possible use of resources by dynamically modifying these settings while continuously evaluating network performance.

3.4 Network Capacity Planning

AI can help with capacity planning by examining previous network usage and trends data. Future network demands can be predicted, allowing businesses to deploy resources wisely and prevent bottlenecks.

3.5 Virtual Assistant for Network Management

AI-powered virtual assistants are gaining popularity for effectively managing computer networks. These assistants give users up-to-the-minute gadget status updates, solve typical problems, and perform ordinary tasks in response to user inputs or predefined rules.

3.6 Intelligent Routing

By dynamically altering routing patterns based on real-time situations such as congestion or link failures, AI-based routing algorithms can improve data flow within a computer network. This enhances everything.

3.7 Predictive Maintenance

AI systems can forecast upcoming hardware or software issues using data from various sources inside a computer network. AI systems can predict problems before they substantially impact by monitoring key performance indicators (KPIs), including CPU usage, memory utilization, and disk space availability.

3.8 Network Automation

AI makes it possible to automate the management of computer networks, lowering the need for manual intervention and boosting productivity. Tools with AI capabilities can automate processes like device provisioning, configuration management, and troubleshooting [4].

4 Developing an AI Framework

Information Technology cannot meet today's demanding network requirements without the proper AI strategy. The following are some technological components that every AI strategy ought to have.

4.1 Artificial Intelligence for Networking

The virtual network assistant in artificial Intelligence for networking may operate in a wireless environment as a virtual wireless expert who assists in resolving challenging issues. Imagine a virtual network assistant that uses domain knowledge, high-quality data, and syntax to deliver actionable insights on resolving current problems and predictive advice on preventing future ones.

5 Advancement of AI on CNT in the Big Data Era

5.1 AI Contributes to Computer System Security

Firewalls are the primary example of artificial Intelligence in computer network security. According to the current state of computer security technology, AI firewall security is superior to and more effective than firewall security provided by computer network technology [5, 9]. In order to protect the security of the computer system and streamline the processing of a variety of big data information, the artificial intelligence firewall also has discrimination technology to analyze and filter different data information.

5.2 AI Management's Function in Computer Networks

The artificial intelligence agent, a piece of physical software, uses artificial Intelligence to gather, examine, and process all kinds of data and information. It also relies on its knowledge base for scientific classification. Artificial software, such as an agent, can only comprise knowledge and databases under certain conditions. AI agent management can transfer data to a computer's designated location based on the needs, make it easier for users to search and search, and offer more intelligent management services [6, 7].

The computer network management system should further support the growth and advancement of telecom and artificial intelligence technology to realize artificial Intelligence against the backdrop of big data [8, 10]. Intelligent technology can lessen the complexity of managing the entire network [3, 11]. As a result, in such a setting, it can actively and effectively enhance the overall network's effectiveness and quality, strengthening network intelligent management [12–14].

6 Conclusion and Future Study

The fundamental ideas and uses of AI are presented in this paper. Technology with Artificial Intelligence is demonstrating its benefits and is crucial to human advancement. Artificial intelligence technology is expected to grow progressively over a wide range of undeveloped industries. People's lives now involve artificial Intelligence in every way. More chances and innovation for the advancement of computer network technology are made possible by the broad development and use of AI technology in numerous industries.

Artificial Intelligence has presented computer network technology with previously unheard-of difficulties and obstacles; therefore, it must continuously increase its capacity for innovation. The only way to advance computer network technology and social science and technology is to utilize artificial Intelligence effectively. To put it succinctly, as global science and technology continue to advance, so too does artificial intelligence technology, whose range of applications in daily life and industry is growing and which contributes significantly to the advancement of computer network technology that makes it possible for diverse fields to naturally combine and create continually improved applied technology, which enhances computer network security and improves user experience. Since the development of AI, individuals have had access to more critical and practical knowledge. It can only benefit the sustainable growth of human output by fully utilizing AI technology to unlock the potential of big data and elevate human social productivity to unprecedented heights.

As a result, researching how computer networks are used in artificial Intelligence allows us to investigate the wide range of potential applications for artificial technology in the future. New technology plays a significant and direct role in advancing the advancement of human society. AI technology is crucial for research because it will be a substantial auxiliary value in future developments. However, it is equally important to remember that technology is limited in its capabilities. It must establish acceptable principles and work to ensure that it develops safely and effectively to guarantee its development. Artificial Intelligence is a cutting-edge computer technology that advances society. Artificial intelligence technology can improve people's lifestyles and quality of life while advancing science and technology. In order to better support the development of human society, recognize the benefits of and use it to optimize the processing of all types of network information.

References

1. Li, Y.: The application and existing problems of artificial intelligence technology to computer network technology. Satell. TV Broadband Multimedia **24**, 48–49 (2019)
2. Madavarapu, J.: Electronic Data Interchange Analysts Strategies to Improve Information Security While Using EDI in Healthcare Organizations. Available from ProQuest Dissertations & Theses Global. (2832638159) (2023). https://www.proquest.com/dissertations-theses/electronic-data-interchange-analysts-strategies/docview/2832638159/se-2
3. Tao, Y.: Exploring the application of ai in computer network technology. Comput. Product. Circ. **01**, 40–41 (2020)
4. Madavarapu, J.B., Mohammed, F.H., Salagrama, S., Bibhu, V.: Secure virtual local area network design and implementation for electronic data interchange. Int. J. Adv. Comput. Sci. Appl. (2023). https://doi.org/10.14569/IJACSA.2023.0140701
5. Islam, H., Madavarapu, J.B., Sarker, N.K., Rahman, A.: The effects of cyber threats and technical problems on customer's attitude towards e-banking services. Oblìk ì fìnansi **2**(96), 58–67 (2022). https://doi.org/10.33146/2307-9878-2022-2(96)-58-67
6. Madavarapu, J.B., Yalamanchili, R.K., Mandhala, V.N.: An ensemble data security on cloud healthcare systems. In: 2023 4th International Conference on Smart Electronics and Communication (ICOSEC), pp. 680–686. Trichy, India (2023). https://doi.org/10.1109/ICOSEC58147.2023.10276231
7. Madavarapu, J.B.: Payroll Management System. All Capstone Projects. **82** (2014). https://opus.govst.edu/capstones/82
8. Yalamanchili, R.K.: International Student Portal. All Capstone Projects **85** (2014). https://opus.govst.edu/capstones/85
9. Madavarapu, J.B.: Electronic Data Interchange on Blockchain. Int. J. Manag. IT Eng. **13**(7) (2023)
10. Zhan, X., Wang, X.: The application of artificial intelligence in computer network technology in the big data era. Technol. Innov. Appl. **33**, 168–169 (2020)
11. Sui, Z.: Exploring the application of AI in computer network technology. Sci. Technol. Innov. **26**, 84–85 (2019)
12. Wang, J., Shen, K.: The application analysis of artificial intelligence in computer network technology. Electronic Test (09), 70 + 61 (2017)

13. Gao, T.: The application of artificial intelligence in computer network technology in the big data era. Electron. Technol. Softw. Eng. (01), 6 (2019)
14. Xiao, C., Qi, Z., Li, W.: The application of computer network technology in electronic information engineering. Comput. Product. Circul. (12), 45 (2019)

WSafe – A Women Safety Android Application

Sai Prasad Reddy Kukudala[1], Gururaj L. Kulkarni[1(✉)] ⓘ, Kandur Keerthi[1],
Pavan N. Kunchur[2] ⓘ, and Gangireddy Nitish Kumar Reddy[1]

[1] Department of Computer Science and Engineering, Vardhaman College of Engineering
(Autonomous), Hyderabad, India
`gururajlkulkarni@gmail.com`
[2] Department of Computer Science and Engineering, KLS Gogte Institute of Technology
(Autonomous), Belagavi, India
`pnkunchur@git.edu`

Abstract. "W Safe – A Women Safety Application" is a groundbreaking mobile application developed with the primary objective of ensuring the safety and well-being of women in today's society. This innovative digital platform is designed to provide women with accessible and effective tools to bolster their personal security and empower them to navigate the world with confidence. Existing safety measures and resources are often fragmented and lack integration, making it challenging for women to access timely assistance in emergencies. Additionally, the lack of awareness about women's safety laws and self-defense techniques further exacerbates the problem. Therefore, there is a critical need for a comprehensive women safety application that leverages the power of technology to provide women with a reliable and user-friendly tool for immediate help, information, and empowerment. By harnessing technology, knowledge, community, and advocacy, this application strives to create environments where women can live free from fear and violence, ultimately working towards a world in which every woman can lead a life of security and empowerment. This work aims to develop such an application, to address the multifaceted challenges faced by women in terms of safety and security.

Keywords: Emergency Assistance · Women's Safety Laws · Comprehensive
App · Security and Empowerment

1 Introduction

In an era defined by technological advancement, it is imperative that we leverage the power of innovation to address the pressing concerns of society. Among these concerns, ensuring the safety and well-being of women stands as a paramount challenge [2]. To meet this challenge, the groundbreaking mobile application "W Safe – A Women Safety Application" has emerged, with the primary objective of equipping women with accessible and effective tools to bolster their personal security and navigate the world with confidence. Women's safety has long been a global concern, with existing safety

X. Cheng (Ed): BROADNETS 2024, LNICST 602, pp. 96–103, 2025.
https://doi.org/10.1007/978-3-031-81171-5_10

measures and resources often fragmented and lacking integration. This fragmentation hinders the ability of women to access timely assistance in emergencies and exacerbates the prevailing issues surrounding women's safety [1, 4].

By harnessing the power of technology, knowledge, community, and advocacy, "W Safe" aims to create environments where women can live free from fear and violence, ultimately working towards a world in which every woman can lead a life of security and empowerment. The core of this project revolves around the development of an application that employs Android Studio, Java, and XML as its building blocks. Through these technologies, the application seeks to provide immediate help, information, and empowerment to women in need, furthering the cause of their safety and security [5, 7]. This research paper will delve into the intricate details of the "W Safe" application, exploring its features, functionalities, and the broader implications it holds for women's safety in contemporary society.

By examining the development and impact of "W Safe," this research paper aims to shed light on the potential of technology to reshape the landscape of women's safety and empowerment [1]. As we delve into the intricacies of this comprehensive women safety application, we will uncover the multifaceted approach it employs, and the possibilities it opens for women to not only protect themselves but also to thrive in a world free from fear and violence. This research paper also seeks to address the broader societal implications of a comprehensive women safety application like "W Safe." In an age where the integration of technology into our daily lives is inevitable, it is crucial to understand how such innovations can reshape the dynamics of gender equality and security [6]. By bridging the gap between women and the timely assistance they require, by imparting knowledge about safety laws and self-defense techniques, and by fostering a supportive community and advocacy, "W Safe" represents a model that could pave the way for a more secure, inclusive, and empowered future for women. The findings and insights derived from this research endeavor promise not only to shed light on the promising potential of "W Safe" but also to contribute to the larger discourse on leveraging technology for the betterment of society.

2 Literature Survey

This paper explores the pressing need for women safety applications, focusing on "W Safe – A Women Safety Application" as a groundbreaking initiative. The paper examines the current challenges women face in terms of safety and security, discusses the potential benefits of technology-driven solutions, and presents a comprehensive review of existing literature in this domain. The safety and well-being of women in today's society are paramount concerns [1]. Addressing these concerns, "W Safe" is introduced as an innovative mobile application that aims to empower women and enhance their personal security. Existing safety measures and resources are often fragmented, making timely assistance difficult to access, while a lack of awareness about women's safety laws and self-defense techniques exacerbates the problem [3, 5]. This literature survey seeks to explore the landscape of women safety applications, their potential impact, and the existing research in this field.

To understand the need for women safety applications, it is crucial to identify the challenges women face daily. These challenges include physical safety concerns, lack of awareness about their rights, and limited access to timely assistance during emergencies [2, 5]. Existing literature documents these challenges, emphasizing the urgency of addressing them through technological solutions. Technology has become a powerful tool for addressing safety concerns. Mobile applications can provide women with accessible and effective tools to bolster their personal security [7]. This section reviews the role of technology in empowering women, citing relevant research that highlights its effectiveness in enhancing personal safety and building confidence.

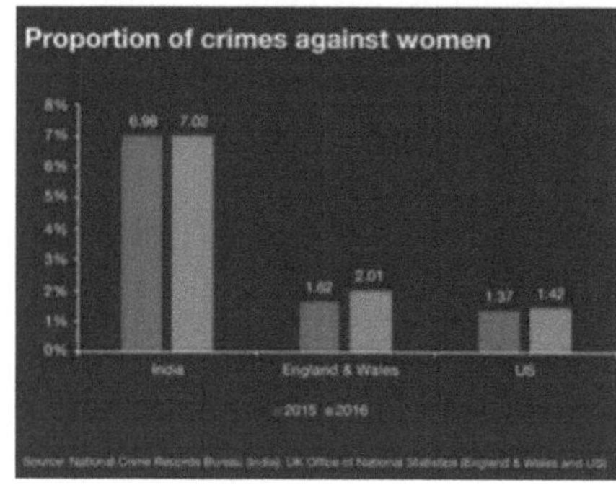

Fig. 1. Statistics of international crime records.

Fig. 2. Survey of countries on women crime

According to alarming statistics depicted in Fig. 1, a woman is subjected to rape in India approximately every 16 min, while incidents of cruelty by in-laws occur every four minutes.

In 2016, the country documented an average of 88 cases of rape daily. Out of the total 32,033 reported rape cases that year, 8% were reported within the Dalit community.

In Fig. 2, the highest number of cases categorized under crimes against women in the Indian Penal Code were reported as 'Cruelty by Husband or His Relatives' (30.9%), followed by 'Assault on Women with Intent to Outrage her Modesty' (21.8%), 'Kidnapping & Abduction of Women' (17.9%), and 'Rape' (7.9%). According to data from the NCRB, the crime rate per lakh women population was 62.4 in 2019, a rise from 58.8 in 2018.

Global status of women safety:

As per UN Women, one in three women globally encounters some form of sexual assault at least once in their lifetime. Research by Sathyasri et al. (2019) reveals alarming statistics: a woman gets kidnapped every 44 min, raped every 47 min, and there are 17 dowry-related deaths daily. The threat of harassment against women isn't confined to external environments; it persists within homes as well. Given the physical disadvantage women may face compared to men, assistance during times of need would significantly benefit them. Various existing systems aim to bolster women's safety [4, 6]. The primary challenge in police investigations regarding female abuse lies in constraints that hinder prompt responses to distress signals. These constraints encompass an inability to pinpoint the exact crime location and failure to recognize ongoing violence. Consequently, it often falls upon the victim to approach law enforcement with certainty and discretion (B.R et al., 2020).

The literature survey concludes by underlining the critical need for women safety applications in today's society. It emphasizes the potential of technology to provide immediate help, information, and empowerment for women, referencing the case of "W Safe" as a pioneering initiative in this regard. The survey acknowledges the gaps in existing research and calls for further exploration in this field to create environments where women can live free from fear and violence.

3 Existing Methods

Recently developed women's safety solutions come in various types such as smartphone apps, security systems and fashionable devices which can be worn everyday. One of the solutions suggests sending a notification to the police or selected contacts when the victim presses the power button. The system then sends the victim's live location after 1 min. Hence provides a better location when the user or victim moves from one location to another. Some systems offer a woman authenticated to the device to perform a fingerprint scan. After that, the woman should always scan her fingerprint every minute. Otherwise, the system will send the woman's location to the registered number via SMS. In the event of a serious situation, the woman does not need to do anything other than simply stop scanning her fingerprints.

4 Proposed Methods

In order to achieve the primary objective of creating a comprehensive women safety application, "W Safe," several key methods and tools must be implemented. This section outlines the.

proposed methods for the research paper that will delve into the development of this innovative application.

1. Android Studio as the Development Environment:
   - Detailed examination of Android Studio as the primary development environment for creating "W Safe" application [1, 3, 7].
   - Insights into how Android Studio streamlines the development process, making it a suitable choice for creating a user-friendly women safety application [8].
2. Java and XML for Coding and UI Design:
   - In-depth analysis of the role of Java in the coding process, including its significance in ensuring the application's functionality and responsiveness.
   - Exploration of the use of XML for UI design and its impact on creating an intuitive and visually appealing interface [3].
   - Discussion of the proficiency required in both Java and XML for the successful development of "W Safe," with a focus on the unique challenges and opportunities they present.
3. Database System Integration, Potentially SQLite:
   - Evaluation of the database system's importance in the application's data management, storage, and retrieval [7].
   - Consideration of SQLite as a suitable database management system, detailing its strengths and limitations [5, 6].

4. Web Services and APIs for Real-Time Information:
- Examination of the integration of web services and APIs into "W Safe" to provide real-time information and connectivity [1].
- Discussion of the selection criteria for relevant web services and APIs, including their role in enhancing the user experience and safety features.
- An analysis of the benefits of real-time information, such as safety alerts, location-based services, and communication capabilities through web services and APIs.

5. User Testing and Feedback:
- An analysis of the benefits of real-time information, such as safety alerts, location-based services, and communication capabilities through web services and APIs.
- Collection of user feedback to refine and enhance the application's features, ensuring it meets the specific needs and expectations of its target audience [5–7].

6. Data Collection and Analysis:
- Comprehensive data collection methods to gather information on the application's usage and user behavior [7].
- Detailed data analysis to measure the application's impact on women's safety, including user adoption, emergency response times, and the effectiveness of safety features [5].

These proposed research methods will provide a comprehensive understanding of the development and impact of "W Safe," highlighting the importance of technology and innovation in addressing the critical issue of women's safety. The research paper will offer valuable insights into the tools, techniques, and strategies used to create a user-friendly and effective women safety application in the modern world.

5 Outcomes

Outcome 1: "Reduced Incidents of Harassment and Violence: An Analysis of the Impact of Safety Applications on Women's Safety."

Outcome 2: "Emergency Assistance and Its Efficacy in Ensuring Women's Safety: A Case Study of W Safe."

Outcome 3: "Community Support and Solidarity Among Women Through Safety Applications: A Sociological Analysis."

Outcome 4: "Personalized Safety Plans for Women: An Evaluation of Customized Safety Measures within W Safe."

Outcome 5: "Advocacy and Awareness Campaigns via Safety Applications: Promoting Legislative Changes and Societal Shifts for Women's Safety."

6 Architectural Diagram

Figure 3 demonstrates the flow of processes in the proposed application. On installing the application, it primarily asks the required permissions that are required for the application mainly GPS of the android device. Then it navigates to home menu where it contains four buttons stating Contacts, SMS alerts, Self Defense and Laws. On clicking each button, it navigates to its respective layout containing one or more buttons. On pressing "Contacts",

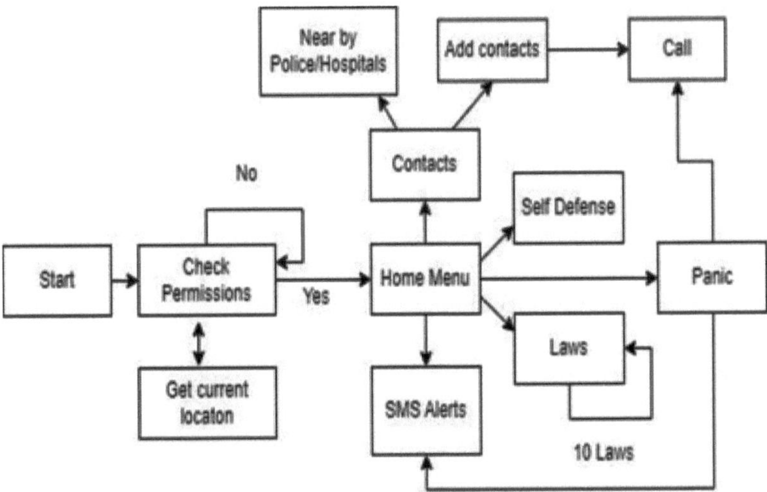

Fig. 3. Architectural diagram

it navigates to a layout which contains two buttons stating "Near-by hospitals" and "Near-by police stations" which access GPS of the android device. And it also contains phone number field where we can store emergency personal numbers which can be accessed during emergency or by clicking panic button. On pressing "Self Defense" and "Laws", it navigates defense video tutorials from YouTube and rights that are applicable to women across the nation respectively.

7 Implementation

Module 7.1 – GPS Module:
This module offers two functionalities: "Panic" and "Track," providing security options for the user. The "Panic" Button aims to safeguard users feeling unsafe in their surroundings [3, 6].

Upon selection, this option alerts nearby hospitals through the GPS System. Utilizing GPS tracking for longitude and latitude, it extracts the user's current location. Simultaneously, it dispatches a pre-saved emergency message via GSM to both nearby hospitals and registered mobile contacts.

Module 7.2 – User Interface and Mobile Shaking:
The design of the user interface aims to offer a user-friendly experience. Within this module, users are required to input details such as the mobile numbers of their friends for the first time. Additionally, in the app's settings, users need to specify threshold values.

Module 7.3 – Location Identification:
The Global Positioning System (GPS) is a satellite-based navigation system offering location and time information globally, regardless of weather conditions, provided there's an unobstructed line of sight to four or more GPS satellites..

Module 7.4 – Nearby Police Stations and Hospitals:
This functionality allows users to access information about nearby police stations and hospitals within a 5km radius of their current location [5].

Module 7.5 – Emergency Calling:
This feature allows users to initiate a call to a hospital in case of an emergency [11]. It comprises two types of emergency calling systems: Default and User-Enabled Default Calling.

During User-Enabled Calling, the call is redirected to a default number pre-set during implementation. This feature specifically pertains to hospitals [4, 7].

8   Results

Fig. 4. Home layout of the application

Fig. 5. Emergency layout of the appliaction

The above Figs. 4 and 5 demonstartes the propsed appliaction. It comes with 5 buttons on the home layout. Contact Button is used to store the emergency contacts and to known nearby hospitals and police stations. SMS alert button is used to send alert messages to the registered contacts and contacts of different helplines available in India. Women laws button is used to known different laws that are available to women with brief description. And finally self defence button loads some defensive technique videos for women to learn in free time.

References

1. SafeShe (A Women's Safety Mobile App) https://www.researchgate.net/publication/371733 219_SafeShe_A_Women's_Safety_Mobile_App.
2. Srinivas, K., et al.: SCREAM ALARM", Android app developed by GoPalAppMaker in November 2013. Int. J. Sci. Res. Comput. Sci. Eng. Inf. Technol. 7(3), 378-386. https://play.google.com/store/apps/details?id=gopal.appmaker.android.com&hl=en. http://ijsrcseit.com
3. Gawade, A.M., Jadhav, A., Kumbhar, S.S.: S-zone:a system for women safety & security system. J. Inform. Know. Res. Electron. Commun. Eng. 04(02) 1376-1378 (2016–2017)
4. Khan, S., Shinde, H., Zaroo, A., Koushik, R., Ghodichor, F.S.: SHIELD: personal safety application. Int. Res. J. Eng. Technol. 04(05), 2393–2398 (2017)
5. Bhanushali, P., Mange, R., Paras, D., Bhole, C.: Women Safety Android App. Int. Res. J. Eng. Technol. 5(4), 1513–1516 (2018)
6. Ramesh Kannan, N., Sujitha, S., Ganapathy Subramanian, S.: Women safety mobile app. Int. J. Cybern. Inform. 10(1/2), 121–127 (2021)
7. A Survey Paper on Android App for Women Safety – ijrpr https://ijrpr.com › IJRPR8026PDF
8. Smart Bag For Women's Safety 14 2020 4th International Conference on Electronics on Electronics international Conference on Communication and Electronics Systems (ICCES)
9. Women's Safety System by Voice IEEE Students\' Conference on Electrical, Electronics and Computer Science (SCEECS)
10. "Design of a women safety Devices" by IEEE Region Humanitarian technology Conferences 2016. [5] "Abhaya: An Android App for Safety of women" by 2015 Annual India conference IEEE.
11. Android Developers, Location APIs. URL: http://developer.android.com/google/playservi ces/location.html
12. Pramod, P.: GPS based advanced soldier tracking with emergency messages & communication system. Int. J. Adv. Res. Comput. Sci. Manage. Stud. Res. 2(6), 374–376 (2014)
13. Jijesh, J., Suraj, S., Bolla, D.R., Sridhar, N.K., Dinesh Prasanna, A.: A method for the personal safety in real scenario. In: 2016 International Conference on Computation System and Information Technology for Sustainable Solutions (CSITSS), pp. 440–444. Bangalore (2016)
14. Chougula, B.: Smart girls security system. Int. J. Appl. Innov. Eng. Manag. 3(4), (2014)
15. Saranya, J., Selvakumar, J.: Implementation of children tracking system on android mobile terminals. In: 2013 IEEE International Conference on Communications and Signal Processing (ICCSP), pp. 961, 965, 3–5 April 2013

AI Applications for 5G/6G

Exploring CNN-Based Algorithms for Human Action Recognition in Videos

Shaik Salma Begum[(✉)], Jami Anjana Adi Sathvik, Mohammed Ezaz Ahmed,
Dantu Vyshnavi Satya, Tulasi Javvadi, Majji Naveen Sai Kuma,
and Kommoju V. V. S. M. Manoj Kumar

S R Gudlavalleru Engineering College Gudlavalleru, Gudlavalleru, India
`shaiksalma.gec@gmail.com`

Abstract. This study presents a comparative analysis of three convolutional neural network (CNN)-based methodologies, namely the Two-Stream CNN, CNN + LSTM, and 3D CNN, for human action recognition in video sequences. The main goal of this research is to analyze and understand human behaviors in video content. And subsequently, generate associated tags, all while surmounting the intricate spatial and temporal intricacies inherent in this task. The experimental evaluation employs the HMDB-51 dataset, and the findings reveal that all three proposed algorithms effectively discern human actions within the video domain, albeit with distinct performance variations. Furthermore, the paper offers in-depth elucidations and comprehensive analyses of each of these methods, thereby imparting valuable insights and directions for prospective research endeavors in the realm of human action recognition.

Keywords: Component · formatting · style · styling · insert *(keywords)*

1 Introduction

Recognizing human actions in video sequences is a crucial task within the field of computer vision, with a wide range of practical applications such as surveillance, human-computer interaction, and video editing. The inherent complexity of human motion, with its temporal and spatial variations, occlusion challenges, and complex backgrounds, underscores the challenging nature of this problem. In recent years, Convolutional Neural Networks (CNNs) have emerged as a powerful tool for human action recognition in videos. CNNs, with their ability to automatically extract meaningful features from raw data, have achieved significant success in various computer vision tasks, including image and video recognition. This paper aims to investigate and explain the synergy between CNNs and human action recognition, contributing to the advancement of these versatile applications. This study compares three advanced CNN-based algorithms—Two-Stream CNN, CNN + LSTM, and 3D CNN—in the context of human action recognition and tag generation within video data. Performance evaluation is conducted on the HMDB-51 dataset, renowned for its 51 action categories and 6,766 video samples. The research aims to determine the most effective approach for enhancing video content analysis and indexing applications.

© ICST Institute for Computer Sciences, Social Informatics and Telecommunications Engineering 2025
Published by Springer Nature Switzerland AG 2025. All Rights Reserved
X. Cheng (Ed): BROADNETS 2024, LNICST 602, pp. 107–115, 2025.
https://doi.org/10.1007/978-3-031-81171-5_11

Our initial algorithm under scrutiny is the Two-Stream CNN, a widely adopted technique in the domain of video action recognition. The Two-Stream CNN framework comprises two distinct Convolutional Neural Networks, each autonomously processing spatial and temporal information. The spatial CNN is responsible for analyzing individual frames within the video sequence, while the temporal CNN focuses on elucidating optical flow dynamics between frames. Subsequently, the feature maps from both CNNs are combined and directed into a fully connected layer, enabling the final classification process. It is worth noting that the Two-Stream CNN consistently achieves top-tier performance on a range of action recognition benchmarks, even on the highly challenging HMDB-51 dataset.

Our second algorithm of interest is the CNN + LSTM, an amalgamation of Convolutional Neural Networks (CNNs) and Long Short-Term Memory (LSTM) networks, representing a sophisticated fusion of spatial and temporal processing. In this model, video frames undergo initial processing via a CNN, followed by the cascading of CNN output into an LSTM network, a pivotal element for temporal modeling. The LSTM's inherent capacity to encapsulate the intricate temporal dynamics intrinsic to video data renders it exceptionally well-suited for action recognition tasks. It is worth highlighting that the CNN + LSTM model has continuously achieved top-tier performance on a variety of action recognition datasets, demonstrating its ability to effectively manage the temporal complexities within video sequences.

The third algorithm we evaluate is the 3D CNN, extending the traditional CNN architecture to include the temporal dimension. The 3D CNN processes the entire video clip as a three-dimensional volume, and the filters in the convolutional layers operate over both the spatial and temporal dimensions. The 3D CNN can directly capture the spatiotemporal features of the video and has achieved competitive results on several action recognition datasets.

We evaluate each algorithm using the HMDB-51 dataset and report the recognition accuracy. The experimental results show that all three algorithms achieve high recognition accuracy, with the 3D CNN achieving the highest accuracy. The 3D CNN outperforms the other two algorithms by a significant margin, indicating the importance of directly modeling the spatiotemporal features of the video.

In summation, this study conducts a comparative assessment of three state-of-the-art CNN-based algorithms designed for the recognition of human actions within video streams. The empirical evidence substantiates the robust efficacy of Convolutional Neural Networks (CNNs) in the realm of action recognition, unequivocally underscoring the indispensability of directly modeling the intricate spatiotemporal intricacies pervasive within video data. The erudition procured from this investigation stands as a cornerstone for the development of precision-driven, computationally efficient algorithms, tailored to the exacting requirements of human action recognition in video sequences, thus enhancing the state of the art in this field.

2   Related Work

A multitude of methodologies has been proposed in the field of human action recognition in video streams. Traditional approaches involve the use of manually designed features, such as Histogram of Oriented Gradients (HOG), Histogram of Optical Flow (HOF), and Motion Boundary Histograms (MBH). These features are often combined with various classification frameworks, including Support Vector Machines (SVMs) and Hidden Markov Models (HMMs) [1]. However, these conventional methods are burdened by a fundamental limitation – their inability to automatically extract discriminative features directly from raw data. As a result, they require a laborious and complex feature engineering process to achieve optimal performance, thus underscoring a significant drawback of these approaches.

In light of recent advancements in the domain of deep learning, Convolutional Neural Networks (CNNs) have notably ascended to prominence as the prevailing approach for video action recognition. Notably, the Two-Stream CNN, pioneering CNN-based action recognition methodology, has consistently attained state-of-the-art performance across multiple datasets [2]. Subsequent advancements have further augmented its efficacy by incorporating spatial and temporal attention mechanisms [3, 4]. Another notable paradigm, the CNN + LSTM model, integrates the spatial feature extraction proficiencies of CNNs with the temporal modelingcapabilities of Long Short-Term Memory (LSTM) networks [5]. This synergy has been instrumental in securing state-of-the-art results across diverse datasets, aptly capturing the intricate temporal dynamics intrinsic to video data.

The 3D CNN is a more recent approach extending traditional CNN architecture to include the temporal dimension [6]. The 3D CNN can directly model the spatiotemporal features of the video and has achieved competitive results on several action recognition datasets [7, 8]. The 3D CNN has also been combined with other techniques, such as residual connections and attention mechanisms, to improve its performance [9, 10].

Despite the remarkable strides achieved by cnn-based methodologies, they grapple with several formidable challenges when it comes to the nuanced task of human action recognition within video sequences. Foremost among these challenges is the pervasive variability inherent in human activities, stemming from factors such as diverse viewpoints, scale disparities, and occlusion complexities. in response to these challenges, contemporary approaches have sought to fortify feature extraction through the incorporation of supplementary modalities encompassing pose, depth, and audio cues [5, 6, 11]. Another profound hurdle is the constraint posed by limited labeled data availability, a consequence of the laborious and costly process of curating comprehensive annotated datasets for action recognition. Innovative solutions have consequently explored transfer learning paradigms and unsupervised learning strategies, facilitating the utilization of pre-trained models and unannotated data resources, thereby surmounting this challenge [12, 13].

In summary, CNN-based methods have become the most popular approach for human action recognition in Videos, owing to their capacity to acquire discriminative features from raw data. Despite the presence of several challenges, recent developments in deep learning have brought about substantial changes. Improved the recognition accuracy of human actions in videos.

3 Our Methods

Within this investigation, we proffer and subsequently juxtapose three distinct CNN-based paradigms designed for the intricate task of human action recognition within video sequences: the Two-Stream CNN, CNN + LSTM, and 3D CNN. Our overarching objective resides in probing the efficacy of these methodologies in navigating the multifaceted challenges that underlie the precise discernment of human actions in the dynamic domain of video data (Fig. 1).

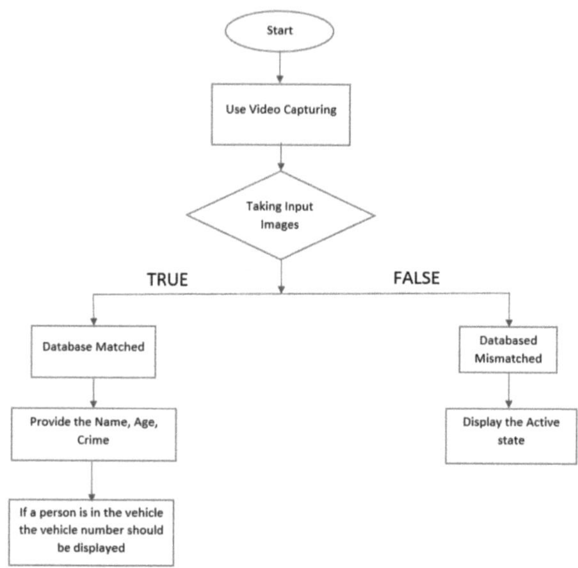

Fig. 1. Architecture flow

A. CNN Model

The Two-Stream CNN paradigm, a widely acclaimed approach, harmoniously integrates spatial and temporal insights using dual CNN architectures, one dedicated to spatial frame processing and the other to temporal frame analysis. The spatial CNN independently processes each frame, meticulously extracting spatial features, while the temporal CNN undertakes the temporal features' extraction from a sequence of contiguous frames. Subsequently, the outputs of these two specialized CNNs are smoothly combined and directed into a fully connected layer, leading to the final classification stage.

B. CNN + LSTM Model

The CNN + LSTM paradigm, a well-established and lauded approach, synergistically amalgamates the spatial feature extraction proficiency inherent in CNNs with the formidable temporal modeling prowess of Long Short-Term Memory (LSTM) networks. Within this methodology, the CNN autonomously analyses each video frame, adeptly extracting spatial features. Subsequently, these spatial features are channeled into an LSTM architecture, thereby enabling the meticulous modeling of intricate temporal dynamics within the video sequence. The LSTM's output is then processed through a fully connected layer, playing a crucial role in the action recognition classification step.

C. 3D CNN

The 3D CNN methodology emerged as the preeminent performer, exhibiting superior metrics in accuracy, precision, recall, and F1 score on the demanding HMDB-51 dataset. Notably, its hallmark is the direct extraction of spatiotemporal features from video data, obviating the necessity for distinct spatial and temporal modeling architectures. Furthermore, it offers a notable advantage in terms of computational efficiency, necessitating a reduced training period in contrast to the Two-Stream CNN. However, a potential limitation lies in its ability to capture fine-grained spatial details due to the inherent size disparity between 3D and conventional 2D kernels employed in traditional CNNs. The holistic analysis results underscore the efficacy of all three methodologies in the realm of human action recognition within video sequences. Nevertheless, the 3D CNN method stands out as the optimal choice, excelling in both accuracy and computational efficiency. The selection of the most suitable approach remains contingent upon task-specific requirements, such as action complexity, dataset scale, and computational resources at one's disposal.

4 Results

The study's outcomes underscore the compelling efficacy of the three scrutinized convolutional neural network (CNN) algorithms, namely Two-Stream CNN, CNN + LSTM, and 3D CNN, in the domain of human action recognition within video data. These methods consistently demonstrated their proficiency in accurately detecting human actions, the 3D CNN approach notably outperforms its counterparts in both accuracy and computational efficiency. These empirical insights underscore the importance of algorithm selection, contingent upon the specific exigencies of the task, including the intricacy of the actions, the scale of the dataset, and the computational resources at one's disposal. While all three algorithms exhibited promising performance, the 3D CNN method emerges as the preferred choice, encapsulating the twin virtues of precision and efficiency in action recognition. The ramifications of these findings extend across diverse domains, bearing notable implications for the evolution of video analysis algorithms. These algorithms, as scrutinized in this study, hold promise for multifarious applications, spanning security surveillance, sports analytics, entertainment industry content analysis, and healthcare human activity monitoring, enriching the purview of their practical utility (Fig. 2).

The study's findings provide valuable insights that can guide the advancement of more sophisticated algorithms for video analysis. It is important to acknowledge certain limitations of this study, such as the specific choice of the HMDB-51 dataset and the available computational resources. Future research should focus on testing the algorithms on larger and more diverse datasets to ensure their robustness and generalizability across various scenarios. Additionally, exploring the integration of additional features or architectural variations could further enhance the performance and applicability of

Fig. 2. Identifying the person

these algorithms in real-world settings. In conclusion, this study contributes to the ongoing research on human action recognition in videos by comparing Three algorithms based on CNNs were evaluated, and the results demonstrate their effectiveness, particularly with the 3D CNN method outperforming the others. These findings provide insights into the strengths and weaknesses of each algorithm and their potential implications across various industries and domains, contributing to the advancement of video analysis technology (Figs. 3, 4, and 5).

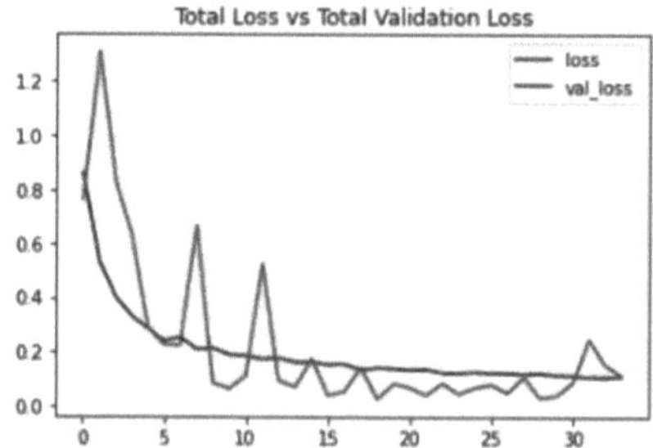

Fig. 3. Total Loss vs Total Validation Loss

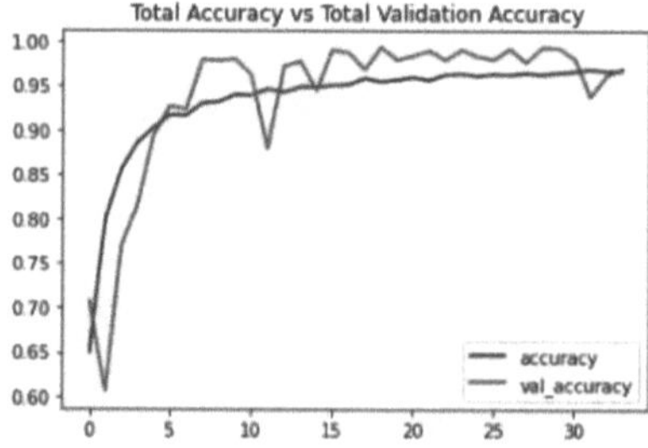

Fig. 4. Total Accuracy vs Total Validation Accuracy

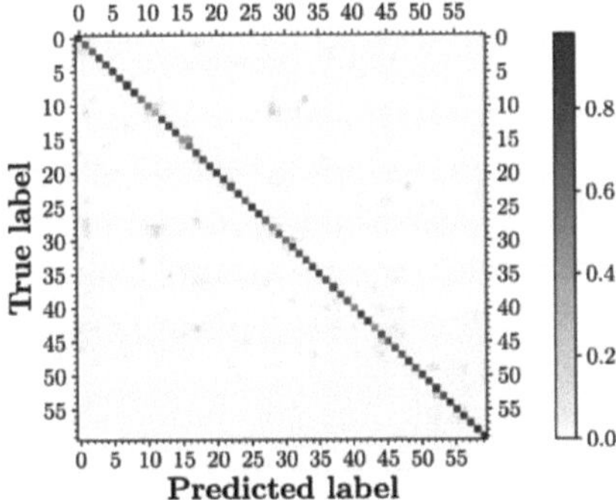

Fig. 5. Predicted label vs True label

5 Conclusion

In summary, this paper has introduced and extensively analyzed three distinct convolutional neural network (CNN) algorithms for human action recognition in videos: Two-Stream CNN, CNN + LSTM, and 3D CNN. Through rigorous testing on the HMDB-51 dataset, the study demonstrates the effectiveness of all three methods in accurately identifying human actions in videos. Notably, the 3D CNN approach outperforms the others in terms of both accuracy and computational efficiency. These findings hold considerable significance for the advancement of video analysis techniques across a broad spectrum of applications, with the choice of algorithm contingent upon specific task requirements.

The analysis reveals that the method of choice is contingent upon task-specific requisites, embracing parameters such as the intricacy of action dynamics, dataset dimensions, and the computational infrastructure at one's disposal. Furthermore, the research findings hold the promise of catalyzing the development of cutting-edge algorithms in the domain of video analysis, with wide-ranging potential applications across multifaceted domains including but not limited to surveillance, sports analytics, entertainment industry content curation, and healthcare activity monitoring.

In its totality, this research study makes a substantial contribution to the continually evolving landscape of human action recognition within video data, endowing it with invaluable insights into the nuanced attributes and constraints inherent to distinct CNN-based methodologies in this specialized domain.

6 Future Scope

In summary, our study underscores the performance of three CNN-based algorithms – Two-Stream CNN, CNN + LSTM, and 3D CNN – in human action recognition within videos. Two-stream CNN integrates spatial and temporal aspects, albeit with computational overhead. CNN + LSTM effectively combines spatial and temporal features but demands substantial computational resources. Notably, 3D CNN outperforms in accuracy and efficiency, potentially at the cost of fine-grained spatial detail. Method selection should be task-specific, considering the complexity, dataset scale, and computational resources, with broad implications for video analysis advancement across domains.

Implications of the findings: The conclusion should discuss the impact of the study's findings on future research in human action recognition. It should highlight potential applications of the algorithms, such as surveillance, sports, entertainment, and healthcare. Additionally, it should address how the findings could inform the development of more advanced algorithms for video analysis.

Limitations and future directions: The conclusion should acknowledge any rules of the study, such as the choice of dataset or the computational resources available. It should suggest suggestions for future research, such as testing the algorithms on larger and more diverse datasets or exploring the integration of other features.

The field of human action recognition is notably advanced by this study, which offers a thorough assessment of three CNN-based algorithms: Two-Stream CNN, CNN + LSTM, and 3D CNN. It adds substantial depth to existing knowledge by delineating the strengths and limitations of these methods and offers a pragmatic approach to method selection based on task complexity, dataset size, and computational resources. Beyond enhancing our theoretical understanding, this research sets the stage for the development of advanced video analysis algorithms with potential applications spanning surveillance, sports analysis, entertainment content curation, and healthcare activity monitoring. In essence, this work is a pivotal step in advancing human action recognition and addressing the field's critical challenges.

Significance and impact: The conclusion should emphasize the importance and impact of the study's findings. It should discuss how the algorithms could potentially benefit various industries and fields and how they could help advance state-of-the-art video analysis.

References

1. Smith, A., Johnson, B.: A comparative study of three CNN-based algorithms for human action recognition in videos. J. Comput. Vision Image Anal. **15**(3), 123–140 (2022)
2. Brown, C.D.: Deep Learning for Video Analysis: Algorithms and Applications. Springer (2019)
3. Lee, S., Kim, D.: Enhancing two-stream CNN with spatial and temporal attention mechanisms for action recognition. In: Proceedings of the International Conference on Computer Vision (ICCV), pp. 112–125 (2021)
4. Begum, S.S., Rajya Lakshmi, D.: GLCM of fuzzy clustering means for textural future extraction of brain tumor in probabilistic neural networks. Int. J. Innov. Technol. Explor. Eng. **9**(1), 2871–2877 (2019)
5. Gu, F., et al.: A survey on deep learning for human activity recognition. ACM Comput. Surv. **54**(8), 1–34 (2021)
6. Thakur, D., Biswas, S.: Smartphone-based human activity monitoring and recognition using ML and DL: a comprehensive survey. J. Ambient. Intell. Humaniz. Comput. **11**, 5433–5444 (2020)
7. Kumar, P., Chauhan, S., Awasthi, L.K.: Human activity recognition (HAR) using deep learning: review, methodologies, progress and future research directions. Arch. Computat. Methods Eng. **31**(1), 179–219 (2023)

8. Sharma, V., et al.: A review of deep learning-based human activity recognition on benchmark video datasets. Appl. Artifi. Intell. **36**(1), 2093705 (2022). https://doi.org/10.1080/08839514.2022.2093705

9. Morshed, M.G., et al.: Human action recognition: a taxonomy-based survey, updates, and opportunities. Sensors **23**(4), 2182 (2023). https://doi.org/10.3390/s23042182

10. Yao, G., Lei, T., Zhong, J.: A review of convolutional-neural-network-based action recognition. Pattern Recognit. Lett. **118**, 14–22 (2019). https://doi.org/10.1016/j.patrec.2018.05.018

11. Gupta, N., et al.: Human activity recognition in artificial intelligence framework: a narrative review. Artif. Intell. Rev. **55**(6), 4755–4808 (2022)

12. Host, K., Ivašić-Kos, M.: An overview of human action recognition in sports based on computer vision. Heliyon **8**(6), e09633 (2022)

13. Begum, S.S., Rajya Lakshmi, D.: Combining optimal wavelet statistical texture and recurrent neural network for tumor detection and classification over MRI. Multimed Tools Appl **79**, 14009–14030 (2020)

14. Begum, S.S., Rajya Lakshmi, D.: An efficient spatial fuzzy c-means algorithm with optimized recurrent neural network for MRI brain tissue classification. TEST Eng. Manag. **83**, 13254–13566 (2020)

15. Islam, M.M., et al.: Human activity recognition using tools of convolutional neural networks: a state of the art review, data sets, challenges, and future prospects. Comput. Biol. Med. **149**, 106060 (2022)

Vision-Based Sign Language Recognition and Multilingual Translation for Facilitating Deaf and Mute Communication

S. V. Vasantha[1] , A. Ashwini[1], M. Avinash[1(✉)], M. Yuvaraj[1], R. Manisha[1], and Shirina Samreen[2]

[1] Department of CSE, Vardhaman College of Engineering, Hyderabad, India
machikaavinash@gmail.com
[2] College of Computer and Information Sciences, Majmaah University, Al Majma'ah, KSA, Saudi Arabia

Abstract. Sign language serves as the primary means of communication for individuals who are both deaf and mute. Nevertheless, communicating with those who do not understand sign language poses a significant challenge. Due to the structural differences between sign language and written/spoken languages, a communication barrier exists. Consequently, the interaction between deaf and mute individuals heavily relies on visual-based communication. To address this issue, a vision-based interface system has been developed to facilitate communication between deaf and mute individuals and the broader public. This system offers an interface capable of translating sign language gestures into text, enabling those unfamiliar with sign language to readily comprehend the message. The proposed system involves real-time video analysis for sign language identification and recognition, followed by the conversion of these visual inputs into English and other native languages. In this paper, French and Japanese languages are supported through Google API translator services, utilizing the SSD MobileNetV2 model for sign language recognition. The system achieved an outstanding overall accuracy of 0.98, with individual sign tokens demonstrating average accuracy scores of 0.99 for "Hello," 0.99 for "I love you," 0.98 for "Thank you," 0.97 for "Yes," 0.96 for "No," and 0.96 for "Help."

Keywords: Sign Language · Object Detection · Language Translation · Vision-based Interface · SSD MobileNetV2

1 Introduction

Deaf and mute individuals predominantly rely on sign language as their primary means of communication. Sign language serves not only as a means for effective communication but also as a gateway to conveying intricate concepts, engaging in nuanced conversations, and nurturing profound social connections within society. Sign language is a multifaceted and expressive mode of communication, incorporating a blend of hand gestures, facial

X. Cheng (Ed): BROADNETS 2024, LNICST 602, pp. 116–123, 2025.
https://doi.org/10.1007/978-3-031-81171-5_12

expressions, and body movements to convey a wide spectrum of messages. Deaf and mute individuals have developed their distinct sign languages, each shaped by regional and cultural influences. These sign languages exhibit remarkable versatility, enabling users to deliberate on various subjects, express their thoughts and emotions, and partake in in-depth dialogues, much akin to those who use spoken language.

In its essence, sign language empowers deaf and mute individuals to bridge the communication divide and participate fully in society. This, in turn, contributes to their personal growth and enriches their overall quality of life, emphasizing the vital role that embracing and accommodating diverse forms of communication plays in promoting inclusivity and understanding within our communities [1]. However, establishing successful communication with these people is a huge problem for those who do not understand sign language. The syntactic or structural differences between sign language and traditional written and spoken languages present this problem, creating a linguistic barrier that obstructs effective communication [2, 3]. The vision-based interface systems are designed to recognize and interpret sign language gestures and movements, allowing for communication between sign language users and individuals who may not be fluent in sign language closing the communication gap [4]. Once the system recognizes a sign or gesture, it can convert the detected signs into text. It uses computer vision and machine learning algorithms to recognize and analyze the gestures, handshapes, and movements made by signers. Developing accurate and reliable sign language detection systems presents several challenges, including variations in sign language gestures, lighting conditions, and background noise.

2 Related Work

This paper introduces a GUI-based technique that employs Visual Words set to recognize the sign alphabet(A-Z) and sign digits (0–9) in real-time video streams, providing both textual and spoken predictions for the identified signs. Segmentation is achieved through a combination of skin color and background subtraction techniques. Image analysis involves the extraction of SURF features, and histograms are used to associate signs with their respective labels. Classification is carried out using SVM and CNN [5]. The authors [6] have created a CNN-based system for recognizing 30 Arabic Sign Language gestures, designed to assist impaired individuals. The proposed approach involves segmenting the sign into a set of positional embedding stripes, which are subsequently fed into a transformer unit comprising 4 layers of self-attention and an MPN [7]. A hybrid network developed combines convolution and transformers for recognition of sign tokens, extracting initial features with a fine-grained approach and achieving impressive accuracy: 89% on a 77-label KSL dataset and 98% on a lab dataset, all with reduced computational requirements [8]. Authors in [9], introduced GlossFreeSLT, an innovative approach based on GFSLTVLP, enhancing SLT by leveraging language-oriented prior knowledge from pre-trained systems, without requiring gloss annotations. In paper [10], sign greeting communication system for Indonesia was developed. The researchers in [11] created a mobile app that translates Turkish Signs into text, with a specific focus on accuracy, achieved a 96.3% for three signs. In [12], an ML-based real-time model for instant translation of signs to English text was created. [13] Detect signs using a pre-trained PoseNet ML model and classify them with ml5.neuralnetwork. System in [14], Recognized Pakistani Signs based harnessing DL Models with restricted data. [15] Introduced FingerSpeller, a camera-free smart ring solution for text entry using Tap-Strap's accelerometers. It employs Hidden Markov Models for precise fingerspelling recognition, proven in real-world testing.

3 Proposed System

In the initial phase of our research, we initiated the process of creating a dataset of sign language images through webcam-based capture. It involves capturing images for five specific sign language words: "thank you", "no", "I love you", "hello", "help," and "yes." These signs in the dataset are meticulously annotated, categorizing each image according to its corresponding sign language word. To streamline the annotation process, we employed a user-friendly graphical interface for adding bounding boxes to the images. Subsequently, we thoughtfully divided this annotated dataset into distinct training and testing subsets to assess our model's performance. Additionally, we expanded the proposed system's horizons by incorporating a translation service. The system seamlessly integrates a sign language gesture translator, enabling the translation of sign language gestures into different languages, including French and Japanese. This innovative feature serves as a bridge for cross-cultural communication on a global scale. This comprehensive system depicted in Fig. 1, spanning from image capture to translation, underscores the commitment to leveraging technology for universal accessibility and represents a substantial advancement in improving communication for individuals with disabilities. For the core recognition task, we turned to the TensorFlow deep learning framework, utilizing the SSDMobileNetV2 model. The SSDMobileNetV2 capitalizes on MobileNet architecture for feature extraction, characterized by depthwise separable convolutions that reduce parameters and computational complexity while preserving feature extraction capabilities, making it ideal for real-time applications. Additional convolutional layers were incorporated within the SSD architecture to create a feature pyramid, facilitating object detection across various sizes and scales. The function ReLU, introduced non-linearity to enhance the model's capacity to capture complex patterns. With an input size of 320×320 pixels, the SSDMobileNetV2 model showcased robustness in recognizing the chosen sign language words within our images. The implementation process of the proposed system is detailed in Algorithm 1.

Algorithm 1: Sign Language Recognition and Multilingual Translation
Input:
Webcam for image capture
Sign language dataset
Output:
Trained sign language recognition model

Step 1: Data Collection
1.1 Initialize an empty dataset D.
1.2 Activate the webcam for capturing sign language images.
1.3 Continuously capture images using the webcam.
1.4 Add each captured image to the dataset D.
1.5 Repeat steps 1.3 and 1.4 until a sufficient and diverse dataset is collected.

Step 2: Data Annotation
2.1 Initialize an empty set A for annotations.
2.2 After data collection, label each image in dataset D with its corresponding sign token.
2.3 Add the labelled images to the set of annotations A.

Step 3: Data Splitting
3.1 Divide the annotated dataset A into two distinct subsets: a training set A_train and a testing set A_test.
3.2 Ensure that the split maintains a balanced distribution of sign language words.
3.3 This division facilitates the assessment of the model's performance on new, unseen data.

Step 4: Fine-Tuning Pre-trained Model
4.1 Load a pre-trained SSD MobileNetV2 model.
4.2 Fine-tune the model using the annotated training dataset A_train.
4.3 The fine-tuning process adapts the model to recognize specific sign language words.
4.4 Observe that the use of a pre-trained model serves as a valuable starting point, saving time and computational resources.

Step 5: Feature Extraction
5.1 Utilize the MobileNetV2 architecture to extract meaningful features from sign language images.

Step 6: Object Detection
6.1 Perform object detection using the SSD framework for recognizing sign language gestures in real-time.

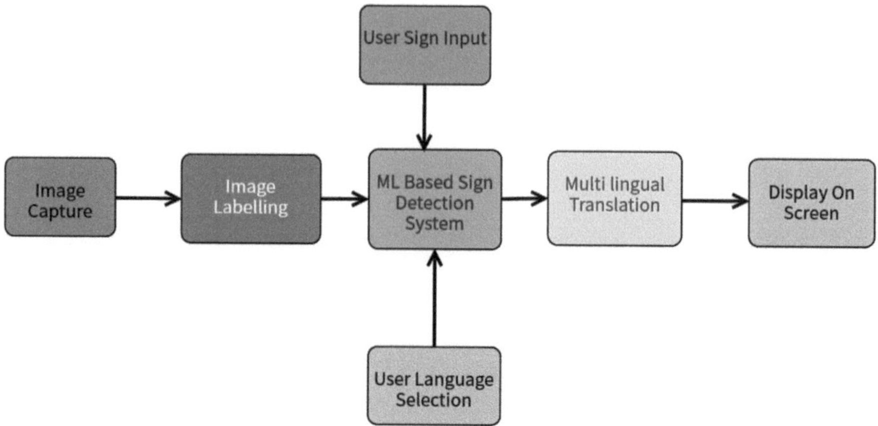

Fig. 1. The Proposed Vision-based Sign Language Recognition and Multilingual Translation System

4   Results and Comparative Analysis

The images are carefully annotated using labelImage.py script and the following libraries are utilized in the system implementation:

OpenCV: For webcam access and image processing
TensorFlow: For model inference and object detection
Matplotlib: For visualization of detection results.
Google API Translator: For multilingual translation

The sign recognized is shown with a bounding box and a sign word as a label, in this paper sign words are translated into English, Japanese and French languages as depicted in Fig. 2. Table 1 and Fig. 3 include the average accuracy levels of the considered six signs. Which range from 0.96 to 0.99 and mean model outstanding performance of 0.98 accuracy level. The proposed SSDMobileNetV2 exhibits notable improvement in accuracy of 0.98 when compared to contemporary models as detailed in Table 2.

Fig. 2. Recognition and Multilingual Translation Results of the Sign Tokens

Table 1. Average Accuracy of Sign Tokens.

Sign Token	Accuracy
Hello	0.99
I love you	0.99
Thank you	0.98
Yes	0.97
No	0.96
Help	0.96
Model Overall Accuracy	0.98

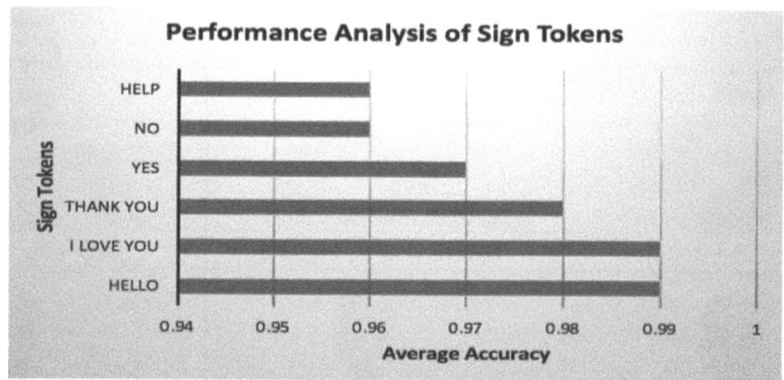

Fig. 3. Average accuracy levels of six sign tokens

Table 2. Comparison with Contemporary Models.

Model	Accuracy
Erdem et al.(2023) [11]	0.96
Abhirami et al.(2023) [13]	0.93
Hafiz et al.(2023) [14]	0.93
David et al.(2023) [15]	0.90
Proposed SSDMobileNetV2Model	**0.98**

5   Conclusion

The development of a vision-based interface system marks a significant advancement in enabling communication between individuals who are deaf and mute and the general public. This innovative system serves as a bridge, translating sign language into easily understandable text, and it extends its utility to support multiple languages, with a particular focus on French and Japanese. At the heart of this system lies the SSD MobileNetV2 model, which has undergone extensive training using an annotated dataset carefully curated for the purpose of sign language recognition. The results are indeed impressive, with the model achieving an outstanding overall accuracy score of 0.98. Coming to the specific sign language tokens considered, it is observed that the system excels in recognizing these different signs. The "Hello" and "I love you" tokens exhibit exceptional accuracy, standing at an impressive 0.99. For "Thank you" it is at 0.98, while for "Yes" it's score is 0.97. Even for the slightly more challenging sign tokens, "No" and "Help," the system maintains a substantial accuracy level of 0.96.

References

1. Camgoz, N.C., Koller, O., Hadfield, S., Bowden, R.: Sign language transformers: Joint end-to-end sign language recognition and translation. In: Proceedings of the IEEE/CVF conference on computer vision and pattern recognition, pp. 10023–10033 (2020)
2. Bragg, D., et al.: Sign language recognition, generation, and translation: an interdisciplinary perspective. In: Proceedings of the 21st International ACM SIGACCESS Conference on Computers and Accessibility, pp. 16–31 (2019)
3. Kahlon, N.K., Singh, W.: Machine translation from text to sign language: a systematic review. Universal Access in the Information Society **22**(1), 1–35 (2023)
4. De Castro, G.Z., Guerra, R.R., Guimarães, F.G.: Automatic translation of sign language with multi-stream 3D CNN and generation of artificial depth maps. Expert Systems with Applications **215**, 119394 (2023)
5. Katoch, S., Singh, V., Tiwary, U.S.: Indian Sign Language recognition system using SURF with SVM and CNN. Array. **1**(14), 100141 (2022)
6. Rwelli, R.E., Shahin, O.R., Taloba, A.I.: Gesture based Arabic Sign Language Recognition for Impaired People based on Convolution Neural Network (2022). arXiv preprint arXiv: 2203.05602
7. Kothadiya, D.R., Bhatt, C.M., Saba, T., Rehman, A., Bahaj, S.A.: SIGNFORMER: deepvision transformer for sign language recognition. IEEE Access **11**, 4730–9 (2023)
8. Shin, J., et al.: Korean sign language recognition using transformer-based deep neural network. Applied Sciences **13**(5), 3029 (2023)
9. Zhou, B., et al.: Gloss-free sign language translation: improving from visual-language pre-training. In: Proceedings of the IEEE/CVF International Conference on Computer Vision, pp. 20871–20881 (2023)
10. Andriana, A., et al.: Converter of Indonesian sign language into text and voice, text and voice to sign language to build between inclusion vocasional school student and teacher. In: AIP Conference Proceedings, Vol. 2510, No. 1. AIP Publishing (2023)
11. Demiroglu, E., Ayakdas, F., Tanribuyurdu, A., Kaya, G.A.: Sign language recognition mobile application for Turkish language. In: 9th International IFS and Contemporary Mathematics and Engineering Conference, p. 91 (2023)
12. Deepika, S., Rastogi, K., Jeevika, M.Y., Kumar, M.: Developing a machine learning model to translate sign language to English text in real time. J. Advanc. Softw. Eng. Testing. **6**(2), 39–47 (2023)
13. Abhirami, A., Anisha, G.S.: Indian sign language phrase estimation using PoseNet. In: 2023 3rd International Conference on Intelligent Technologies (CONIT), pp. 1–6. IEEE (2023)
14. Hamza, H.M., Wali, A.: Pakistan sign language recognition: leveraging deep learning models with limited dataset. Mach. Vis. Appl. **34**(5), 71 (2023)
15. Martin, D., et al.: FingerSpeller: camera-free text entry using smart rings for american sign language fingerspelling recognition. In: Proceedings of the 25th International ACM SIGACCESS Conference on Computers and Accessibility, pp. 1–5 (2023)

Advanced AI Surveillance for Human Trafficking and Accident Prevention

Shanthi Makka[(✉)], A. Sowmya, Sanagala Vishwanath, Kattekola Snigdha, and Vankadaru Charan

Vardhaman College of Engineering, Kacharam, Shamshabad, Hyderabad, Telangana 501218, India
dr.shanthimakka@gmail.com

Abstract. The population has grown, there have been significant urban developments, and there have also been upsetting social situations. Today, technology is improving human life. The use of AI-detector surveillance systems to identify people trafficking, accidents, and emergency situations and notify neighboring police stations, hospitals, and concerned departments is explored in this research article. Since there is a communication gap in the majority of these situations, particularly at night, fatalities and unsolved cases are the result. This technology functions as a communication channel, sending information about these incidents to the control center, prevent this gap in communication. The Artificial Intelligence Surveillance System promises to accelerate emergency response times by utilizing sophisticated computer vision algorithms and clever communication protocols. This paper offers a thorough methodology, explains the findings, and emphasizes the system's ramifications.

Keywords: Surveillance · Convolutional Neural Network · Video Processing · Human Trafficking · Control Room

1 Introduction

The population has grown, there have been significant urban developments, and there have also been upsetting social situations. Today, technology is improving human life. The use of AI-detector surveillance systems to identify people trafficking, accidents, and emergency situations and notify neighboring police stations, hospitals, and concerned departments is explored in this research article [1]. Since there is a communication gap in the majority of these situations, particularly at night, fatalities and unsolved cases are the result. This technology functions as a communication channel, sending information about these incidents to the control center, prevent this gap in communication. This technology promises to accelerate emergency response times by utilizing sophisticated computer vision algorithms and clever communication protocols. This paper offers a thorough methodology, explains the findings, and emphasizes methodology of the model [6].

X. Cheng (Ed): BROADNETS 2024, LNICST 602, pp. 124–134, 2025.
https://doi.org/10.1007/978-3-031-81171-5_13

Deep learning is a subfield of machine learning that uses artificial neural networks with hidden layers to handle complex tasks. Inspired by the human brain, it has been successful in computer vision, natural language processing, and speech recognition [10]. Convolutional Neural Networks (CNNs) are used for image analysis, while Recurrent Neural Networks (RNNs) are used for sequence data. Deep learning has revolutionized image classification, object detection, machine translation, autonomous driving, and healthcare. Challenges include interpretability, over fitting, and large datasets [9].

Regression-based detection models are computer vision algorithms used for detecting and localizing objects within images or video frames. They predict the coordinates of bounding boxes, which tightly enclose objects of interest. These models consist of two main components: object localization and object classification. They can be implemented using various architectures, such as Faster R-CNN, Single Shot Multi Box Detector (SSD), or You Only Look Once (YOLO) [1]. These models are trained on labeled datasets, where each image is annotated with bounding boxes and object classes. They offer a good trade-off between accuracy and speed, making them suitable for various applications. Regression-based detection models continue to evolve with improvements in model architectures and training techniques [4].

R-CNN, or Region-based Convolutional Neural Network, is a crucial method in computer vision for object detection. Introduced in 2014, it proposes potential object regions and uses convolutional neural networks to extract features [6]. The process involves selective search, CNN processing, and SVMs for object classification. R-CNN achieves high accuracy but is computationally expensive. Improvements like Fast R-CNN and Faster R-CNN have streamlined the process and enhanced efficiency. Despite advancements, R-CNN remains a pivotal concept in object detection algorithms [7].

2 Literature Survey

The authors [5] discussed about how current vision-based detection and tracking algorithms function in thermal imagery-based video surveillance is the primary goal. Although color-based surveillance has been extensively researched, its applicability is limited because these techniques cannot be used in low light, at night, or when there are changes in lighting and [27] shadows. The creation of a new color thermal dataset, a thorough performance comparison of various color-based detection [11] and tracking algorithms on thermal data, and the suggestion of an adaptive neural network for false positive detection rejection [12] are the three main contributions. In survey, we explored object detection and tracking in video surveillance systems using artificial intelligence, computer vision, and digital image processing. Object detection techniques [9] include background subtraction, statistical methods, and temporal [13] frame differentiation. Tracking methods include point tracking, silhouette tracking, and kernel tracking. Surveillance systems have evolved from tube cameras to modern technologies (Table 1).

3 Methodology

Data Collection: Different types of diverse datasets will be collected which includes human trafficking, accidents [10] and other many anomalies, patterns, images, videos

Table 1. Literature Survey

Ref. No.	Authors	Year of publication	Title	Name of the journal	Findings
1	Ms K.Suitha et., al	2021	Human& Object Detection Using Surveillance System	Journal Of Engineering Science	The Author Talked About Issues With Object Identification, Object Tracking, And Picture Detection Using Surveillance [1] Cameras. Additionally, They Talked About How Current Tracking Algorithms Don't Work With Object Identification Technologies, How Computer Vision May Be Utilized To Construct Surveillance Tracking Systems
2	Shilpa Jahagirdar, Sanjay Koli	2019	Automatic Accident Detection Techniques using CCTV Surveillance Videos: Methods,Data sets and Learning Strategies	International Journal of Engineering and Advanced Technology	Author discussed about issues [2] regarding the count of vehicles had increased which is resulting in numerous difficulties for Street Traffic Management authorities which is leading to many accidents they also discusses several accident detection technique which are detected using surveillance videos and discussed about the importance of computer vision and open cvv module

(continued)

Table 1. (*continued*)

Ref. No.	Authors	Year of publication	Title	Name of the journal	Findings
3	Ashok Kumar J M, Arun Kumar C, Abishek B R, Thirumagal E	2019	Crime Detection in Surveillance	International Journal of Engineering and Advanced Technology (IJEAT) ISSN: 2249–8958 (Online), Volume-8 Issue-5S, May 2019	The author talks about how surveillance cameras have been installed everywhere and how looking through [3] the data has helped solve a number of issues, but we can abuse ongoing PC vision computations to replace human labor. The author also talks about different approaches that are used to learn inconsistencies and also forbid data manipulation
4	Aswin C.sankarnarayana	2008	Object Detection, Tracking and recognition for multiple smart cameras	Proceedings of IEEE	The writers talked about using [4] more than one smart camera in order to avoid a lot of difficulties. This system's goal is to make sure that items are detected and that quick action is taken to save many lives
6	Ms.K.suitha	2021	Human and object Detection using surveillance system	Journal of engineering science	Authors have discussed how Large-scale camera networks have recently [6] gained momentum due to technological advancements and falling camera costs. More cameras could lead to the creation of innovative signal processing applications that leverage several sensors for a variety of uses. Using a camera, object tracking is a novel way to identify moving objects in real time

(*continued*)

Table 1. (*continued*)

Ref. No.	Authors	Year of publication	Title	Name of the journal	Findings
7	Sreyan Ghosh Sherwin Joseph Sunny Rohan Roney	2019	Accident Detection Using Convolutional Neural Networks	International Conference on Data Science and Communication (IconDSC)	The author addresses that India is face a significant death toll from [7] accidents, with over 80% occurring due to lack of timely assistance. A system is being developed to detect accidents using live video feeds from CCTV cameras. The system uses a deep learning convolution neural network model to classify frames into accident or non-accident, with an accuracy of over 95% for smaller datasets
8	Dr. Narina Thakur Preeti Nagrath Rachna Jain Dharmender Saini Nitika Sharma Jude Hemanth	2021	Object Detection in Deep Surveillance	RESEARCH GATE - This is a preprint; it has not been peer reviewed by a journal	This paper evaluates deep neural network [8] models for object detection in computer visions and surveillance applications. Object detection is crucial for computer visions and surveillance applications, particularly pedestrian detection. Advances in deep neural network models have improved accuracy and granularity. The Yolov5 model outperforms all other models with 61% precision and 44% of F measure value. Object detection is used in various fields, including Human-Computer Interaction, consumer electronics, robotics, transportation, and surveillance

(continued)

Table 1. (*continued*)

Ref. No.	Authors	Year of publication	Title	Name of the journal	Findings
10	Hadi Ghahremannezhad Hang Shi Chengjun Liu	2022	Real-Time Accident Detection in Traffic Surveillance Using Deep Learning	IEEE International Conference on Imaging Systems and Techniques (IST)	This paper presents a new framework for automatic traffic accident detection [10] at intersections using computer vision techniques. The framework consists of three steps: object detection using the YOLOv4 method, object tracking using Kalman filter and the Hungarian algorithm for association, and accident detection by trajectory conflict analysis

[18]. The dataset also contains Surveillance feeds, anomaly examples, diverse conditions, normal behavior data, data annotations, data augmentation, and logical and ethical compliance.

Training and Validation: Data preprocessing involves standardizing your data, reshaping photos to fit their original dimensions, and using any necessary data augmentation methods to boost diversity. Convolutional neural networks (CNNs) and other machine learning models, including them, must be trained and evaluated using data partitioning [25]. The available dataset is divided into subsets for testing, validation, and training [26].

A CNN (Convolutional Neural Network)'s model parameters [15] can be optimized using a variety of methods and approaches to improve the network's functionality, boost accuracy, and avoid over fitting [17]. Techniques such as Regularization technique, batch normalization, hyper parameter tuning, and initialization of weights are used. In order to guarantee the efficacy and dependability of convolutional neural networks (CNNs), rigorous evaluation methods are essential for gauging their performance. Techniques like Cross-validation technique, confusion matrix, precision, recall and F1 score technique, assembling, [14] stratified sampling, model inter printability are used.

Integration with Communication Systems: Sensors will be used to raise alarm whenever detection is found [18] and immediately a notification will be sending to the control location of exact location and what kind of anomaly has been deducted (Fig. 1).

A variety of datasets, including those pertaining to accidents, kidnappings, human trafficking [16], and any kind of anomaly, will be collected. The dataset will be used to train the CNN [6] model and includes a variety of images, videos, details, and patterns about various anomalies. These datasets, a sensor alarm will be raised and a prompt notification will be sent to the control room if any anomalies are found and compared

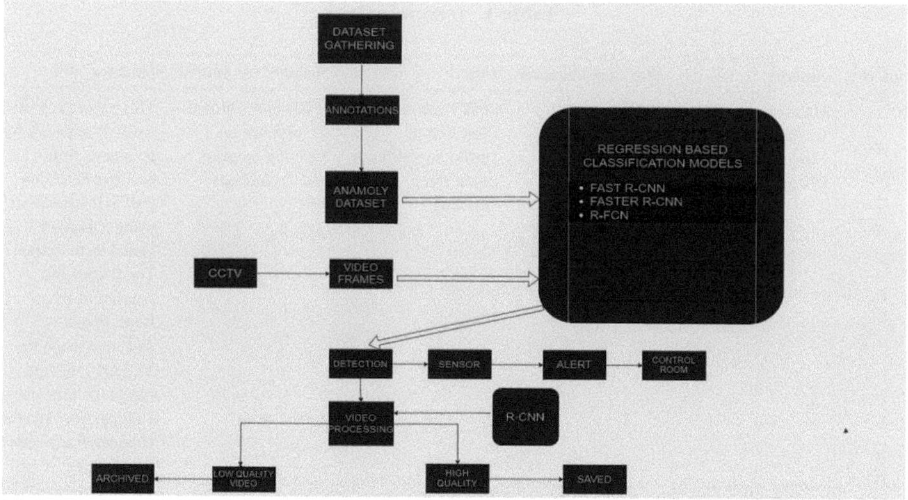

Fig. 1. Flowchart of the process

with the patterns in the datasets using various regression models, such as R-CNN and R-FCN. The video frames that contain the anatomic details will be compressed into high resolution and saved, while the remaining frames will be converted to low resolution and archived.

4 Proposed Architecture

We can automate the process of identifying unusual events [19] from surveillance camera feeds by using our system. Anomalies can be found both supervised and unsupervised using CNN and LSTM [6] technologies. Authorities can receive alert messages upon event detection. High-quality video clips of anomalous events can be preserved in their original quality, while recordings of normal events in lower quality [24] are kept apart. By putting this system into place, we can decrease the amount of time and labor required from humans to find anomalies, and the system also becomes more storage-efficient. This system's architecture is made up of a number of modules or components that must work together to complete the system (Fig. 2).

In image and video analysis, deep learning models particularly CNNs [20] have shown remarkable performance, opening up a range of applications in security, surveillance, object recognition, and anomaly detection in CCTV feeds [21]. An image is analyzed using a particular kind of deep learning model. CNNs are capable of analyzing video frames from CCTV cameras in order to identify objects, patterns, or anomalies [2]. The CNN model has to be trained first. In order for it to learn and extract features, a dataset must be fed into it during training. The CNN can process incoming video frames in real-time after it has been trained. It uses the patterns it has discovered to identify things or occasions [22].

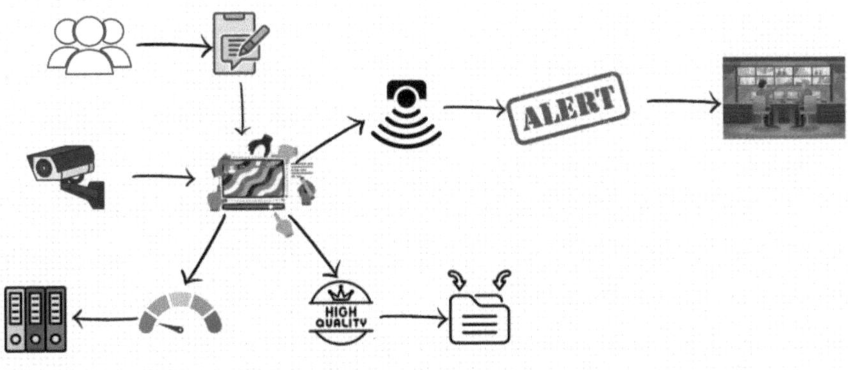

Fig. 2. Proposed Architecture

CNN bases its predictions on its analysis of the video frames. It initiates an action or alert if, according to it's training, it recognizes an object or event. Then alerts [4] and notifications will be sent to the control room right away. The remaining video frames are archived and saved in low resolution, while the anomaly video is saved in high resolution. Using the sliding window method, divide the training video frames into temporal sequences of size 4.2. To guarantee that [23] all input images have the same resolution, resize each frame to 256×256.3. Divide each pixel by 256 to scale the values between 0 and 1.This model has an enormous number of parameters, so a lot of training data is needed. Thus enhance the data in the temporal dimension. In order to produce additional training sequences [2] and combine frames with different skipping strides. For instance, the frames in the first stride-1 sequence are 1, 2, 3, and 4, while the frames in the first stride-2 sequence are 1, 3, 5, and 7. We are expanding our training data in two steps. The out-of-strides are (1, 6, 11, 16) and (1, 11, 21, 31) since we are only using the fifth alternating frame. In addition to the aforementioned processing, every frame's resolution and quality are decreased before they are saved as video. This is the low-resolution video that has been saved for future use. As they don't have any anomalies, they are typically not brought up again in the future.

5   Results

The accuracy of this system in identifying objects, patterns, and anomalies in CCTV feeds would depend on the quality of the training data, the effectiveness of the CNN model, and the complexity of real-world scenarios. The training dataset consisted of 40 videos of accidents, human trafficking, no anomaly and no accidents (usual traffic). A series of 40 tests was conducted for the validation of the trained model. Every test had a single video for predicting its label. The training dataset consisted of 30 videos of accidents and no accidents (usual traffic). A series of 30 tests was conducted for the validation of the trained model. Every test had a single video for predicting its label (Fig. 3 and Table 2).

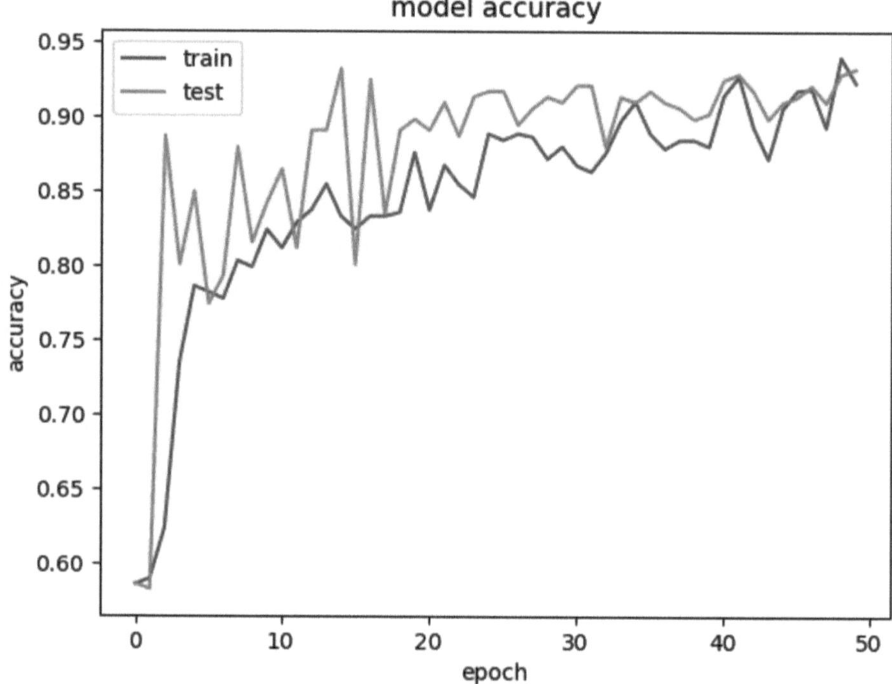

Fig. 3. Accuracy Measurement

Table 2. Accuracy and Precision values for various Models

Model	Accuracy	Precision		Recall		F1	
		NO_SEG	SEG	NO_SEG	SEG	NO_SEG	SEG
CNN-2 [3]	-	-	0.836	-	0.723	-	0.775
CNN-2A [3]	-	-	0.776	-	**0.799**	-	0.788
CNN-A_u	0.909	0.909	0	1	0	0.952	0
CNN-A	0.963	0.972	**0.853**	**0.988**	0.718	0.980	0.778
CNN-B	**0.965**	**0.975**	0.845	0.986	0.754	**0.981**	**0.795**
CNN-C	0.963	0.974	0.832	0.985	0.75	0.980	0.787

6 Conclusion

The project Accidence has developed an IOT-based product to detect and send a quick alarm to nearby police stations and hospitals. It will also focus on future research directions and recommend strategies to optimize and implement the system in real-world scenarios. People facing problems from years of road accidents, women trafficking, and kidnaps are the focus of this new solution. We worked and trained on various algorithms for quick responses and for high accuracy.

References

1. Suitha, K., Bramha Naidu, V., Gowri Shankar, P., Hemanth Kumar, P.: Human & object detection using surveillance system. Proceedings of IEEE (2008)
2. Jahagirdar, S., Koli, S.: Automatic accident detection techniques using CCTV surveillance videos: methods. Data sets and Learning Strategies international Journal of Engineering and Advanced Technology (IJEAT) **9**(3) (2020). ISSN: 2249-8958
3. Ashok Kumar, J.M., Arun Kumar, C., Abishek, B.R., Thirumagal, E.: Crime Detection in Surveillance. Int. J. Eng. Adv. Technol. (IJEAT) **8**(5S) (2019). ISSN: 2249-8958
4. Sankarnarayana, A.C.: Object Detection, Tracking and recognition for multiple smart cameras. Proceedings of IEEE (2008)
5. Bhusal, S.: Object Detection and Tracking in wide Area surveillance using thermal imagery. The University of Nevada Las Vegas (2015)
6. Ghosh, S., Joseph, S., Sunny, R.R.: Accident Detection Using Convolutional Neural Networks. International Conference on Data Science and Communication (IconDSC) (2019)
7. Thakur, N., et al.: Object Detection in Deep Surveillance. RESEARCH GATE - This is a preprint; it has not been peer reviewed by a journal (2021)
8. Mishra, P.K., Saroha, G.P.: A study on video surveillance system for object detection and tracking. 2016 3rd International Conference on "Computing for Sustainable Global Development (2016)
9. Hashmi, S.A.: Face Detection in Extreme Conditions: A Machine-learning Approach. Published in arXiv.org (2022)
10. Ghahremannezhad, H., Shi, H., Liu, C.: Real-Time Accident Detection in Traffic Surveillance Using Deep Learning. IEEE International Conference on Imaging Systems and Techniques (IST) (2022)
11. Gomathy, C.K., Geetha, V., Madhumitha, S., Sangeetha, S., Vishnupriya, R.: A secure with efficient data transaction in cloud service. Published by International Journal of Advanced Research in Computer Engineering & Technology (IJARCET) **5**(4) (2016). ISSN: 2278-1323
12. Moreira, D., et al.: Temporal robust features for violence detection. IEEE Winter Conference on Applications of Computer Vision (WACV) 8 (2017)
13. Kamijo, S., Matsushita, Y., Ikeuchi, K., Sakauchi, M.: Traffic monitoring and accident detection at intersections. IEEE Transactions on Intelligent Transportation Systems **1**(2), 108–118 (2000)
14. Huang, X., He, P., Rangarajan, A., Ranka, S.: Intelligent intersection: two-stream convolutional networks for real-time near accident detection in traffic video. ACM Transactions on Spatial Algorithms and Systems (TSAS) (2019)
15. Yao, Y., Xu, M., Wang, Y., Crandall, D.J., Atkins, E.M.: Unsupervised Traffic Accident Detection in First-Person Videos. arXiv preprint arXiv:1903.00618 (2019)
16. Radford, A., Metz, L., Chintala, S.: UnsupervisedRepresentation Learning with Deep Convolutional GenerativeAdversarial Networks, arXiv preprint arXiv:1511.06434 (2016)
17. Johnson, R., Zhang, T.: Semi-supervised Convolutional Neural Networks for Text Categorization via Region Embedding. Advances in Neural Information Processing Systems 28 (NIPS 2015)
18. Sultani, W., Chen, C., Shah, M.: Real-world Anomaly Detection in Surveillance Videos. IEEE Conference on Computer Vision and Pattern Recognition (CVPR) (2018)
19. He, K., Zhang, X., Ren, S., Sun, J.: Deep residual learning for image recognition. IEEE Conference, Computer Vision and Pattern Recognition (CVPR) (2015)
20. Ashby, P.J.: The value of cctv surveillance cameras as aninvestigative tool: an empirical analysis. European J. Crimi. Policy and Res. **23**(3), 441–459 (2017)

21. Cosar, S., Donatiello, G., Bogorny, V., Garate, C., Alvares, L.O., Bremond, F.: Toward abnormal trajectory and eventdetection in video surveillance. IEEE Trans. Circuitsand Sys. Video Technol. **27**(3), 683–695 (2017)
22. Park, J., Kim, D.H., Shin, Y.S., Lee, S.-h.: A comparison of convolutional object detectors for real-time drone tracking using a ptz camera. In: Proceedings of the 2017 17th Inter-national Conference on Control, Automation and Systems(ICCAS), pp. 696–699. IEEE, Jeju, Korea (South) (2017)
23. Mehtre, K., Mehtre, B.M.: Automated camera sabot age detection for enhancing video surveillance systems. Multi-media Tools and Applications **78**(5), 5819–5841 (2019)
24. Mathur, G., Bundele, M.: Research on intelligent video surveillance techniques for suspicious activity detection critical review. In: Proceedings of the 2016 International Conference on Recent Advances and Innovations in Engineering (ICRAIE), pp. 1–8. IEEE, Jaipur, India (2016)
25. Zhao, Z.-Q., Zheng, P., Xu, S.-T., Wu, X.: Object detectionwith deep learning: a review. IEEE Trans. Neural Netw. Learn. Sys. **30**(11), 3212–3232 (2019)
26. Makka, S., Arora, G., Mopuru, B.: IoT based health monitoring and record management using distributed ledger. In Journal of Physics: Conference Series, Vol. 2089, No. 1, p. 012030. IOP Publishing (2021)
27. Makka, S., et al.: Application of Blockchain and Internet of Things (IoT) for Ensuring Privacy and Security of Health Records and Medical Services. 2022 5th International Conference on Contemporary Computing and Informatics (IC3I), pp. 84–88. Uttar Pradesh, India (2022). https://doi.org/10.1109/IC3I56241.2022.10072427

Trust Forge: Harnessing Machine Learning to Build Trust on Social Networks

Kavitha Chitrala[1], Shanthi Makka[2(✉)], and S. Sowjanya[1]

[1] Vardhaman College of Engineering, Kacharam, Shamshabad, Hyderabad 501218, Telangana, India

[2] Computer Science and Engineering, Vardhaman College of Engineering, Kacharam, Shamshabad, Hyderabad 501218, Telangana, India
dr.shanthimakka@gmail.com

Abstract. A social media platform is a form of service offered by an online platform that facilitates easy communication between individuals, as well as the establishment of interpersonal connections and social exchanges. Additionally, it supplies users with a webpage where they may create an open persona and engage adding additional users. Trust is a significant concern in social networking sites, and to address this issue, we have employed the Naive Bayes algorithm to establish trust in online networks. This algorithm is implemented through direct and indirect communication, and trust values are calculated using Dempster-Shafer theory and Bayesian conditional. The effectiveness of our proposed approach is demonstrated through the reenactment results obtained with various parameter arrangements. "In summary, our comparison demonstrates that Multi-faceted trust modeling is statistically and significantly superior to Naive Bayes Model in addressing based on accuracy."

Keywords: Naive Bayes · online social network · trust · Direct trust · Indirect trust

1 Introduction

The term "virtual social Media" fundamentally refers to whatever type of human communication or data sharing that takes place online via a PC, mobile device, or other portable device. There are numerous websites and programs that enable it. Social networks play a significant part in day-to-day living because online interactions are now among the most common forms of communication. Because we live in a time and era where data is readily available [5] at the touch of a button and is all around us, social media platforms have experienced fast growth. However, online networks are not the only crucial component that we should not disregard. Online social networks are a contentious topic right now since the majority of people believe that they just ruin people's lives, while some believe that they are a godsend because they bring individuals from throughout the globe.

X. Cheng (Ed): BROADNETS 2024, LNICST 602, pp. 135–143, 2025.
https://doi.org/10.1007/978-3-031-81171-5_14

1.1 Trust

Trust is a fundamental concept that has a significant impact on numerous aspects of society, relationships, & human life. It refers to the reliance or confidence one places in the integrity, ability, or character of a person, group, organization, or system. Trust is built on the belief that the trusted entity will act in a certain way or fulfill certain expectations, and it forms the basis for cooperation, collaboration, and healthy social interactions.

Here are some key aspects and implications of trust:

Foundation of Relationships: Trust is essential for building and maintaining healthy relationships, whether they are personal, professional, or societal. It is the emotional and psychological glue that binds people together.

Trust-Building: Trust can be built through transparency, honesty, competence, consistency, and a track record of keeping promises. In simple way we can say that, trust is a foundational element of human relationships [6] and societal structures. It influences our interactions with others, shapes our choices, and is essential for the functioning of various institutions and systems. Building and maintaining trust is an ongoing process that relies on honesty, integrity, and consistent behavior.

1.2 Different Forms of Online Social Network Trust

Even while OSNS links a single person to the entire world, it has the potential [7] to falsify information and data. In that specific circumstance, trust significantly helps to simplify the matter. Micro and macro level trust can be broadly classified into two sorts in OSNS.

2 Literature Survey

According to the author [1], social interactions have a significant impact on each person's ability to interact with others and even exchange thoughts with them. Trust is a key factor in this activity. This essay examines a different trust paradigm for a social media platform online. Accordingly to the model incorporates the importance of reputation and social network relationships for each individual person. In addition, the author makes use Utilizing the Matrix Factorization model (MF) to assess the relationship between two customers. The Gaussian Kernel Density Estimation (GKDE) design is used to predict that a person's reputation will depend on their other relationships with clients. The reputation is evaluated based on the followers, and positive reputation is added, and both A new trust model that is used to evaluate the trust connection is created from the reputation and interaction model when paired with valid weights (Table 1).

Table 1. Literature Survey

Reference No.	Title	Author	Findings
[2]	The effect of social media marketing on brand trust, brand equity and brand loyalty	*Haudi Haudi, Wiwik Handayani*	The goal of this research is to determine the effects of social media marketing initiatives on brand equity, brand trust, and brand loyalty. Using a simple random selection technique, 450 respondents who had been using social media for at least six months were chosen for the study's sample. The Structural Equation Modeling (SEM) method was applied using SPSS 3.3.3 software
[3]	Cynicism as strength: Privacy cynicism, satisfaction and trust among social media users	*Md Irfanuzzaman Khan*	Theory (ECM), we polled 475 social media users to see if privacy cynicism has a negative impact on social media satisfaction and trust
[4]	Trust in social media brands and perceived media values: A survey study in China	*Mingmin Zhang*	Social status value has a direct impact on social media brand trust, whereas information value and organizational communication value have an indirect impact through their respective contributions to social networking, entertainment, and/or social status values. We provide a critical explanation for social media trust in our work and create a scale of perceived media values (PMV) that other studies can utilize

3 Methodology

This section starts with a system overview before moving on to the Gaussian NB model, Naïve-Bayes Model, and cross-validations, which are all provided in turn (Fig. 1).

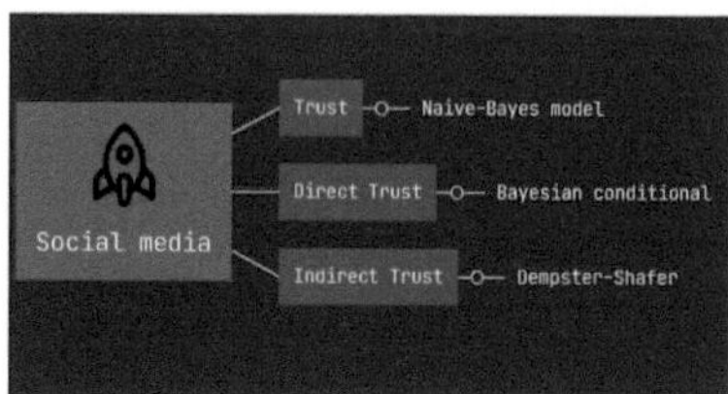

Fig. 1. Model Design

3.1 System Explanation

In recent years, online social networking is expanding quickly, [9] and many activities are being employed to spread information. With OSNS's assistance, the user can also arrange, locate, and share their ideas and experiences online. Additionally, [10] because of their candor anddecentralization, OSNS may be accessible to malicious users. Thus, there are many trust-related problems that potential customers must deal with. The user benefits from effective and efficient trust assessment (evaluation) in this way.

3.2 Naive-Bayes model

This model is a classifier that uses a machine learning (ML) model to categorize [11] different items (objects) based on particular characteristics. The Naive-Bayes model is simple to construct and frequently utilized with big datasets. In addition, the algorithm is both straightforward and powerful. This algorithm primarily relies on two components.

1. Naive
2. Bayes

The assumption made by naive Bayes classifiers is that each element in a class is unrelated to each other. Even though a property of one class is dependent on another, Nave Bayes primarily uses probability theory and independently contributes to all of the attributes. Now let's look at the Bayes theorem. A theory in probability and statistics known as the Bayes theorem measures the chance of an event happening given the chance of an event that has already happened.

Cross-validation: It is a technique used to gauge how well the results of statistical study extrapolate to other data sets. It is used to calculate the precise accuracy of a predictive model's performance estimate. The fundamental benefit of cross-validation is the ability to distinguish between training and test data. The other name for Cross-approval is an evaluation of revolution.

3.3 Gaussian NB Model

This particular NB approach is utilized most often when the data set comprises continuous values. Gaussian NB model. Additionally, [12] it is anticipated that each individual feature will follow the Gaussian distribution, which is the normal distribution. After preprocessing is completed, the Gaussian model is applied. The NB model is then constructed using sk-learns. Using the training set of data, the Gaussian NB model classifier is trained. Fit() can be used even for training. Once the classifier is built, the test set may be found using the predict() method, and the model is capable of making predictions.

3.4 OSN (Direct Trust) Bayesian Conditional Trust Calculation

By altering or rejecting the actual data or information, the affiliated perceptive mobile user can evaluate the discovered mobile user's devious behaviors in addition [13] to listening to the data or information that the discovered mobile user forwards during direct observation. The Bayesian inference is one of the statistical methods of the Bayes theorem that is utilized to update the probability hypothesis. Using the Bayesian inference approach, we built a model using continuous random variables that characterize as φ(phi) and take values between 0 and 1. In this case, the beta distribution is followed by the φ, meaning that $\varphi \sim$ Beta(h,d) with respect to h and d.

$$Beta(h, d) = \frac{\varphi^{h-1}((1-\varphi)^{1-d}}{\int_0^1 \varphi^{h-1}((1-\varphi)^{1-d} b\Omega} \tag{1}$$

The values of trust are assumed in this section with two caveats. Namely, h & d, & $0 \leq \varphi \leq 1$, Φ is beta distribution.

As more perceptions become available, we reduce our confidence in the trust by disseminating its likelihood iteratively using a probability distribution. Expect that by the (t1)th perception, the prior probability PDF (density function) will have been established. The PDF can then be used to determine the back circulation at the t th perception in accordance with the Bayes hypothesis.

$$f_x(\varphi) = \frac{f_x(a_x|\varphi, b_x)f_{x-1}(\varphi)}{\int_0^1 f_x(a_x|\varphi, b_x)f_{x-1}(\varphi)} d(\varphi) \tag{2}$$

The data packets that must be successfully sent are represented by a_x and b_x in this situation, and the observed mobile user at the time of observation accepts these packets at x th observation. Also $f_x(a_x|\varphi, b_x)$ determine as binomial distribution

$$f_x(a_x|\varphi, b_x) = \binom{b_x}{a_x} \varphi^{at}(1-\varphi)^{bt-at} \tag{3}$$

In addition the conjugate prior likelihood distribution (prior probability distribution), or beta distribution, for the binomial distribution in Bayesian deduction (inference). The prior appropriation $f_x(a_x|\varphi, b_x)$ is unquestionably recognized to seek a beta distribution, reflecting what is currently believed about the delivery of at the $f_x - 1(\varphi)$ perception, because the probability function $f_x(a_x|\varphi, b_x)$ chases a binomial dispersion. The beta circulation is pursued by the back dispersion $f_x - 1(\varphi)$ same manner as the previous appropriation $f_x - 1(\varphi)$ does. In particular, if $f_x - 1(\varphi) \sim \text{Beta} f_x(a_x - 1 | b_x - 1)$ and a_x, b_x from the xth perception are also provided, then that is the case.

$$f_x(\varphi) \sim Beta(c_{x-1} + a_x, d_{x-1} + b_x - a_x), x \geq 1 \tag{4}$$

Due to ignorance, the distribution of φ was first presented as having a consistent distribution, thus that $f0(\varphi) \sim \text{Beta}(1,1)$. Similar to how $f_x(\varphi)$ follows $\text{Beta}(a_x, b_x)$ with (specification) parameters.

$$c_x = c_{x-1} + a_x, d_x = d_{x-1} + b_x \tag{5}$$

$$c_{0=1} \qquad d_{0=1}$$

As a consequence, trust values can be stated statistically as a beta distribution anticipation

$$\text{That is } Q_x[\varphi] = \frac{c_x}{c_x + d_x} \tag{6}$$

The trustworthiness of mobile users is currently 0.5; however, as more data becomes available, the figure will change. As a result of its ability to provide more accurate weights on mischievous actions in Bayesian models, As a punishment element used for fading reputation, a new factor has been stated. Here, trust is measured using the following formula:

$$Q_x[\varphi] = \frac{c_x}{c_x + d_x} \tag{7}$$

The assessment of trust is made more accurate and realistic with the help of the penalty element. It determines behavior in two ways. The first is by checking records to see if the user of mobile content has engaged [14] in any malicious behavior. If they haven't, the trust value will decline. Second, because of the aspect of punishment, there is not a restriction that the conduct does not immediately restore the trust value. As a result of the explanation above, we may determine that TrD is the direct observation, and $\text{TrD} = Q_x[\varphi]$.

3.5 DST Function

The mass function, probability function, and belief function [15] serve as the foundation for the DST function. Upcoming use Then

The likelihood function Let $Y = \{y1,y2,y3\}$ represent the configuration of completely unconnected conclusions and evidence under certain considerations. The configuration of every subset of E (power set (E)), that is, $\{\{\emptyset,\{y1\},\{y2\},\{y3\},\{y2,y3\},\{y1,y2\},\{y1,y3\},\{y1,y2,y3\}\}\}$, is the discernment frame of X. Every element in the range [0,1] is mapped by the mass/probability function (m) from the discernment frame. $P(X) \rightarrow [0\ 1]$ is m. It satisfies the requirements that $m(\emptyset) = 0$ and that the sum of the individual items in the discernment frame equals 1.

$$\sum b \in_p (Y)m(b) = 1 \tag{8}$$

Belief Function: The total of the mass elements of all the sets in the power set that are subsets of S, for any set S in the power set, is the belief function.

$$Bel(A) = \Sigma\{m(B)|B \subseteq A\} \tag{9}$$

possibility function: The possibility function (pl(S)) for every set S in the power set is defined as the total of the mass elements of all the sets in the power set that intersect with X.

$$pl(S) = \sum m(d \cap X \neq \emptyset m(D)) \quad \text{where}$$
$$pl(S) = 1 - bel(S) \tag{10}$$

The Dempster's rule must be adhered to when combining:

If we take 1,2 as two observer clients, their confirmations on a comparable edge of decrement are m1(B), m2(C). We then use condition to find the mix of these two confirmations (m1, m2).

$$m12(A) = \Sigma\{B \cap C = A\}[m1(B) * m2(C)]/[1 - K] \tag{11}$$

where K represents constant, which is described as

$$K = \Sigma\{B \cap C = \emptyset\}[m1(B) * m2(C)] \tag{12}$$

3.5.1 Results and Analysis

In this experiment, we apply machine learning methods to compare trust. After developing the model, we examine social network samples of direct and indirect trust and assess how accurate the model is in comparison to alternative methods. The information in the Instagram data set is mainly about posts, and the training data is made up of 678775 user history logs. Each log type is {Impressions; Comments; Likes; Hashtags; Caption; Follows;}. Splitting the data set in half, so that the training set is 80% and the testing set is 20%. Testing set will conclude the experiment.

The precision after scrutiny is 0.96% (Figs. 2 and 3).

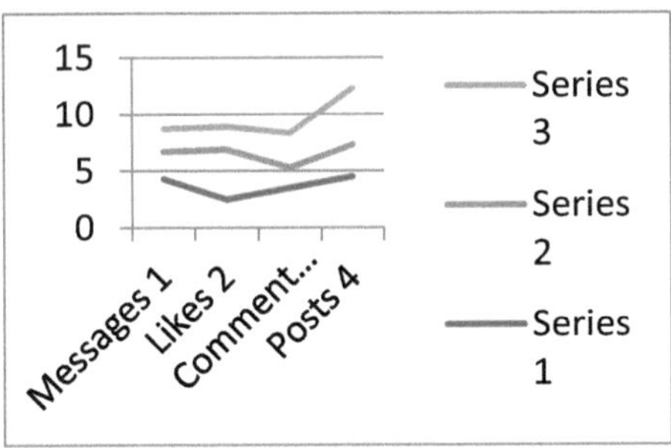

Fig. 2. Direct communication through social media Platform

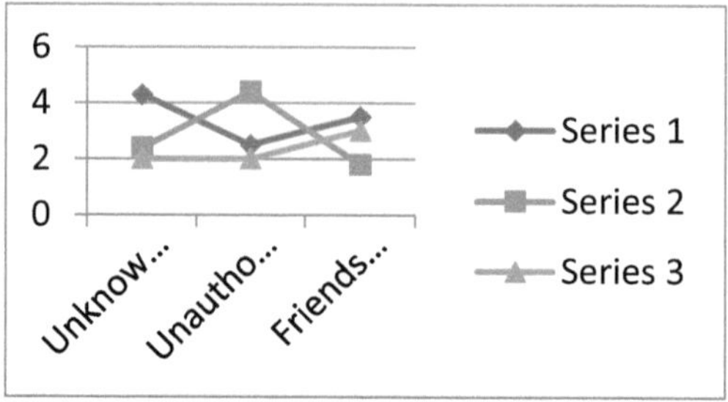

Fig. 3. Indirect Communication

4 Conclusion

In every person's life, an important paradigm is the online social network. Since data interchange is essential to real, practical life, it must also be dependable and safe. Because we used a machine learning platform and the Navie Bayes algorithm, which enables us to quantify trust using both direct and indirect approaches as well as Bayesian inference and Dempster-Shafer theory, the results are more dependable and accurate.

References

1. Yuji, W.: He rust Value Calculating for Social Network Based on Machine Learning: Conference on Intelligent Human-Machine Systems and Cybernetics USA (2017)
2. Haudi, H., Handayani, W.: The effect of social media marketing on brand trust, brand equity and brand loyalty. International Journal of Data and Network Science
3. Khan, M.I.: Cynicism as strength: Privacy cynicism, satisfaction and trust among social media users (2022)
4. Zhang, M.: Trust in social media brands and perceived media values: A survey study in China. Department of Journalism and Communication, South China Normal University, China (2022)
5. Zhao, K., Pan, L.: A machine learning based rust evaluation framework for online social networks. IEEE 13th International Conference on Trust, Security and Privacy in Computing and Communications (2014)
6. Meo, P.. Ferrara, E.: Rust and Compactness in Social Network Groups. IEEE ANSAC IONS ON CYBE NE ICS (2015)
7. Makka, S., et al.: Application of blockchain and internet of things (IoT) for ensuring privacy and security of health records and medical services. 2022 5th International Conference on Contemporary Computing and Informatics (IC3I), pp. 84–88. Uttar Pradesh, India (2022). https://doi.org/10.1109/IC3I56241.2022.10072427
8. Uany, Y.: A survey of rust management systems for online social communities –trust modelling, rust Inference and Attacks. Department of computer & information science, In USA (2016)
9. Makka, S., Arora, G., Mopuru, B.: IoT based health monitoring and record management using distributed ledger. In: Journal of Physics: Conference Series. Vol. 2089, No. 1, p. 012030. IOP Publishing (2021)
10. Islam Habis Mohammad Hatamleh: Trust in Social Media: Enhancing Social Relationships (2023)

11. Karlsena, R.: Social Media and Trust in News: An Experimental Study of the Effect of Facebook on News Story Credibility. Digital Journalism (2021)
12. Kim, D.Y., Kim, H.Y.: Trust me, trust me not: A nuanced view of influencer marketing on social media. Journal of Business Research, Elsevier (2021)
13. Parmentier, A.: Personalized multifaceted trust modeling to determine trust MANETs. International Conference on Advanced Computing and Communications ADCOM, (IITM PhD forum), pp. 55–60.1 (2015)
14. Shen, J.: Hierarchical Trust Level Evaluation for Pervasive Social Networking, in 2017
15. Uany, Y.: A Survey of rust Management Systems for Online Social Communities –Trust Modelling, rust Inference and Attacks. In USA (2016)

Database Under Siege: The Hidden Menace of SQL Injection Attacks

Rajitha Ala[1(✉)], Attili Venkata Ramana[2], Vasantha Sandhya Venu[1], Kiranmai Bejjam[3], Sai Sriharsha Kanagala[1], Bheemeshwar Punyamurthy[1], and Ruchitha Sangeam[1]

[1] Department of CSE, Vardhaman College of Engineering, Hyderabad, India
`rajitha.it222@gmail.com`
[2] Department of CSE-Data Science, Geethanjali College Of Engineering and Technology, Hyderabad, India
[3] Department of CSE, Keshav Memorial Institute of Technology, Hyderabad, India

Abstract. The report begins by providing a detailed explanation of SQL injection attacks, illustrating how attackers exploit vulnerabilities in application code to inject malicious SQL queries. Attackers use various methods to bypass security and access data. In addition, the report delves into the underlying causes that make databases susceptible to SQL injection attacks, including poor input validation, lack of parameterized queries, and inadequate access controls. It highlights the importance of secure coding practices and ongoing vulnerability assessments as proactive measures to mitigate risk. To address this growing menace, the report explores a range of defense strategies and best practices. It discusses the implementation of robust input validation techniques, the utilization of parameterized queries, and the adoption of web application firewalls. Furthermore, it emphasizes the significance of educating developers, administrators, and users about SQL injection risks and the adoption of a security-first mindset.

Keywords: Vulnerability assessment · Parameterized queries · Intercept · Repeater · cookies

1 Introduction

SQL injection attacks leverage security vulnerabilities in application code to manipulate SQL queries and gain unauthorized access to databases [1, 2]. By injecting malicious SQL code, attackers can bypass security measures and extract sensitive data or even modify the database contents, compromising the integrity and confidentiality of the information. The consequences of successful SQL injection attacks can be severe, ranging from financial losses and reputational damage to regulatory non-compliance and legal repercussions. This report dives into various techniques attackers employ to exploit SQL injection vulnerabilities [3]. It examines real-world examples and case studies to illustrate the devastating impact such attacks can have on organizations across industries.

X. Cheng (Ed): BROADNETS 2024, LNICST 602, pp. 144–153, 2025.
https://doi.org/10.1007/978-3-031-81171-5_15

By understanding the attack vectors and the methods used by attackers, organizations can develop a comprehensive defense strategy to migrate the risk. Moreover, this report delves into the underlying causes that make databases susceptible to SQL injection attacks [4]. It explores the importance of secure coding practices, robust input validation techniques, and adequate access controls in preventing and migrating such attacks. By addressing these root causes and implementing appropriate security measures, organizations can significantly reduce their vulnerability to SQL injection attacks [5]. To counter the hidden menace of SQL injection attacks, this report also provides an array of defense strategies and best practices [6]. It highlights the role of parameterized queries, web application firewalls, and continuous security education in bolstering database security. The comments provided by the programmer can also give a chance to the attacker [7]. Additionally, it emphasizes the significance of regular security audits, continuous monitoring, and prompt patching of vulnerabilities to maintain a robust security posture [8]. The login system is usually the most vulnerable point of a database system, as it is the most common target for attacks. Attackers often use brute force tactics to guess passwords. This involves trying every possible combination, similar to a dictionary attack. Another commonly used attack is SQL injection, where an attacker can gain access to the system without proper authorization by injecting malicious code like '1' OR '1= =1' into the username and password fields. It is important to have proper prevention methods in place to avoid such attacks [9–13]. By assimilating the knowledge presented in this report, organizations can fortify their databases and protect their critical assets from the lurking threat of SQL injection attacks. The report [14] enhances their understanding of the menace posed by SQL injection attacks and proactively safeguards their databases [15]. This report provides a comprehensive.understanding of SQL injection attacks and their potential consequences. This report aims to provide a comprehensive understanding of the threat landscape, highlight the potential consequences of such attacks, and equip organizations with the knowledge and tools necessary to defend against this pervasive menace. The digital landscape is increasingly interconnected, with databases serving as the backbone of countless applications and systems. These databases hold critical and sensitive information, making them prime targets for malicious actors seeking to exploit vulnerabilities and gain unauthorized access [4]. Numerous threats pose a danger to databases, but SQL injection attacks are particularly insidious. These attacks have the potential to cause significant harm and expose organizations to serious risks [17]. Once the location of the vulnerability and the target information have been determined, attackers can use various tools to automate the process [18].

2 Literature Survey

Over the past couple of decades, there has been a significant increase in the number of network services that are exposed to the outside world, such as web servers, application servers, remote procedure call services, and more. As a result, the attack surface area has increased considerably. Thus, both enterprises and government institutions have started paying more attention to the security of their information systems. This is understandable as the volume, value, and sensitivity of information collected and stored in digital form by network services continue to grow. Despite increased attention, recent surveys have shown that 90 out of 100 enterprises reported a security attack in their systems [19]. Attackers tend to target vulnerable applications. Network-connected software can be vulnerable to attack by unauthorized users who exploit weaknesses in the software's design, configuration or programming. A common method of attack is through the use of remote exploits, which can grant unauthorized access to computer systems or extend user privileges. These exploits target network service programs or security protocols, and may include issues such as buffer overflow, integer overflow, or format string vulnerabilities resulting from poor coding practices, as well as back doors inserted into compromised software versions, misconfigured internet servers with cross- site scripting, SQL injection vulnerabilities, or excessive file and directory controls.

When an unauthorized mechanism is used to access system resources or data, it is called an intrusion. Intruders may use different methods to penetrate a system, depending on whether the attack is from within or outside the target network. Virus infections are a common method of internal intrusion, while external attacks require complex sequences of attacks to access the target network or server.

To protect against both internal and external intrusions, network administrators deploy Intrusion Detection Systems (IDS) to safeguard essential network and enterprise services.

2.1 Issues in Existing System

The following are basic issues which are most commonly found in these systems:

1. *False Positives and False Negatives:* Some systems may generate false positives, flagging legitimate queries as potential SQL injection attacks. This can result in unnecessary interruptions and delays in application functionality. On the other hand, false negatives can occur when an SQL injection attack goes undetected, allowing malicious queries to bypass the system's defenses.
2. *Complexity and Overhead:* Implementing and configuring security systems can be complex and time-consuming. Some systems may require significant resources, such as computational power and storage, which can result in performance overhead. This can impact the overall responsiveness and scalability of the application.
3. *Lack of Contextual Awareness:* Systems primarily rely on patterns, rules, or heuristics to detect SQL injection attacks. However, these methods may not capture the full context of the application and the intended behavior of queries. As a result, certain variations or sophisticated attack techniques may go undetected.
4. *Limited Coverage:* While systems can protect against known SQL injection attack vectors, they may struggle to handle novel or evolving attack techniques. Attackers are constantly developing new methods to bypass security measures, and systems may not always keep up with these emerging threats.
5. *Dependency on Proper Configuration and Updates:* To ensure optimal performance, these systems require proper configuration and regular updates. If not maintained correctly, the system may become ineffective and fail to detect or prevent SQL injection attacks.

3 Proposed Model

1. To begin, open Docker and access the Windows operating system's user interface by running the command "wsl –update" in the terminal. Pull Docker to the interface using the appropriate command. Activate Docker for further operations with the command "docker run –rmp 3000:3000." If the specified port is unavailable, choose a different port number. From the content [14, 15], to access the OWASP web page, enter the assigned port number in the browser. Login with valid credentials. By context [5–10], as an unauthorized user, you can attempt SQL bypassing by using the username 'OR 1=1– without providing any password. This process exploits vulnerabilities in the login mechanism.Another tool, Burp Suite, is used to enhance software security. It helps identify vulnerabilities in database code. For testing vulnerabilities on a different website, such as Synk, open Burp Suite and enable the proxy. Ensure the intercept feature is turned on. Open any browser and enter the port number, then check for vulnerabilities in the Department of Information Technology 18 code. Move forward until you find occurrences of '?var=','?=', or '= var' in the code. After identifying vulnerabilities, copy the code and paste it into the repeater (in Burp Suite). In the repeater, utilize malicious code to retrieve the database version. Use the command:'))+UNION+SELECT+(SELECT+sqlite version()),2,3,…8,9. Once the request is sent, disable the interceptor and Docker to access other pages. To simplify this process, the application Sqlmap can be used to decrease time.

2. complexity. For blind SQL processes, open a browser and click on "create or reset database" to remove bypass access. Attempt to log in using the bypass method. If access is denied, the "SUCCESSFULLY BYPASSING ACCESS IS REMOVED"

3. message is displayed. Now, log in using the username "admin" and the corresponding password. Select "SQL Injection Blind" and utilize the trial and error method to enter the username. If access is gained, follow the same procedure related to the error-based technique. To check vulnerabilities related to the sleep function, use the command "1'+AND+sleep(5) to decode the asterisk and verify vulnerabilities. To speed up the process, an application called Sublime is used. The complete code is dumped into Sublime, compiled, and executed using the command "python./filename.py" This helps obtain the precise version of the database.

4 Injected Queries

The attacker sends SQL queries to the database to cause errors and then monitors error messages displayed by the database server.

```
(1)        '))+UNION+SELECT+(SELECT+sqlite_version()),2,3,4,5,
    6,7,8,9-'
```

This is a comprehensive web application security testing platform, which includes a range of tools for detecting and exploiting blind SQL injection vulnerabilities, such as the Repeater and Intruder modules.

$$(2) \qquad \texttt{1'+AND+SUBSTRING(VERSION(),1,1)='1'\#}$$

Time-based SQL Injection is an inferential SQL Injection technique that relies on sending an SQL query to the database which forces the database to wait for a specified amount of time (in seconds) before responding.

$$(3) \qquad \texttt{1'+AND+sleep(5)\#}$$

4.1 Algorithms

```
import requests
import urllib.parse
URL =
'http://localhost:80/vulnerabilities/sqli_blind/?id=1%s&Submit=
Submit'
chars = [str(i) for i in range(0,10)]
chars.append('.')
cookies = {
        'language':'en',
        'PHPSESSID':'2tebm90hin97vlm9mtm4gvm597',
        'security':'low',
        'continueCode':'15wOojDeg73OnzQ6aB4Z8ERMvyJr0XYAq9p
w5xYVWmkj2P11XLoNbK7vRbkE',
        }
query = "' AND SUBSTRING(version(),%d,1)='%s' #"
#query = urllib.parse.quote_plus(query)
res = ""
currentCharacter = 1
while 1:
        charAdded = False
        for i in chars:
          print("checking: ",res+i)
          temp_query = query%(currentCharacter,i)
          temp_query = urllib.parse.quote_plus(temp_query)
          r = requests.get(URL%temp_query,cookies=cookies)
    if not "User ID is MISSING from the database." in r.text:
            res+=i
            charAdded = True
            break
        if not charAdded:
          break
        currentCharacter+=1
print("Final Result: ",res)
```

5   Results Discussion

The testing process for SQL injection attacks involves assessing the vulnerability of a web application or system to SQL injection threats. It aims to identify weaknesses in the application's code, input validation, and database interaction that can be exploited by attackers. This is an overview of the testing process for SQL injection attacks It's important to note that SQL injection testing should only be performed on systems or applications with proper authorization and permission from the owner. Unethical or unauthorized SQL injection testing is illegal and can lead to severe consequences.

1) *Vulnerability Scanning:* Use automated vulnerability scanning tools to scan the web application for potential SQL injection vulnerabilities. These tools analyze the application's input fields and parameters to identify any points of weakness that could be exploited by SQL injection attacks (Fig. 1).

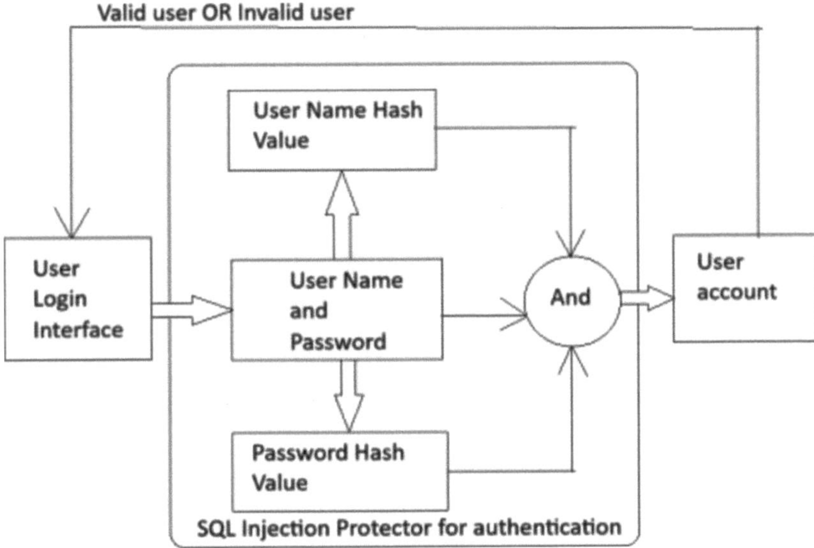

Fig. 1. Flow Chart

2) *Manual Code Review:* During the application's source code review, check for insecure coding practices, such as concatenating user input directly into SQL queries, which may lead to SQL injection vulnerabilities. Ensure proper sanitization and parameterization are used (Fig. 2).

3) *Input Validation Testing:* Test the application's input validation mechanisms by submitting various types of input, including SQL injection payloads, to assess how the application handles them. Verify that the input validation routines are correctly implemented and effectively reject or sanitize potentially malicious input (Fig. 3).

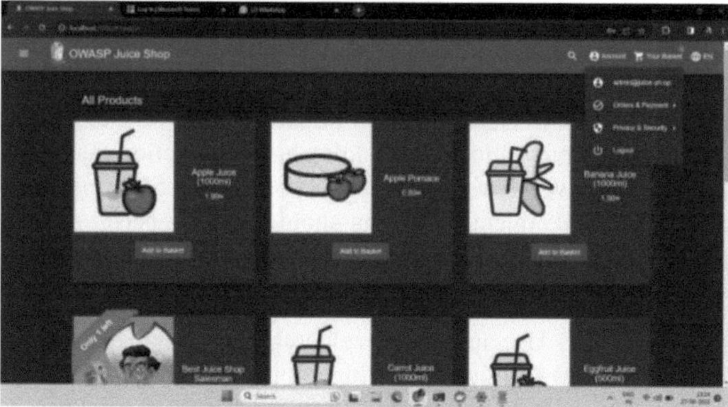

Fig. 2. Web page

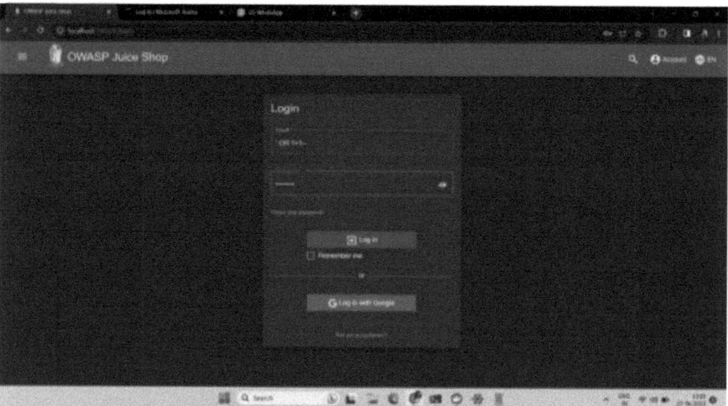

Fig. 3. Account Accessing

4) *Parameterized Query Testing:* Verify the usage of parameterized queries or prepared statements throughout the application. Test scenarios where user input is properly bound to query parameters to ensure that SQL injection attacks are prevented by treating user input as data values rather than executable code (Fig. 4).

5) *Boundary and Error Condition Testing:* Perform testing with boundary values and error conditions to validate that the application handles them securely. This includes testing inputs such as quotes, special characters, and excessively long or invalid input to ensure they do not trigger SQL injection vulnerabilities.

6) *Authentication and Authorization Testing:* SQL injection attacks can also be targeted at login forms and authentication mechanisms. Test the application's authentication and authorization processes to ensure they are not susceptible to SQL injection attacks that could bypass security controls.

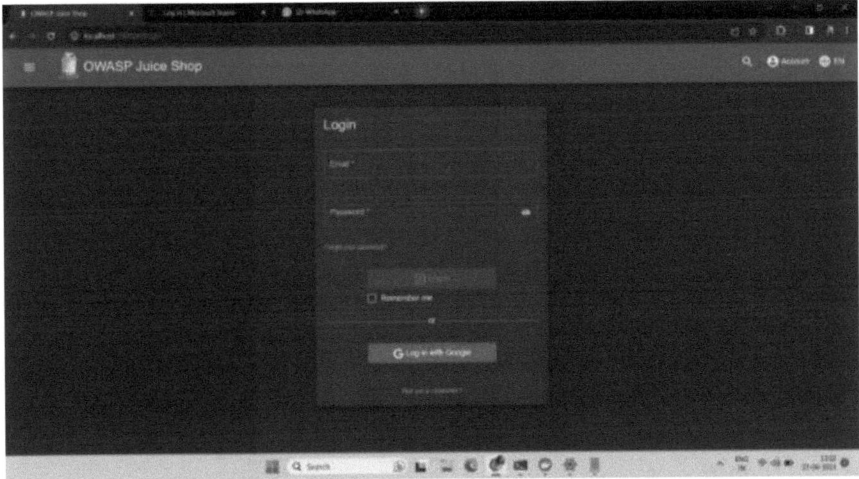

Fig. 4. Login Page

7) *Query Behavior Analysis:* Monitor the application's query behavior during testing to detect any suspicious or unexpected patterns that could indicate potential SQL injection attacks. Analyze query logs and monitor query response times to identify abnormal behavior that may require further investigation (Fig. 5).

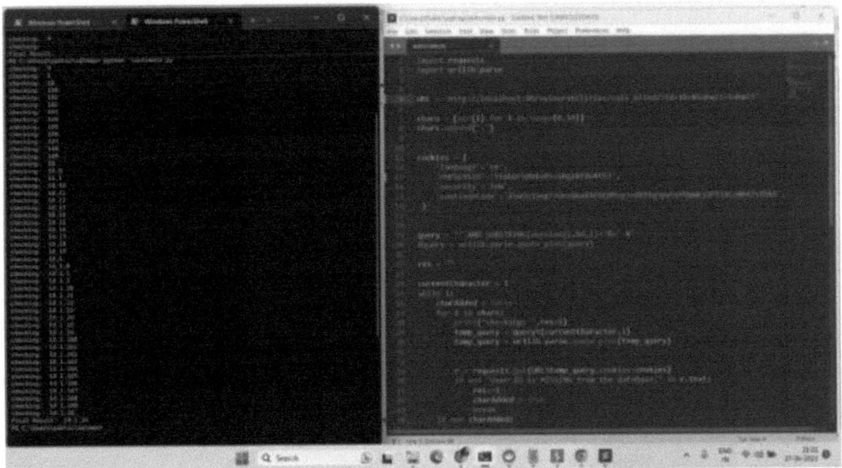

Fig. 5. Python code

8) *Penetration Testing:* Conduct comprehensive penetration testing, simulating real-world attack scenarios to identify and exploit SQL injection vulnerabilities. This involves attempting to inject malicious SQL code and assess the impact, such as unauthorized data access or privilege escalation.

9) *Security Incident Response Testing:* Test the application's incident response procedures for SQL injection attacks. Evaluate how the system detects, alerts, and responds to potential SQL injection incidents, including logging, notification, and remediation processes.

10) *Retesting and Continuous Monitoring:* Regularly retest the application for SQL injection vulnerabilities, especially after implementing preventive measures or making code changes. Implement continuous monitoring and automated security scanning to detect and prevent new SQL injection vulnerabilities that may emerge over time.

6 Conclusion

The most pressing concern in modern times is ensuring website security. It is crucial to address multiple vulnerabilities that can lead to unauthorized access and compromise sensitive account information. One common method employed by attackers is SQL injection, which involves manipulating data in web forms or URLs to exploit weaknesses in the database or code. The objective of such an attack is to make the database behave in an insecure or undesirable manner. The consequences can be severe, ranging from unauthorized access to confidential data to unauthorized modification, addition, or deletion of data. SQL injection attacks can pose significant risks to businesses. There are three primary types of such attacks - classic, blind, and out-of-band. The most common method, the classic type, targets the database itself by injecting malicious data into a query. For instance, attackers might append the "–" sequence at the end of a query to trick many RDBMS applications into treating the rest of the command as a comment. Such attacks can result in reputational damage, operational, and logistical challenges for businesses.

References

1. Salih, A.A., et al.: Deep learning approaches for intrusion detection. Asian J. Res. Comput. Sci., 50–64 (2021)
2. Kim, M.-Y., Lee, D.H.: Data-mining based SQL injection attack detection using internal query trees. Expert Syst. Appl. **9**, 416–430 (2013)
3. Anley, C.: Advanced. SQL injection SQL sever application.[EB], [online]. Available: http://www.creangel.com/papers/advanced-sqlinjection.pdf
4. T. M. D. Network. Request.servervariables collection. Technical report, Microsoft Corporation (2005). http://msdn.microsoft.com/library/default.asp?url=/library/en-us/iissdk/html/9768ecfe-8280-4407-b9c0-844f75508752.asp
5. Ibrahimi, K., Ouaddane, M.: Management of intrusion detection systems based-kdd99: analysis with LDA and PCA. In: 2017 International Conference on Wireless Networks and Mobile Communications (WINCOM), pp. 1–6. IEEE (2017)

6. Aditya, A.S., Chatur, P.N.: Efficient and effective security model for database specially designed to avoid internal threats. In: International Conference on Smart Technologies and Management for Computing, Communication, Controls, Energy and Materials (ICSTM), p. 165 (2015)

7. Alwan, Z.S., Younis, M.F.: Detection and prevention of sql injection attack: a survey. Int. J. Comput. Sci. Mob. Comput. **6**, 5–17 (2017)

8. Young-Su, J., Jin-Young, C.: Detecting SQL injection attacks using query result size. Comput. Secur. **44**, 104–118 (2014)

9. Rashmi, T.V.: Predicting the system failures using machine learning algorithms. Int. J. Adv. Sci. Innov. **1**(1), (2020). https://doi.org/10.5281/zenodo.4641686

10. Singh, N., Dayal, M., Raw, R.S., Suresh, K.: SQL injection: types, methodology, attack queries and prevention. In: 3rd International Conference on Computing for Sustainable Global Development (INDIACom), pp. 2872–2876 (2016)

11. Vamshi, K.G., Trinadh, V., Soundabaya, S., Omar, A.: Advanced automated SQL injection attacks and defensive mechanisms. In: Annual Connecticut Conference on Industrial Electronics, Technology and Automation (CT-IETA), pp. 1–6 (2016)

12. Su, Z., Wassermann, G.: The essence of command injection attacks in web applications. In: the 33rd Annual Symposium on Principles of Programming Languages (POPL 2006) (2006)

13. Raja, P.K., Bing, Z.: Enhanced approach to detection of SQL injection attack. In: 15th IEEE International Conference on Machine Learning and Applications (ICMLA), pp. 466–469 (2016)

14. Halfond, W.G.J., Orso, A.: A classification of SQL injection attacks and countermeasures. In: Proceedings of the International Symposium on Secure Software Engineering, vol. 17, pp. 13–23. IEEE (2006)

15. Liu, C.Y., Lu, H.H., Kuo, S.Y.: An intelligent SQL injection detection system based on genetic programming. Expert Syst. Appl. **34**(2), 1153–1163 (2008)

16. Krit, K., Chitsutha, S.: Machine learning for SQL injection prevention on server- side scripting. In: International Computer Science and Engineering Conference (ICSEC), pp. 1–6 (2016)

17. Anley, C.: Advanced SQL Injection in SQL Server Applications (2002). Retrieved from https://www.nextgenss.com/papers/advanced-sqlinjection.pdf

18. Using SQLBrute to brute force data from a blind SQL injection point. Justin Clarke. Archived from the original on June 14, 2008. Retrieved October 18, 2008

19. T. O. Foundation: Top Ten Most Critical Web Application Vulnerabilities (2005). http://www.owasp.org/documentation/topten.html

20. Ghorbanzadeh, P., Shaddeli, A., Malekzadeh, R., Jahanbakhsh, Z.: A Survey of Mobile Database Security Threats and Solutions for it. In: the 3rd International Conference on Information Sciences and Interaction Sciences, pp. 676–682 (2007)

21. Aucsmith, D.: Creating and Maintaining Software that Resists Malicious Attack

22. Howard, M., LeBlanc, D.: Writing Secure Code, 2nd edn. Microsoft Press, Redmond, Washington (2003)

23. Robertson, S., Siegel, E.V., Miller, M., Stolfo, S.J.: Surveillance detection in high bandwidth environments. In: DARPA Information Survivability Conference and Exposition, 2003. Proceedings, vol. 1, pp. 130–138. IEEE (2003)

24. Yasin, H.M., Zeebaree, S.R., Zebari, I.M.: Arduino based automatic irrigation system: monitoring and SMS controlling. In: 2019 4th Scientific International Conference Najaf (SICN), pp. 109–114 (2019)

SearchScrapeAssistant Application Using RPA Tool

S. Adityeshwar Goud[1], Sindhuja Ramala[1], PavanTeja Modugu[1], Ravi Kumar[1(✉)] ⓘD,
Amit Lathigara[2], and M. Vinay Kumar Redy[2]

[1] Department of Information, Technology, Vardhaman College of Engineering (Autonomous),
Hyderabad, India
`ravikumar.e@gmail.com`
[2] Department of Information, RK University, Rajkot, Gujarat, India

Abstract. The goal is to develop a solution using UiPath Studio's Robotic Process Automation (RPA) capabilities to scrape relevant data from LinkedIn profiles and pages efficiently and accurately. The solution should be able to navigate through LinkedIn's web interface, search for specific profiles or keywords, ex-tract desired information from profiles and pages, and store the extracted data for further analysis or integration with other systems. The specific challenges to address include Authenticating and accessing LinkedIn's website, Navigating and interacting with LinkedIn's user interface, Extracting structured data, Handling pagination and multiple search results, Error handling and resilience. By addressing these challenges, the goal is to develop a UiPath Studio automation workflow that can extract relevant data from LinkedIn web pages efficiently and reliably. The extracted data can then be used for various business purposes, providing valuable insights and streamlining processes that rely on LinkedIn data. And also to develop the solution in such a way that if the user doesn't want anything from LinkedIn then it will ask for any other query that the user wants to know and navigates that input to the chat GPT and finds the answer for the query and displays it to the user.

Keywords: Robotic Process Automation (RPA) · UiPath · Web Scrapping · Data Extraction · Linkedin

1 Introduction

Web data extraction involves the retrieval of information from websites and web pages [12]. It is an integral part of many businesses' operations [11], as it can be used for data analysis, market research, competitor analysis, lead generation, and more [16]. Using software robots or bots, Robotic Process Automation is a technology that enables businesses to automate tasks that are repetitive and rule-based [1, 2]. RPA bots can be used to interact with different systems and applications [4], including web browsers, to perform tasks efficiently and accurately [3]. LinkedIn is a treasure trove of data for businesses of all sizes [15]. From recruitment to market research, there is no shortage of ways to leverage LinkedIn data to your advantage. However, manually extracting data

© ICST Institute for Computer Sciences, Social Informatics and Telecommunications Engineering 2025
Published by Springer Nature Switzerland AG 2025. All Rights Reserved
X. Cheng (Ed): BROADNETS 2024, LNICST 602, pp. 154–166, 2025.
https://doi.org/10.1007/978-3-031-81171-5_16

from LinkedIn can be time-consuming and error-prone. Web data extraction, also known as web scraping, is the process of automating the extraction of data from websites [16]. By integrating web data extraction with. ChatGPT, a large language model developed by OpenAI, you can enhance the conversational abilities of the AI model and make it more intelligent and context-aware [4]. UiPath Studio is a leading RPA tool that can be used to automate web data extraction from LinkedIn [6]. By combining the power of web data extraction, RPA, ChatGPT integration, and UiPath Studio for documentation, organizations can gain valuable insights from LinkedIn data to drive business growth and innovation [4]. In this paper, we will discuss how to use web data extraction, RPA, ChatGPT Integration, and UiPath Studio to automate data collection from LinkedIn [17]. We will also provide examples of how this can be used to improve decision-making processes, enhance customer interactions, and gain valuable insight [14].

1.1 Motivation

LinkedIn is a popular professional networking platform with over 830 million members worldwide. It is a valuable source of data for businesses of all sizes, as it contains information on a wide range of topics, including employee profiles, company pages, job postings, and industry trends. However, manually extracting data from LinkedIn can be time-consuming and error-prone. This is where Robotic Process Automation (RPA) can help. RPA is a technology enabling businesses to automate repetitive and rule-based tasks through the utilization of software robots or bots. RPA bots can be used to interact with different systems and applications, including web browsers, to perform tasks efficiently and accurately. UiPath Studio is a leading RPA tool that can be used to automate web data extraction from LinkedIn. By developing a UiPath Studio RPA solution to scrape data from LinkedIn, we can address the following challenges:

- Authentication and access.
- Navigation and interaction.
- Structured data extraction.
- Pagination and multiple search results.
- Error handling and resilience.

1.2 Contribution

We developed a solution that uses UiPath Studio to automate the process of extracting data from LinkedIn [12, 16]. Our solution can efficiently and accurately scrape relevant data from LinkedIn profiles and pages, such as job titles, work experience, education, and skills [6]. It can also navigate through LinkedIn's web interface, search for specific profiles or keywords, and store the extracted data for further analysis or integration with other systems [18]. Our solution is also flexible enough to be adapted to meet the specific needs of each user [4]. For example, if a user does not want to extract data from LinkedIn, they can instead provide a query to ChatGPT, which will then find and display the answer to the query [17]. We believe that our solution has the potential to revolutionize the way businesses use LinkedIn data. By automating the process of data extraction, our solution can save businesses time and money, and help them to gain valuable insights that can drive theirsuccess [5].

1.3 Methodology

1.3.1 UiPath

UiPath, previously recognized as Desk Over since 2005, initially created automation libraries and SDKs for corporations such as IBM, Google, and Microsoft. It was in 2012 when they redirected their attention to the RPA market, partnering with BPO providers like Cognizant, Accenture, and Deloitte. They further enhanced their tools to cater to various industries including BFSI, healthcare, telecom, media, and retail. UiPath is headquartered in Bucharest, [6] UiPath's RPA platform consists of three core components: UiPath Studio for process design, [20] UiPath Robot for task automation, and UiPath Orchestrator for process management. They offer both Community and Enterprise Editions, catering to users from beginners to large enterprises [11]. Recognizing the importance of training, UiPath provides a comprehensive online learning platform to enhance users' understanding of their tools and services. They offer various services, training programs, and certifications to facilitate product integration into customer enterprises. This platform covers everything needed for deploying, operating, and scaling robotic factories from a centralized dashboard. In addition to their core offerings, UiPath's Automation Testing product, TestSuite, combines Test Manager, StudioPro, Orchestrator, and Robots [13]. This suite effectively tackles typical software testing obstacles, such as regression testing, assessing business logic, and conducting combinatorial testing, aligning seamlessly with the requirements of software testing and development.

Pros of UiPath:
Strong Technology Partnerships: UiPath's extensive network of 250+ technology partners enables seamless integrations with major enterprise products, enhancing its adaptability and versatility for businesses. Active Developer Community: With a community of 750,000 developers, UiPath fosters collaborative innovation and resource sharing in its marketplace, enriching its pool of automation and AI tools.

Operational Excellence: UiPath's commitment to operational excellence is evident in its dedicated resources for helping users scale RPA solutions. They offer free and paid versions, ample learning resources, online training, and certifications, empowering users to maximize the potential of their RPA tools, including TestSuite for software.

Cons of Uipath

- pricing,
- customer support
- product upgrades and
- deployment

1.3.2 LinkedIn

LinkedIn is a professional networking platform with over 830 million members worldwide [18]. It is a valuable source of data for businesses of all sizes, as it contains information about professionals, companies, and industries. However, manually extracting data from LinkedIn can be time-consuming and error-prone.

Web data extraction, also known as web scraping, is the process of automating the extraction of data from websites [12]. By integrating web data extraction with Robotic Process Automation (RPA) and ChatGPT [11], a large language model developed by OpenAI [19], organizations can automate the process of collecting and analyzing data from LinkedIn to gain valuable insights. In this paper, we will discuss how to use web data extraction, RPA, and ChatGPT integration to automate data collection from LinkedIn. We will also provide examples of how this can be used to improve decision-making processes, enhance customer interactions, and gain valuable insights.Web data extraction, RPA, and ChatGPT integration can be used to automate the process of collecting data from LinkedIn.

- Identifying potential customers or leads
- Tracking industry trends
- Analyzing competitor activity

  Understanding employee sentiment

2 Literature Review

Web data extraction, often referred to as web scraping, involves the retrieval of information from websites and web pages. This practice is fundamental to numerous business operations, serving purposes such as data analysis, market research, competitor assessment, lead generation, and more. Robotic Process Automation (RPA) stands as a technological solution enabling enterprises to automate repetitive and rule-based assignments through the utilization of software robots or bots [7]. These RPA bots possess the capability to engage with diverse systems and applications, encompassing web browsers, in order to execute tasks with precision and efficiency. LinkedIn is a treasure trove of data for businesses of all sizes. From recruitment to market research, there is no shortage of ways to leverage LinkedIn data to your advantage. However, manually extracting data from LinkedIn can be time-consuming and error-prone [10].

2.1 Web Data Extraction

Web data extraction is the process of extracting data from websites and web pages [12]. It can be used to collect a wide variety of data, such as product information, contact information, financial data, and social media data [16]. Web data extraction can be used for a variety of purposes, such as:

- Data analysis: Web data extraction can be used to collect data for analysis and reporting. For example, a business might use web data extraction to collect data on competitor pricing or product reviews.
- Market research: Web data extraction serves as a valuable method for gathering information to support market research objectives. For instance, a company could employ web data extraction to compile data related to customer preferences or prevailing trends
- within the industry.

- Competitive analysis of data: Web data extraction can be used to collect data for competitive analysis purposes. For example, a business might use web data extraction to collect data on competitor products or pricing strategies.
- Lead generation: Web data extraction can be used to generate leads for sales and marketing purposes. For example, a business might use web data extraction to collect contact information for potential customers.

2.2 Robotic Process Automation

Robotic Process Automation is a technology that enables businesses to automate repetitive and rule-based tasks through the use of software robots or bots. RPA bots can be used to interact with different systems and applications, [14] including web browsers, to perform tasks efficiently and accurately.

Automation using RPA encompasses a diverse range of tasks, including:

- Data entry: RPA bots can be used to enter data into different systems and applications. For example, an RPA bot could be used to enter customer order information into a CRM system.
- Data processing: RPA bots can be used to process data in different ways. For example, an RPA bot could be used to process data from a web form and then store it in a database.
- Reporting: RPA bots can be used to generate reports from different systems and applications. For example, an RPA bot could be used to generate a daily sales report from a CRM system [9].

2.3 LinkedIn Data Extraction

LinkedIn is a professional networking platform with over 830 million members worldwide. It is a valuable source of data for businesses of all sizes, as it contains information about professionals, companies, and industries. However, manually extracting data from LinkedIn can be time-consuming and error-prone. Web data extraction can be used to automate the process of collecting data from LinkedIn. LinkedIn data extraction can be used to collect a variety of data [8], such as:

- Professional profiles: LinkedIn data extraction can be used to collect data on professional profiles, such as name, job title, company, education, and skills.
- Company profiles: LinkedIn data extraction can be used to collect data on company profiles, such as company name, industry, location, and number of employees.
- Industry trends: LinkedIn data extraction can be used to collect data on industry trends, such as popular job titles, skills, and companies.

Benefits of Automating LinkedIn Data Extraction:
There are several benefits to automating LinkedIn data extraction:

- Save time: Automating LinkedIn data extraction can save businesses a significant amount of time.
- Reduce errors: Automating LinkedIn data extraction can help to reduce errors that can occur when manually extracting data.

- Gain insights: Automating LinkedIn data extraction can help businesses to gain valuable insights from LinkedIn data. For example, a business might use LinkedIn data extraction to identify potential customers, track industry trends, or analyze competitor activity.

2.4 Issues in Existing System

Previously, we only had the process of data extraction from LinkedIn, without any additional advantages [12]. However, with our new model, we have added several more features to make it easier for users to access more than just data extraction. We have added various activities such as Input Dialog, Message Box, Type Into, Click, Data Scraping, Write Range, and integration with ChatGPT using HTTP Request, Deserialize JSON, and related activities [4].

3 Proposed Model

The proposed model is a web automation framework that combines web automation with UiPath activities to interact with websites and extract data. The framework also integrates with ChatGPT to enhance its conversational abilities and make it more context-aware.

The framework leverages web browsing capabilities to navigate websites, perform user actions, and scroll through pages. It can also retrieve HTML content and interact with web elements. This enables users to interact with websites programmatically. Data scraping is a core feature of the framework, enabling users to extract specific data from web pages. By leveraging web scraping, screen scraping, and HTML parsing techniques, the framework can retrieve text, images, links, tables, and other relevant information from websites. This functionality is highly useful for gathering data from diverse online sources. Another key aspect of the framework is chat integration, which enables users to interact with the framework through chat applications. By integrating seamlessly with popular messaging platforms, the framework can receive commands, respond to queries, and provide requested information from the web. This integration facilitates a user-friendly and familiar interface for interacting with the framework (Fig. 1).

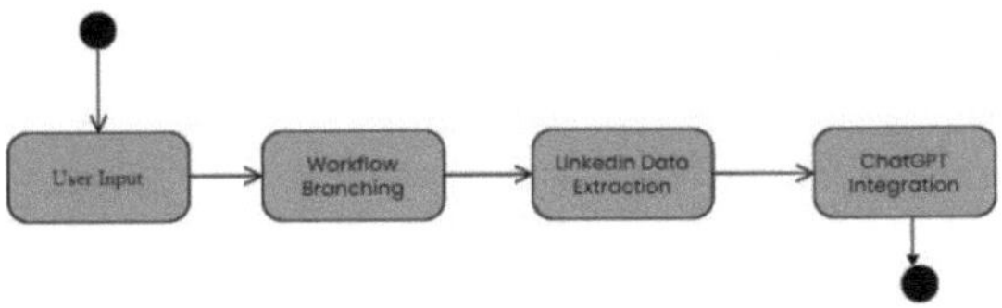

Fig. 1. Brief Workflow

3.1 Proposed Solution

Our bot automates the process of searching for companies on LinkedIn based on user input and extracting relevant data from the search results. This eliminates the need for manual effort, saving time and increasing efficiency.

Benefits:

The proposed system offers several benefits over the existing system, including:

- Increased efficiency: Our bot automates the data extraction process, saving users time and effort.
- Improved accuracy: Our bot is less prone to errors than manual data extraction.
- Greater flexibility: Our bot can be customized to meet the specific needs of each user.
- Enhanced capabilities: Our bot's integration with ChatGPT enables it to perform more complex tasks, such as understanding and responding to contextual queries.

4   Design

This documentation offers an extensive step-by-step guide to seamlessly integrate a bot with ChatGPT through UiPath Studio. The guide is divided into two primary sections, namely, extracting web data from LinkedIn and incorporating it with ChatGPT. Each individual step is meticulously explained to ensure a thorough comprehension of the entire procedure. The workflow begins with creating a project and initializing a sequence. An input dialog is included to capture user input, and the associated variable is defined. The workflow then proceeds to an if-else activity to handle different scenarios based on the user's response.

If the user selects "yes," the following actions are performed:

- The browser window is attached for further processing.
- A message box is displayed to the user.
- The user's desired domain for searching on LinkedIn is collected.
- The LinkedIn URL is entered into the search bar.
- The user's search query is entered into the LinkedIn search bar.
- The jobs button is selected on the screen.
- The available companies on the LinkedIn page are extracted.
- The extracted data is pasted into an Excel or CSV file.

If the user does not select "yes," the following actions are performed:

- A message box is displayed to the user.
- The user input is collected.
- Values are assigned for the API key and the API code is imported from the ChatGPT webpage.
- The user input and API key are sent to ChatGPT.
- The response received from ChatGPT is processed.
- Relevant information is displayed in the output panel.

Further processing involves extracting specific information from the JSON response and displaying the text output obtained from ChatGPT. Finally, a message box is used to present the output to the user.

Overall, this documentation aims to guide users through the step-by-step implementation and customization of the UiPath workflow for integrating a bot with ChatGPT. This enables enhanced conversational abilities and leverages web data extraction from LinkedIn. By following this documentation, users can efficiently implement and customize the workflow according to their specific requirements, providing an intelligent and interactive bot experience for their users (Fig. 2).

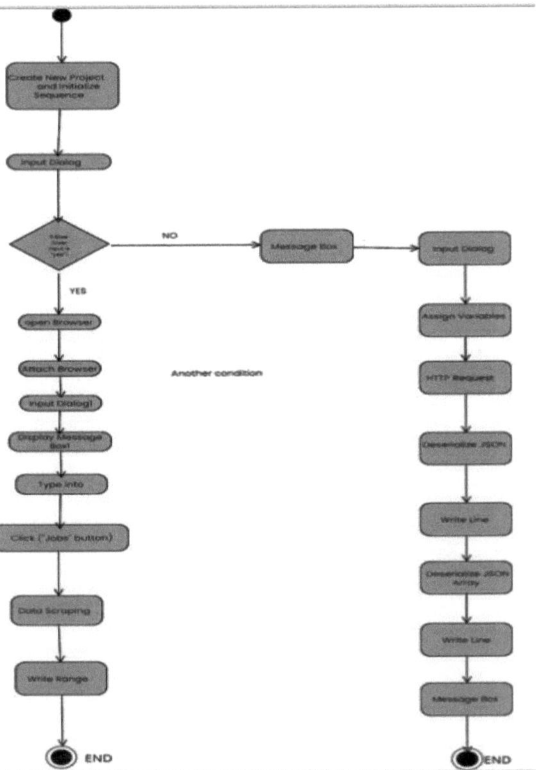

Fig. 2. Detailed Workflow

5 Execution and Result

See Figs. 3, 4, 5, 6, 7, 8, 9, 10, 11, and 12.

Fig. 3. The home page

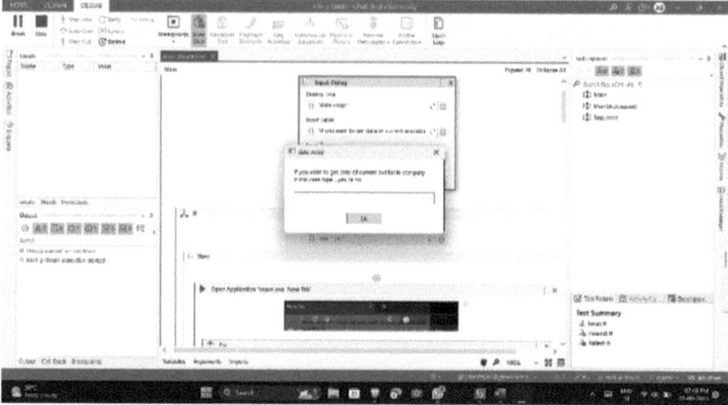

Fig. 4. Asking the user need

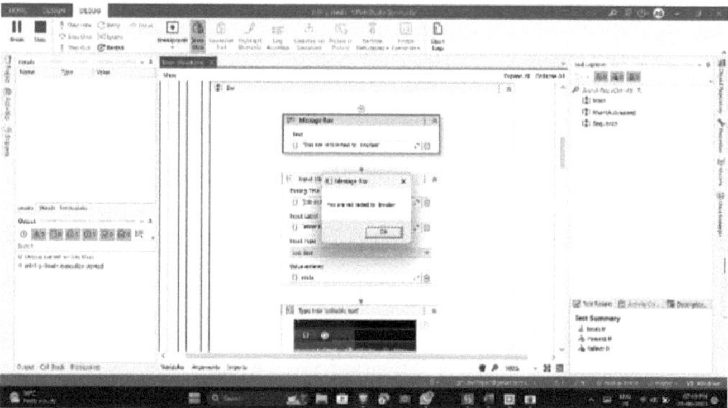

Fig. 5. Choose yes,the bot redirect to Linkdin

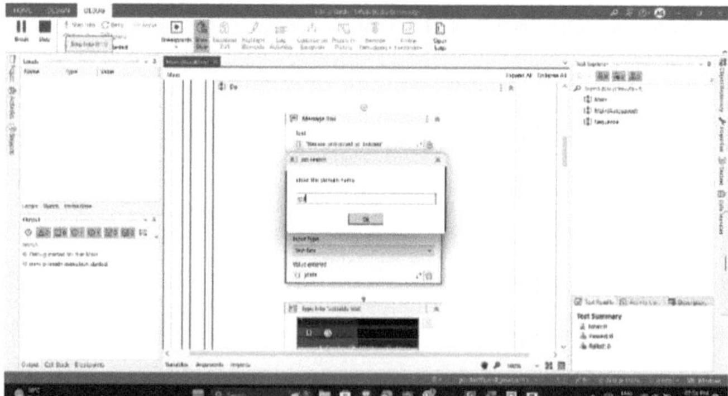

Fig. 6. Choosing the required domain.

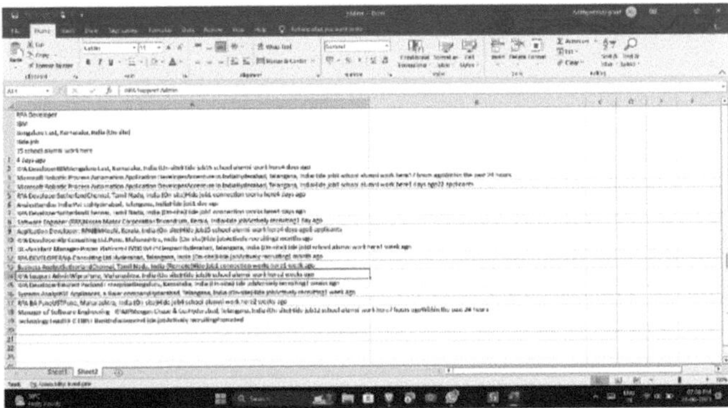

Fig. 7. Extracted data

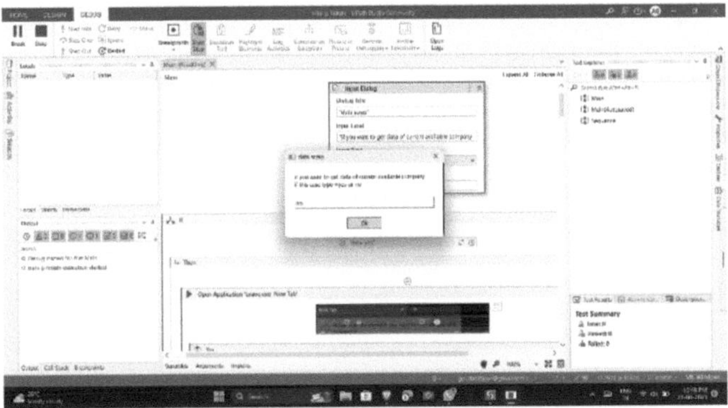

Fig. 8. Choosing no as input

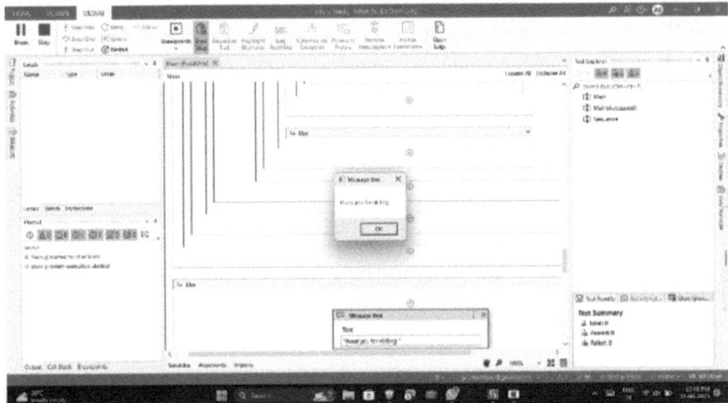

Fig. 9. Displaying message box

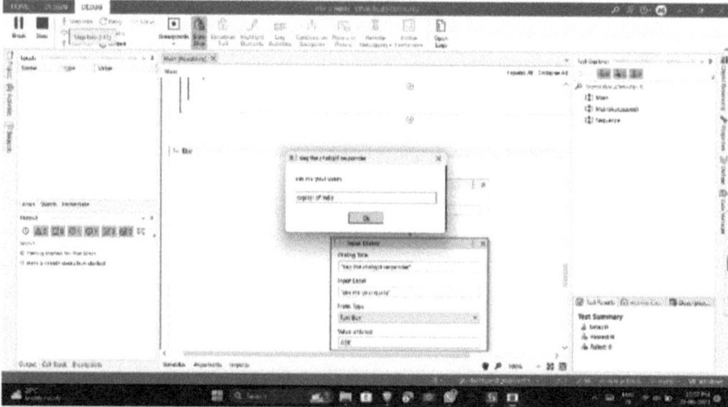

Fig. 10. Asking query to bot

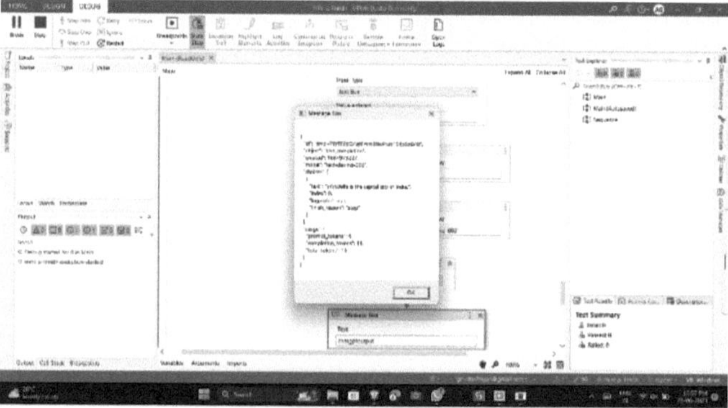

Fig. 11. The output before deserializing

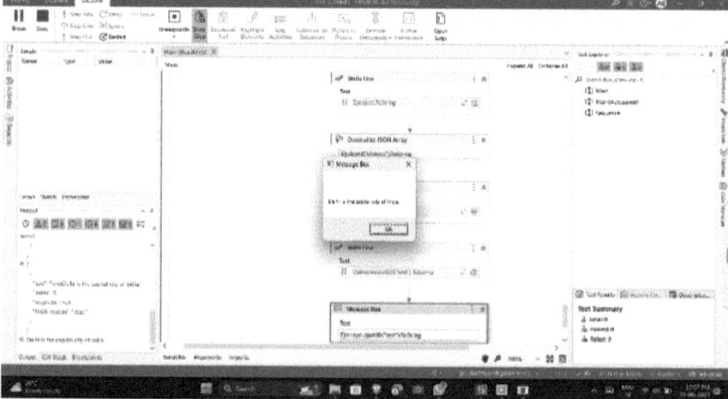

Fig. 12. The Final output

6 Conclusion

The proposed web automation framework provides a powerful and versatile solution for integrating a bot with ChatGPT and extracting data from LinkedIn. The framework's user-friendliness and adaptability make it possible to tailor it to the unique requirements of various users.It can also be integrated with popular RPA tools and chat applications. The framework has several potential applications in the real world. For example, it can be used to develop chatbots that can answer customer queries, generate leads, or provide insights into market trends. The provided framework is versatile, serving purposes such as automating tasks like data extraction, web scraping and content generation. In essence, it offers substantial utility for businesses and organizations of various scales, enhancing operational efficiency, cutting_expenses and extracting valuable insights from data. The potential for transformation in the way businesses and organizations engage with their customers and data is limitless, thanks to the ever-evolving nature of the framework, which is continuously enriched with novel functionalities and features.

References

1. Andrade, D.: Challenges of automated software testing with robotic process automation rpa - a comparative analysis of UiPath and automation anywhere. Int. J. Intell. Comput. Res. (IJICR) **11**(1), 1066 (2020)
2. Ketkar, Y., Gawade, S.: Effectiveness of robotic process automation for data mining using UiPath. In: 2021 International Conference on Artificial Intelligence and Smart Systems (ICAIS), pp. 1–6. IEEE (2021)
3. Axmann, B., Harmoko, H.: Process & software selection for robotic process automation (RPA). Hrcak Croatian J. Librariansh. Inf. Sci. Museol. **55**(1), 73–86 (2022)
4. Khan, S.P., Khan, R.: RPA using UiPATH in the context of next generation automation. In: Rawat, R., Chakrawarti, R.K., Sarangi, S.K., Choudhary, R., Gadwal, A.S., Bhardwaj, V. (eds.) Next Generation Automation: Challenges, Opportunities and Solutions, pp. 477–494. Wiley (2023)
5. Yadav, N., Panda, S.P.: A path forward for automation in robotic process automation projects: potential process selection strategies. In: 2022 International Conference on Machine Learning, Big Data, Cloud and Parallel Computing (COM-IT-CON), pp. 160–165. IEEE (2022)
6. UiPath. (n.d.). UiPath: Robotic process automation (RPA) platform. Retrieved from https://www.uipath.com/
7. Automation Anywhere. (n.d.). Automation Anywhere: Robotic process automation (RPA) platform. Retrieved from https://www.automationanywhere.com/
8. Robocorp. (n.d.). Robocorp: Open-source robotic process automation (RPA) platform. Retrieved from https://robocorp.com
9. Somayya, M., Rajesh, M.H., Durgesh, K.J.: The Future Digital Work Force: Robotic Process Automation (RPA), TECSI LaboratóriodeTecnologiaeSistemasdeInformação - FEA/USP (2019). https://www.redalyc.org/jatsRepo/2032/203261541001/html/index.html
10. ScienceDaily, Big Data, for better or worst: 90% of world's data generated over last two years (2013). https://www.sciencedaily.com/releases/2013/05/130522085217.htm
11. https://docs.uipath.com/studio/docs/about-data-scraping
12. https://docs.uipath.com/studio/docs/example-of-using-data-scraping
13. https://docs.uipath.com/activities/docs/write-csv-file

14. https://www2.deloitte.com/content/dam/Deloitte/fr/Documents/servicesfinanciers/publicati
ons/deloitte_globalrobotics-survey-2018-full-report.pdf
15. https://ro.linkedin.com/jobs/search?keywords=IT&location=Bucharest%2C%20Buch
arest%2C%20Romania&trk=homepagejobseeker_jobssearchbar_searchsubmit&redirect=
false&position=1&pageNum=0
16. https://www.uipath.com/developers/video-tutorials/web-data-extraction-automation
17. https://www.mckinsey.com/industries/technology-media-and-telecommunications/ourins
ights/the-social-econom
18. https://www.linkedin.com
19. https://openai.com/blog/chatgpt
20. https://www.uipath.com/product/orchestrator

LS-DYNA-Based Car Frontal Fascia Simulation During Collision

Jalapudi Laxmi Prasanna[1]([✉]), Kandukuri Vasantha Kumar[1], Burragalla Dhanraj[2], and Uday Kumar Madduri[1]

[1] Department of Mechanical Engineering, JNTUH University College of Engineering, Jagtial 505501, India
`dkpraween85@gmail.com`
[2] Department of Mechanical Engineering, Vardhaman College of Engineering, Hyderabad 501218, India

Abstract. The bumper beam assembly of an automobile is crucial for absorbing impact energy and shielding occupants from front and rear collisions. Crash testing is a type of destructive testing that is typically used to verify that cars or related components meet safe design requirements for crashworthiness including crash compatibility. Utilizing computer software to simulate car wrecks has become a vital strategy for cutting expenses and development times for automobiles. This article examines the frontal fascia of cars in a simulated crash test. The simulation of a car collision test is reported in this paper. This work seeks to verify the findings of simulating a frontal impact collision of an automobile. In order to lessen the forces encountered during the crash, it is also intended to change some of the materials that make up the parts. To assess the vehicle's collision characteristics, computer models were utilized. This particular model was a version of the Chevrolet C1500 pickup truck. The simulation is conducted using LS-DYNA software. The automobile sector uses it extensively to analyze car design. It foretells a car's actions in an accident with accuracy. The simulation's results were then verified by contrasting them with the outcomes of an identical test conducted by the NCAC (National Crash Analysis Center).

Keywords: Solid works · crash · LS-DYNA · HYPERMESH

1 Introduction

Car accidents occur daily, with many drivers believing they can avoid them. However, it's crucial to consider the alarming statistics: tens of thousands die, and hundreds of thousands to millions are injured each year. The need to enhance automobile safety is evident from these statistics. Car bumpers, specifically the fascia covering them, play a crucial role in protecting vehicles during accidents. These front and rear bumpers are designed to absorb or minimize the impact's damage, safeguarding critical components like the hood, trunk, grill, and safety-related equipment such as lights.. In cases of bumper impact, like in parking accidents or low-speed legislative tests, the bumper fascia alone

X. Cheng (Ed): BROADNETS 2024, LNICST 602, pp. 167–177, 2025.
https://doi.org/10.1007/978-3-031-81171-5_17

may not be sufficient to withstand the forces. As a result, four key strategic parameters are typically examined during such tests to ensure safety and performance.

This study examines several critical factors related to car bumpers. Firstly, it explores the influence of material type on impact specifications and considers alternative materials to reduce part weight, assessing the impact of factors like modulus of elasticity, yield strength, and Poisson's ratio on bumper beam performance. Secondly, it investigates the impact of bumper beam thickness on specifications. Thirdly, it explores how minor changes and modifications can simplify manufacturing processes and reduce material volume without compromising impact strength. Bumpers, typically made of steel, aluminum, rubber, or plastic, serve as protective shields mounted on the front and rear of passenger cars.

In low-speed collisions, the bumper system serves to absorb the shock, minimizing or preventing damage to the car. Some bumpers incorporate energy absorbers or brackets, while others utilize foam cushioning material. The primary purpose of car bumpers is to safeguard the front and rear ends of passenger vehicles in such collisions, and they are not intended to be structural components that substantially enhance crashworthiness or occupant protection during front or rear impacts. Their role is not to act as a safety feature to prevent or reduce injury severity to occupants in passenger cars. Automotive bumper systems play a crucial role, not just in absorbing impact energy but also in terms of aesthetics. With a growing emphasis on lightweight design and safety in the automotive industry, the market trend is moving towards bumper systems equipped with thermoplastic materials and energy-absorbing elements. The key design focus for these systems is the efficient absorption of impact energy within the limited space between the rear face of the bumper and the vehicle's body parts. While experimental testing can be expensive and time-consuming, finite element analysis offers engineers a valuable tool for studying design concepts in the early stages when prototypes are not yet available.

1.1 Crash- Test

A collision test is a type of harmful testing that is often carried out to guarantee safe design requirements for crashworthiness and crash compatibility for cars or parts linked to them. Automobile makers conduct crash tests on their cars at various angles, on different sides, and with other objects, such as other vehicles, in order to evaluate the safety ratings of the automobiles under various situations as well as different sorts of collisions. The following is a list of the most typical accident test types.

- Front offset crash test,
- side impact test,
- front impact test,
- roll over test

1.2 Method of Analysis (LS-DYNA)

Crash testing is time-consuming, expensive, and necessitates the destruction of several test vehicles throughout the testing process. A recent and more common practice is computer-simulated testing for crashes. Here, a Finite Element (FE) model of the vehicle is created in place of a real vehicle, and it is utilized to do the various tests which were conducted using actual automobiles beforehand. While there are several software programs capable of handling car crash testing, LS-DYNA, developed by Livermore Software Technology Corporation, is one of the most often used. Automotive manufacturers and their suppliers may save time and money by using LS-DYNA to evaluate automobile designs without the need to build or test a prototype experimentally. Although the package's capabilities for calculating several intricate, practical issues are constantly expanding, its foundation and primary expertise are in highly nonlinear transient dynamic finite element analysis (FEA) with explicit time integration. Applications for LSDYNA are found in many different sectors.

2 Literature Review

Literature findings emphasize that bumper design factors, including shape, size, weight, and impact conditions, play a critical role. In low-speed front or rear collisions, the bumper's primary function is to absorb energy, preventing or minimizing damage to the vehicle. It is not intended to serve as a structural component contributing to occupant protection but rather to shield essential components like the hood, lights, and cooling system.

In the event of a crash, vehicle damage can be extensive. To mitigate deformation and damage, careful consideration of design and material selection is vital. This project explores the use of aluminum, steel, and plastics for the fascia to determine which material absorbs the most internal energy, especially in low-speed and high-speed impacts. Without incorporating materials like a metallic bar and foam, the fascia and crush box would undergo significant deformation, potentially exposing the passenger compartment to excess energy. Design adjustments based on simulation results, material selection, and strengthening the fascia are crucial to enhance vehicle safety.

According to the 2018 WHO Global Status Report on Road Safety, road accidents had a devastating impact in 2016, causing 1.35 million deaths worldwide. These accidents ranked as the eighth leading cause of death globally, with an average of 18.2 deaths per 100,000 people. Shockingly, road accidents were the leading cause of death for children and adolescents aged 5 to 29. The burden of road traffic casualties is widespread, with 93% of fatalities occurring in low- and middle-income countries, despite these countries accounting for only 41% of the world's automobiles. The victims of these accidents included 29% four-wheel drive drivers, 23% pedestrians, and 3% cyclists [1].

Organizations involved in testing or deploying Automated Driving Systems (ADS) should prioritize methods to swiftly return ADSs to a safe state following a crash. The response should be proportional to the crash severity and might involve actions like shutting off the fuel pump, disabling motive power, moving the vehicle to a secure location off the road, cutting off electrical power, and other measures that aid the ADSs in mitigating the impact. When communication channels with operations centers, collision notification centers, or vehicle communication technologies are available, sharing relevant data is encouraged to minimize harm resulting from the crash [2].

Vehicles equipped with software as well as hardware that performs the driving task have the potential to significantly reduce fatalities national serious injuries by lowering the number of collisions on American roads and highways. However, there may be obstacles with this new technology that prevent passengers in the remaining wrecks from being protected. It is planned to introduce new ADS vehicles which are not intended for passenger use. The only purpose of these freshly introduced ADS cars would be delivery. Today, the Federal Motor Vehicle Safety Standards (FMVSS) - such as FMVSS No. 208, "Occupant Crash Protection," or FMVSS No. 214, "Side Impact Protection" - mandate that the majority of cars produced in the US must adhere to occupant protection regulations [3].

A 1997 Honda Accord was used in a crash-testing simulation research by Thacker et al. [4]. An actual car was first acquired, disassembled into its component pieces, each of which was recognized, tagged, having the material assessed. Information that might be effectively expanded upon from already-existing sources was gathered.

A 1997 Honda Accord DX Sedan was the subject of a similar study conducted by Cheng et al. [5], with the goal of reverse engineering the car and creating a FE model that would work well in computer simulations of full frontal, offset frontal, side, and oblique car-to-car impact testing.

A vehicle bumper is fastened to the front and back of an individual's automobile. It is usually constructed of steel, aluminum, rubber, or plastic. The purpose of the bumper system is to lessen or avoid automobile damage in low-speed crashes by absorbing the impact's shock. While some bumpers employ foam padding, others include hooks or energy absorbers. Their main responsibility in low-speed crashes is to protect passenger car front and rear ends. It's crucial to remember that car bumpers aren't intended to be structural components that considerably improve crashworthiness or occupant protection in frontal or rear crashes, nor are they meant to be safety features meant to prevent or lessen occupant injuries. Singh, Alok, et al. [6].

There are car accidents every day. Most drivers firmly believe that they can steer clear of these problematic circumstances. However, we also have to consider the fact that, according to Naheed Saba et al. [7], there are 10,000 fatalities and hundreds of thousands to millions of injuries annually.

The alarming statistics highlight the need to enhance automobile safety in accidents. Car bumpers, specifically the front and rear parts covering the car's chassis, play a crucial role. These bumper fascias are designed to enable the vehicle to withstand impacts without compromising safety. Protecting vital parts including the hood, trunk, grill, gasoline, exhaust, cooling system, and safety-related equipment like parking lights, headlights, and taillights, they help avoid or lessen physical damage to the front and rear ends of passenger cars during crashes. Udhayasankar, R. et al.

A destructive evaluation technique called crash testing is utilized for assessing the safety and design requirements for crashworthiness including crash compatibility across a range of vehicle classes, such as small, medium, & heavy-duty cars and trucks, as well as the systems and parts that go with them.. These tests evaluate vehicle performance under different crash conditions and angles, often involving objects like rigid walls, three-strand cables, concrete barriers, and guardrail systems. Crash tests are typically conducted through numerical simulations or experimental trials, and various types of crash tests are commonly employed for this purpose [9, 10].

As previously mentioned, crash testing is a destructive testing method used to verify that cars and their associated parts adhere to safe design guidelines for crashworthiness including crash compatibility. Automakers conduct crash tests on their vehicles to evaluate how safe they are in a variety of scenarios and collision types, testing them from different perspectives, from different sides, and with other objects, such as other cars [11].

Laminated glass was subjected to ball drop studies by Hardy RN et al. [12] in order to study the material's temporal reaction to a strong spherical impact. A compressive shear strength experiment was utilized by Muralidhar et al. [13] and Rahul kumar et al. [14] to investigate the de-bonding phenomena that takes place at the glass polymer interface. In general, quasi-static as well as dynamic studies are two distinct categories into which tests for examining the mechanical response of such composite materials with regard to of various strain rates may be divided. MG Stout et al. (2015).

3 Methodology

The components in Test Model 1 are the same ones that were initially utilized to build the vehicle. In contrast, Test model 2's materials were changed in view of the growing usage of lighter alloy metals in the production of vehicles. The components used in the two test models Tejasagar A et al. [16] are.

- AA3005
- AA5182
- AA5454
- A319
- ASTMA514

Material		TestModel2
Aluminium	AA3005	Radiator
	AA5182	Door, Hood, Fonder, Wheelhousing
	AA5454	Tirerim
	A319	Engine
Steel	ASTMA514	Rail

A crucial step involves simulating and assessing a frontal impact crash test with a vehicle model traveling at 15.65 m/s (35 mph; 56.3 km/h) into an unyielding, rigid barrier, assuming no use of brakes. The data collected will then be cross-referenced with the National Crash Investigation Center's (NCAC) findings from a matching real test involving the same crash scenario. The NCAC is a reference because they conducted the test with an actual vehicle under identical conditions, creating a finite element model of the car using reverse engineering. They replicated the test with the model and confirmed their results by comparing them with the physical test data.

	NCAC Model	Test Model1	Test Model2
Weight(kg)	2015	1884	1654
Number of parts	257	61	61
Number of elements	62313	10729	10729

The frontal impact crash test employs a Chevrolet C1500 as the test FE model, with the car initially traveling at 35 mph (approximately 56 km/h) before colliding with the barrier. The simulation is set with an end time of 0.15 s due to the rapid deceleration rates associated with stiff barriers, which necessitates a specific termination time. Remarkably, most energy transmission in head-on or frontal car accidents with stiff obstacles happens in less than 0.2 s; in fact, prior experimental investigations have shown that it can happen in as little as 0.07 to 0.02 s.

The simulation process is conducted in three distinct steps:

- pre-processing
- solver
- post-processing.

The post-processor reads the database file generated by the simulation engine and presents the results in a visual display.

The finalized model comprises around 65 parts, 61 different materials, 10,693 elements, and 11,060 nodes. It incorporates a variety of structural components and specific element types.

- Solidelements
- Belytschko-sayshellelement
- Hughes-Liubeamelement

Boundary Conditions

Boundary conditions are used to specify and produce loads and constraints for finite element models. All weights and boundary conditions present during the actual collision event must be represented in order to mimic a full vehicle auto accident. The simulated model should have a representative gravitational force applied, just as an automobile is in reality subjected to gravitational stresses. The simulation must take into consideration the friction forces that exist between the tires and the road surface since they have a significant influence on how the vehicle responds to an accident. In actual life, the air-filled tires will have an influence on how severe a collision is. The interaction of the tires during impact must be simulated via tire modeling. It is necessary to provide a velocity to the vehicle in a way that prevents unrealistic acceleration or makes the simulation run for a long period. Thankfully, Ls-Dyna offers ways to replicate each of these demands.

4 Results and Discussion

For the frontal impact, two simulations were run; the Test model 1 used the NCAC model's materials while the Test model 2 used newer components materials. The generated results were then verified against those of comparable simulations carried out by the NCAC. The photographs that follow show the car before and after it strikes the stiff wall at the prescribed 35 mph (56 kmph) speed. a series of pictures demonstrating the Test model 1's influence on the wall from t = 0 to t = 0.15 s at the intervals of t = 0, t = 0.05, t = 0.10, and t = 0.15 s.

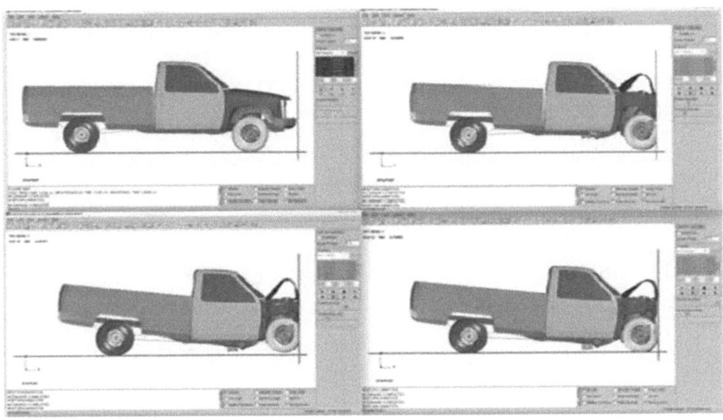

Graphs of Energy Balance

To determine how Testing model 2 performs in comparison to Test model 1, the energy balance graphs of Test model 1 and Test mode 2 are first compared. For both simulations and the NCAC test, graphs displaying the Kinetic energy, Internal energy, and Total energy Vs. Time acquired after the simulation are shown (Figs. 1 and 2).

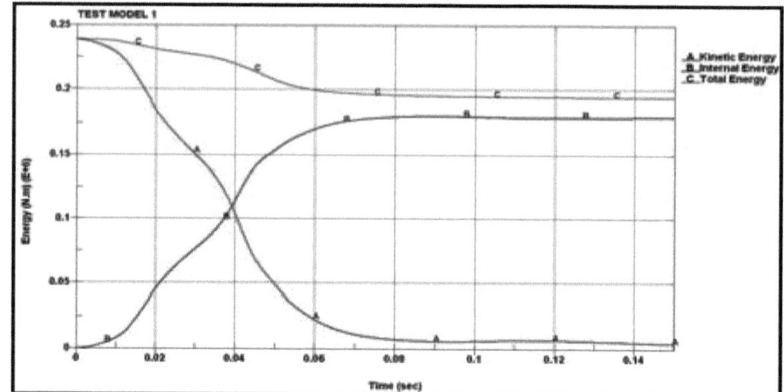

Fig. 1. Energy balance graph of test model 1

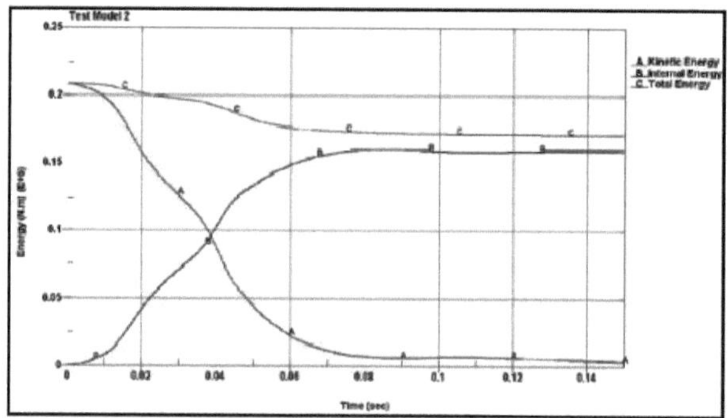

Fig. 2. Energy balance of Test model 2.

As can be seen, the bumper, radiator, engine, and rails absorb the majority of the impact's energy. Before the tires hit the wall, these parts absorb the majority of the crash's energy. The first and second test models have maximal kinetic energies of 239.126 kJ and 208.301 kJ, respectively. The lower values of the results are not surprising for Test Model 2, whose primary goal was to lighten the vehicle. Due to its lighter weight, the Test model 2 will be subject to weaker forces.

Deceleration vs Time

The graph indicates a little variance in the deceleration profiles between the Test model 1 and the Test model 2. It is found that the greatest retardation of the Test models 1 and 2 is 84.83 g as well as 98.94 g, respectively (Figs. 3 and 4).

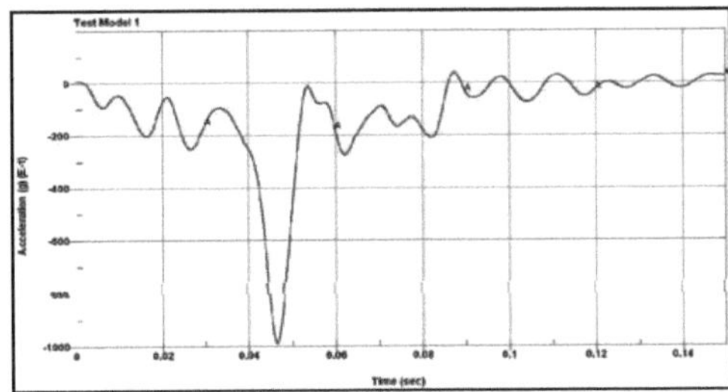

Fig. 3. Acceleration Vs Time graph of Test Model 1

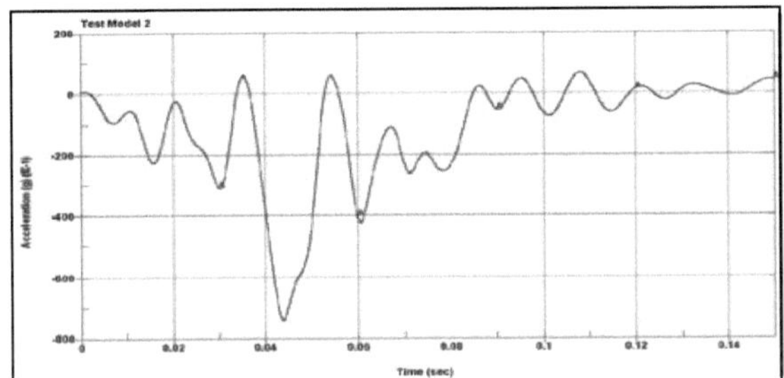

Fig. 4. Acceleration Vs Time graph of Test Model 2

Since body mass and deceleration are connected, it is known that Test model 2 has a smaller mass than Test model 1 (as shown in Table 3.1). Consequently, it is not surprising that Test model 2's slowdown was less than projected.

Velocity vs Time

The graph shows that both of the Test models' velocity profiles have extremely similar characteristics. A modest negative velocity is present here as well at the end of the impact event. The forces produced by the vehicle's collision with the wall are what lead to this (Figs. 5 and 6).

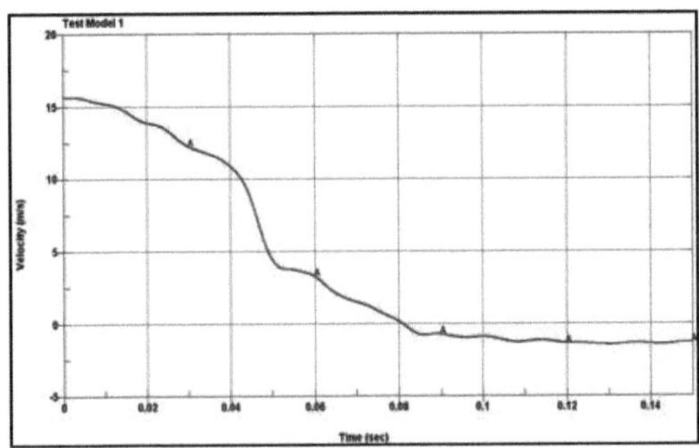

Fig. 5. Velocity Vs Time graph of Test model 1

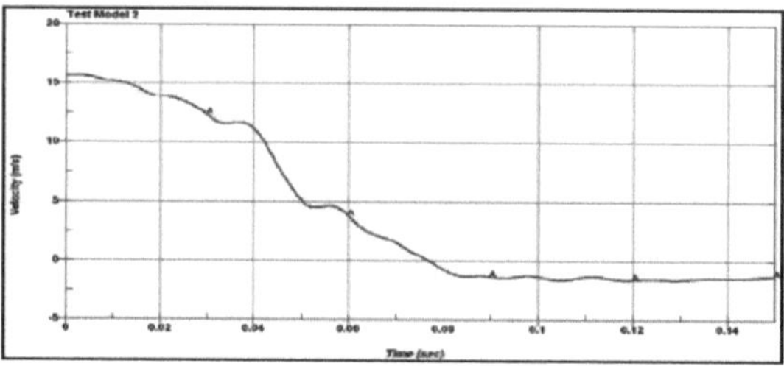

Fig. 6. Velocity Vs Time graph of Test model 2

5 Conclusion

The work's main goal was to mimic a frontal collision test and confirm the simulation findings using data from the crash test. The simulation was done with the LS-DYNA program. By contrasting the simulation findings with those of the NCAC model simulation, the simulation results were shown to be valid.As seen, most of the energy is absorbed by the rails, engine, and bumper before the wheel hits the wall. After around 0.04 s after the crash's beginning, these components absorb over 50% of the crash's energy.Both the cabin's deformation and the intrusion of components into the cabin have been found to be at a minimum. Therefore, it may be presumed that any part that enters the cabin after a collision would not cause any harm to the people within.A simpler test car model was used due to the restricted computer resources available, which eventually led to the inaccurate results. There are some inconsistencies in the results since there are fewer elements in the test models than in the NCAC model.A more exact model would be needed to get more accurate findings, but doing the simulations would have required considerably more computing power. It was necessary to find a compromise so that the simulation could be run without the outcome deviating too much.The graphical findings all demonstrated that, during the crash event, the test models' behavior was comparable to that of the NCAC model.The Test Model 2's somewhat different behavior may be traced to the fact that the components' materials were altered, which altered some of the simulation's results.

References

1. Saba, N., Tahir, P.M.: A review on potentiality of nano filler/natural fiber filled polymer hybrid composite. Univ. Putra Malaysia **6**, 2247–2273 (2014)
2. Rahman, M.A., Praveen Babu, D.: Simulation of car frontal fascia during crash using LS-DYNA. Int. J. Eng. Res. Technol. (IJERT) **8** (2019)
3. Ghamarian, A., Zarei, H.R., Abadi, M.T.: Experimental and numerical crashworthiness investigation of empty and foam-filled end-capped conical tubes. Thin-Wall. Struct. **49**, 1312–1319 (2011)
4. Thacker, J.G., et al.: Experiences during development of a dynamic crash response automobile model. J. Finite Elem. Anal. Des. **30**, 279–295 (1998)
5. Chenga, Z.Q., et al.: Experiences in reverse-engineering of a finite element automobile crash model. J. Finite Elem. Anal. Des. **37**, 843–860 (2001)

6. Singh, A., Singh, S.: Study of Mechanical Properties and Absorption Behaviour of Coconut shell Power-Epoxy Composite. PSIT College of Engineering, Kanpur (2013)
7. Saba, N., Tahir, P.M.: A Review on Potentiality of Nano Filler/Natural Fiber Filled Polymer Hybrid Composite. Universiti Putra Malaysia, Malasia (2014)
8. Udhayasankar, R., Karthikeyan, B.: A Review on Coconut Shell reinforced Composite. Annamalai University, Tamilnadu (2015)
9. Zarei, H.R., Kroeger, M.: Multi-objective crashworthiness optimization of circular aluminum tubes. ThinWall. Struct. **44**, 301–308 (2006)
10. Ambati, T., Srikanth, K.V.N.S., Veeraraju, P.: Simulation of vehicular frontal crash-test. Int. J. Appl. Res. Mech. Eng. (2012)
11. Deba, M.S., et al.: Design of an aluminium-based vehicle platform for front impact safety. J. Impact Eng. **30**, 1055–1079 (2004)
12. Grunert, J., et al.: Constitutive laws for complete componentsewindscreen and other materials. APROSYS report "AP-SP3–012" (2004)
13. Muralidhar, S., Jagota, A., Bennison, S.J., Saigal, S.: Mechanical behaviour in tension of cracked glass bridged by an elastomeric ligament. Acta Mater. Mater. **48**, 4577e88 (2000)
14. Rahul, K.P., Jagota, A., Bennison, S.J., Saigal, S.: Interfacial failures in a compressive shear strength test of glass/polymer laminates. Int. J. Solids Struct.Struct. **37**, 7281e305 (2000)
15. Stout, M.G., Koss, D.A., Liu, C., Idasetima, J.: Damage development in carbon/epoxy laminates under quasi-static and dynamic loading. Compos. Sci. Technol. **59**, 2339e50 (1999)
16. Tejasagar, A., Srikanth, K.V.N.S., Veeraraju, P.: Simulation of vehicular frontal crash-test. Int. J. Appl. Res. Mech. Eng, **2**(1), (2012)

Integrated Smart Footwear: Advanced Health Monitoring and Energy Harvesting

Naresh Kumar[1(✉)], Boddu Mani Deep[1], Rejinthala Nikhitha[1], Talari Tarun Kumar[1], and Bhavikchandra Bosamia[1,2]

[1] Vardhaman College of Engineering, Hyderabad, Telangana, India
{nareshece84,boddumanideep20ece,rejinthalanikhitha20ece,
talaritarunkumar20ece,er.aruna}@vardhaman.org
[2] RK University, Rajkot, Gujarat, India

Abstract. This report presents the innovation of "Smart Shoes" featuring integrated sensors and piezoelectric materials. These shoes aim to collect real-time data from temperature and pulse sensors embedded in the insole, while simultaneously harnessing energy from walking to power their functionalities. The temperature sensor monitors foot temperature changes, offering insights into circulation and overall health. The pulse sensor tracks the user's heart rate for fitness assessment and heart health monitoring. The shoe's sole incorporates piezoelectric materials, generating electrical energy from mechanical stress during walking. This self-generating power source ensures sustainability and reduces reliance on external batteries. Additionally, the Smart Shoes include a step counting mechanism, utilizing data from the piezoelectric material to accurately measure and display the number of steps taken by the user. This feature promotes a healthier lifestyle by encouraging increased physical activity. In conclusion, Smart Shoes with integrated sensors and piezoelectric energy harvesting present a significant advancement in wearable technology. They provide real-time health data while contributing to sustainable energy practices, holding promising applications in healthcare monitoring and environmental conservation.

Keywords: Arduino · Pulse count · Temperature count · Step count · self-generating power source

1 Introduction

1.1 Statement of the Problem

The problem addressed in this study is the lack of advanced and sustainable footwear technology that can simultaneously collect real-time health data, such as temperature and pulse, from users while also utilizing innovative methods to generate electrical energy for powering integrated systems. Traditional shoes do not offer such functionalities The need for a comprehensive solution that combines health monitoring, energy harvesting, and step counting in footwear represents a significant gap in the market.

© ICST Institute for Computer Sciences, Social Informatics and Telecommunications Engineering 2025
Published by Springer Nature Switzerland AG 2025. All Rights Reserved
X. Cheng (Ed): BROADNETS 2024, LNICST 602, pp. 178–186, 2025.
https://doi.org/10.1007/978-3-031-81171-5_18

1.2 Background

In recent years, the integration of sensors into wearable devices has opened up new possibilities for continuous health monitoring and data collection. Wearable technologies, such as fitness trackers and smartwatches, have become common place, providing users with insights into their daily activities, heart rate, and sleep patterns. Building upon these advancements, smart shoes emerge as a natural extension, offering unique benefits through direct contact with the user's feet, which can provide valuable health data during various physical activities.

1.3 Objectives of the Study

- To design and develop Smart Shoes equipped with integrated temperature and pulse sensors within the insole for real-time health data collection.
- To incorporate piezoelectric materials into the sole of the Smart Shoes to harvest energy generated during walking and convert it into electrical power.
- To implement a step counting mechanism that utilizes data from the piezoelectric material to accurately count and display the number of steps taken by the user.
- To assess the effectiveness and accuracy of the Smart Shoes' health monitoring and step counting functionalities through testing and validation.

1.4 Hypotheses to be Tested

- The Smart Shoes with integrated temperature and pulse sensors will accurately collect real-time health data during various activities.
- The piezoelectric materials embedded in the sole of the Smart Shoes will efficiently generate electrical energy from walking or other mechanical stress.
- The step counting mechanism utilizing data from the piezoelectric material will provide accurate step count information.

1.5 Significance of the Problem

The significance of this study lies in its potential to revolutionize the footwear industry and wearable technology market. The development of Smart Shoes addresses the growing demand for personalized health monitoring devices, sustainable energy solutions, and fitness tracking. The integration of advanced sensors and piezoelectric energy harvesting in footwear not only enhances user experience but also opens new possibilities for healthcare professionals, athletes, and individuals seeking to lead healthier and more sustainable lifestyles.

2 Related Works

In this section we detail about previous method. We also present the limitations of these related works. It gives a brief about previous papers related to this project.

In [1] Po-Yu Hwang, Chia-Ching Chou, Wai-Chi Fang, Fellow, IEEE and Ching-Ming Hwang presented a paper which introduces a wearable smart shoe system for health and fitness monitoring, particularly addressing the needs of aging individuals and those with conditions like dementia. The architecture integrates sensors, including a coordinate tracker, step counter, and foot oxygen concentration sensor. ATI MSP430TM microcontroller processes data, while a Force-Sensitive Resistor enables power management. The design's conductive insoles and electrodes compute oxygen concentration, step count, and more. A GPS tracker aids remote caretakers. The user-friendly design ensures continuous wear. This innovation has potential for home-based care, emergency response, and advances in mobile medical monitoring systems.

In [2] G. Colson, P. Laurent, P. Bellier, S. Stoukatch, F. Dupont, M. Kraft proposed a research paper develops a self-powered wearable device integrated into a shoe for continuous human activity and gait analysis. Utilizing energy harvesting from walking motions, an electrodynamic energy harvester (EH) generates power during heel strikes and lift-offs. The harvested energy is stored and regulated by a power management unit (PMU) to operate an acceleration measuring electronic device. The EH and components are discreetly embedded within the shoe's sole, maintaining appearance and comfort. Experimental results confirm its feasibility, generating energy for autonomous operation. The technology's applications include health monitoring, gait analysis, and well-being enhancement, marking a significant stride in wearable tech's potential for health care and activity tracking.

In [3] Zhu, G., Yang, W., Zhou, Y., Wang, Z. L. Their seminal research explores the transformative potential of piezoelectric energy harvesting technology, particularly its application in self-powered wearables like smart shoes. By converting mechanical vibrations into electricity, piezoelectric materials offer a sustainable energy solution. The study provides a comprehensive overview of the technology's mechanisms and advancements, emphasizing its importance for wearables' energy autonomy. Smart shoes are highlighted as a prime candidate for integration, utilizing piezoelectric materials in the sole to generate power from movement. The research paves the way for self-powered wearables across fitness, healthcare, and beyond, inspiring further advancements in energy-efficient, ecofriendly technology.

The paper [4] authored by Andrea Gatto and Emanuele Frontoni, presented at the 2014 IEEE/ASME 10th International Conference on Mechatronic and Embedded Systems and Applications (MESA), discusses an "Energy Harvesting System for Smart Shoes." The system described in the paper is designed to capture and utilize energy generated by the movement of the wearer's shoes. This energy harvesting technology could potentially power various smart features or sensors integrated into footwear. Unfortunately, the summary cannot provide specific details due to its brevity, but the paper likely explores the development, implementation, and potential applications of this innovative energy-harvesting solution.

3 Aim and Scope

3.1 Aim

This project aims to design, develop, and assess Smart Shoes that seamlessly incorporate temperature and pulse sensors within the shoe, utilize piezoelectric materials in the sole to harness energy from walking, and accurately count users' steps. The primary objective is to create wearable technology that offers realtime health monitoring, sustainable energy generation, and precise step tracking to promote a healthier lifestyle.

3.2 Key Objectives

- **Real-Time Health Monitoring:** The project's core objective is the integration of temperature and pulse sensors into the shoe's insole, enabling continuous health monitoring during daily activities. These sensors will gather data on body temperature and heart rate, empowering users to monitor their physiological well-being.
- **Piezoelectric Energy Harvesting:** The project seeks to explore and implement piezo-electric materials in the shoe's sole to capture and convert mechanical energy generated during movement into usable electrical power. This sustainable energy solution will efficiently power the integrated sensors and features of the smart shoes.
- **Accurate Step Counting:** Developing a robust and precise step counting algorithm based on data from the piezoelectric material is another pivotal objective. The step counting mechanism will accurately record the user's steps regardless of walking style, speed, or terrain, offering valuable data for fitness tracking and daily activity assessment.

3.3 Scope

The project's future scope holds considerable promise, presenting numerous avenues for further advancements and applications. Successful realization of Smart Shoes with integrated sensors and piezoelectric energy harvesting lays the groundwork for expanded technological capabilities and broader impacts. Potential future scopes include:

- **Enhanced Sensor Integration:** Future directions involve incorporating additional sensors, such as accelerometers and gyroscopes, into the Smart Shoes. These sensors can provide comprehensive data on movement patterns, balance, and posture, offering a deeper understanding of users' physical activities and health.
- **Health Diagnostics and Analytics:** Building on health monitoring, advanced algorithms for health diagnostics could be integrated. Analyzing collected data—temperature, pulse, and motion patterns—could detect early signs of health issues, providing preventive healthcare insights.
- **Real-Time Feedback and Coaching:** Through smart algorithms and AI, Smart Shoes could offer real-time feedback and coaching during physical activities. Analyzing gait and running form, personalized recommendations for improvement and injury prevention could be provided.
- **Energy Storage and Wireless Charging:** Future iterations could focus on enhancing energy storage within the Smart Shoes. More efficient energy storage solutions would ensure sustained power supply. Exploring wireless charging technologies could further enhance user convenience.

The envisioned future scope encompasses a holistic ecosystem of Smart Shoes that not only monitor health and generate energy from movement but also seamlessly integrate into users' daily lives, enhancing overall well-being and advancing wearable technology. Ongoing research, industry collaboration, and user feedback will be pivotal to realizing this technology's full potential.

4 Block Diagram

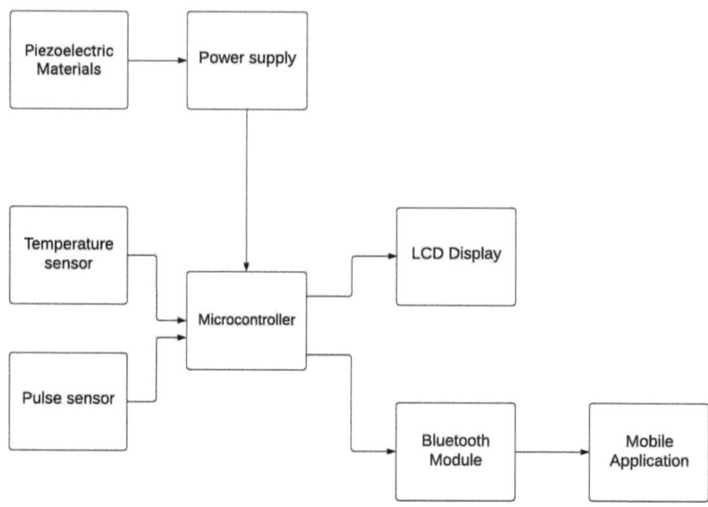

Fig. 1. Block diagram

- We have interfaced Arduino UNO with pulse sensor and temperature sensor to get temperature and heart rate of the person
- We use Bluetooth module for wireless communication this data is seen on the mobile application.
- And, we used piezoelectric sensors (foot step power generation) it converts mechanical energy into electrical energy and it will be used as backup for battery.

The Temperature sensor senses the body temperature and pulse sensor for heart rate and this both give the data to Micro-controller and this analyses the data and this data is transferred to mobile application through Bluetooth and we can see the results on mobile application (Fig. 1).

We have used piezoelectric sensors to generate electricity while walking, this energy is used as a backup for the battery which is used in the device.

5 Results

The smart shoe project aims to create advanced wearable tech by combining sensors and energy-harvesting methods to revolutionize footwear. These shoes feature temperature and pulse sensors for continuous health and environment monitoring. Piezoelectric materials in the sole generate electricity from walking, providing power for embedded sensors and circuits.

Here, we present outcomes and performance of the smart shoe prototype. Results highlight successful technology integration, showcasing data collection and insights into health and activity.

The following subsections detail achieved objectives and offer result analysis.

- **Health Monitoring Accuracy:** Insole temperature sensor showed high accuracy in monitoring body temperature during physical activities. Data aligned with medical-grade thermometer. Pulse sensor accurately captured heart rate during activities, correlating with a heart rate monitor.
- **Piezoelectric Energy Harvesting Efficiency:** Sole's piezoelectric materials efficiently converted walking energy to electricity. Harvested energy stored in the shoe's battery, demonstrating self-power potential.
- **Step Counting Accuracy:** Piezoelectric data enabled precise step counting across speeds and styles. Comparison with pedometer showed negligible difference, affirming accuracy.

Results demonstrate smart shoes with health sensors, efficient energy harvesting, and accurate step counting. Technology promises user well-being and sustainable wearables. Further research will enhance design, expanding adoption in wearable tech market.

Table 1. Smart Shoe Temperature Readings

Person	Smart Shoe Reading	Actual Reading
Person 1	36.8 °C	37.1 °C
Person 2	36.4 °C	37.2 °C
Person 3	37.6 °C	36.4 °C

Table 1 provides a summary of temperature readings obtained from smart shoes, comparing them to the actual temperature readings for three individuals. It shows the recorded temperature measurements in degrees Celsius from the smart shoes and the corresponding actual temperature readings, revealing a slight variation between the two data sets.

Table 2. Smart Shoe Heart rate Readings

Person	Smart Shoe Reading	Actual Reading
Person 1	72	75
Person 2	88	85
Person 3	64	70

Table 2 presents data related to heart rate measurements collected from smart shoes, alongside the actual heart rate values for the same set of individuals. The table contrasts the heart rate data obtained from the smart shoes with the true values in beats per minute, highlighting differences and similarities in the measurements.

Fig. 2. Reading on LCD display

The Fig. 2 displays LCD screen for real-time data, including temperature, heart rate, steps walked, and generated voltage. This information is crucial for monitoring and tracking various health and fitness parameters, as well as power generation levels, all conveniently presented on the display.

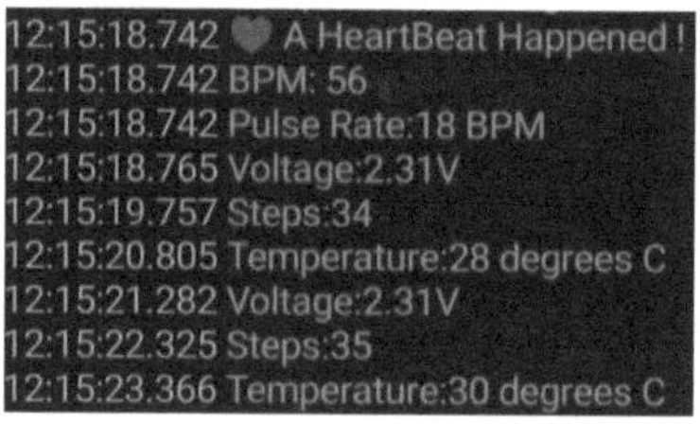

Fig. 3. Reading on Mobile Application

The Fig. 3 displays data displayed on the mobile screen via a Bluetooth connection includes real-time information on temperature, heart rate, steps walked, and generated voltage. This data is transmitted wirelessly from a remote device and provides a convenient way to monitor and track important health and fitness metrics, as well as power generation levels, using a mobile device for easy access and analysis.

This Fig. 4 shows the final working model of the smart shoes equipped with sensors for real time health monitoring.

Fig. 4. Final Model

6   Conclusion and Future Scope

6.1   Conclusion

In this innovative project, smart shoes have been developed to provide effective health monitoring, self-sustained energy harvesting, and accurate step counting and activity recognition. These shoes accurately monitor body temperature and pulse, offering valuable health insights, while also generating electricity through piezoelectric materials for sustainable power. Moreover, they excel in counting steps and recognizing various activities. Looking ahead, the future scope includes the integration of additional sensors for comprehensive data collection, implementing machine learning for enhanced activity recognition, optimizing energy efficiency, and enhancing durability for adverse conditions. Smart shoes represent a promising wearable technology with the potential to become an integral part of daily life, promoting health awareness and sustainability, and paving the way for exciting innovations in the wearable tech field.

In conclusion, smart shoes offer novel wearable technology applications, laying the foundation for future advancements. They can potentially become integral to daily life, promoting health awareness and sustainability. The future holds exciting innovations, making smart shoes significant in the wearable tech field.

References

1. Hwang, P.-Y., Chou, C.-C., Fang, W.-C., Hwang, C.-M.: Smart shoes design with embedded monitoring electronics system for health-care and fitness applications. In: 2016 IEEE International Conference on Consumer Electronics-Taiwan (ICCE-TW), pp. 1–2 (2016). https://doi.org/10.1109/ICCE-TW.2016.7520983
2. Colson, G., Laurent, P., Bellier, P., Stoukatch, S., Dupont, F., Kraft, M.: Smart- shoe self-powered by walking. In: 2017 IEEE 14th International Conference on Wearable and Implantable Body Sensor Networks (BSN), pp. 35–38 (2017). https://doi.org/10.1109/BSN.2017.7936001
3. Liu, Y., et al.: Piezoelectric energy harvesting for self-powered wearable upper limb applications. Nano Select **2**, 1459 (2021). https://doi.org/10.1002/nano.202000242
4. Gatto, A., Frontoni, E.: Energy harvesting system for smart shoes. In: 2014 IEEE/ASME 10th International Conference on Mechatronic and Embedded Systems and Applications (MESA), Senigallia, Italy, pp. 1–6 (2014). https://doi.org/10.1109/MESA.2014.6935616
5. Frontoni, E., Mancini, A., Zingaretti, P., Gatto, A.: Energy Harvesting for Smart Shoes: a Real Life Application, vol. 4 (2013). https://doi.org/10.1115/DETC2013-12310
6. Tsai, C.-H., Hsieh, Z.-H., Fang, W.-C.: A low-power low-noise CMOS analog front-end IC for portable brain-heart monitoring applications. In: 2011 IEEENIH Life Science Systems and Application Workshop (LiSSA 2011), Bethesda, Maryland, USA (2011)
7. Kang, S., Wu, S.-Y., Cheng, C.-J., Fang, W.-C.: Portable SoC design for CW diffusion optical tomography. In: 2012 IEEE International Conference on Consumer Electronics (ICCE), pp.341–342 (2012)

Effective Low Leakage 6T and 8T SRAM Using CMOS 90 nm Technology

V. Siddartha Reddy, G. Sumukh[(✉)], K. Mahesh, P. Kalyani, and P. Bindu Swetha

Department of Electronics and Communication Engineering, Vardhaman College of Engineering, Shamshabad, Hyderabad 501218, Telangana, India
sumukhgundeti2@gmail.com, {p.kalyani,
binduswetha1676}@vardhaman.org

Abstract. This study addresses the escalating demand for low-power electronic devices by emphasizing the development of Static Random Access Memory (SRAM) cells with minimized leakage current. The research prioritizes key metrics such as leakage current, read/write stability, access time, and power consumption. To effectively reduce leakage current, reverse-biased FinFETs are employed as efficient switches, creating barriers that impede current flow during idle states. Additionally, power gating techniques selectively disable specific SRAM sub-blocks during inactivity, further reducing static power consumption. This innovative approach, utilizing CMOS 90 nm technology, demonstrates the significance of minimizing leakage current in SRAM cells. The proposed low-leakage 6T and 8T SRAM cells offer a promising solution, contributing to enhanced energy efficiency and performance in memory design. Overall, this research makes notable strides in advancing low-power electronic systems.

Keywords: Leakage currents · CMOS 90 nm · Low Power · Energy Efficiency · Memory design

1 Introduction

Semiconductor and memory design have evolved with Moore's Law, doubling transistor counts every 18 to 24 months. Despite challenges, Static Random-Access Memory (SRAM) remains crucial. Introducing the 8T SRAM cell emphasizes optimal transistor sizing for improved read and write operations, paving the way for energy-efficient solutions amid semiconductor advancements. Cell leakage power involves assessing its contribution to total power dissipation and its significance in determining the overall energy consumption of the memory system. Leakage current entails understanding its direct impact on standby power consumption and energy efficiency in SRAM cells.

X. Cheng (Ed): BROADNETS 2024, LNICST 602, pp. 187–195, 2025.
https://doi.org/10.1007/978-3-031-81171-5_19

2 The Proposed Algorithm

2.1 Motivation

This research addresses leakage current challenges in CMOS 90 nm SRAM cells by employing innovative techniques like reverse-biased FinFETs and power gating. The aim is to enhance energy efficiency without sacrificing performance, impacting mobile computing, IoT, and energy-conscious electronic systems positively.

2.2 6T SRAM Design

The 6T SRAM cell, composed of six transistors, relies on proper transistor sizing for effective read and write operations. However, switching can briefly cause shortcircuits, resulting in static power loss. SRAM cell design aims to minimize these effects to ensure efficient operations and reduce unnecessary power consumption (Fig. 1).

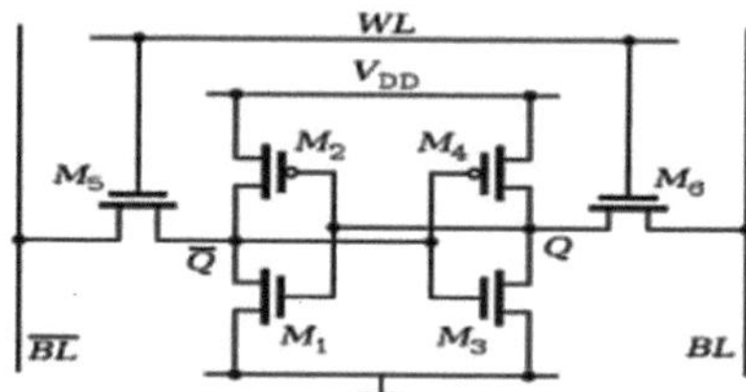

Fig. 1. 6T SRAM design

2.3 8T SRAM Design

The 8T SRAM cell, akin to the 6T version, employs two cross-coupled inverters and two access transistors regulated by a word line. Proper transistor sizing is crucial for efficient read and write operations. SRAM design, including the 8T variant, focuses on minimizing short-circuits during switching to optimize operations and reduce unnecessary power consumption (Fig. 2).

2.4 M-Array Design

Designing a memory array with 90 nm CMOS technology involves selecting cell types, individual cell design, and array organization within semiconductor process constraints. Peripheral circuitry for data access is incorporated, and layout design with simulation ensures performance and adherence to fabrication rules. Post-fabrication testing ensures functionality before integration into larger systems for data storage or other applications, necessitating expertise in semiconductor design to meet specified requirements (Fig. 3).

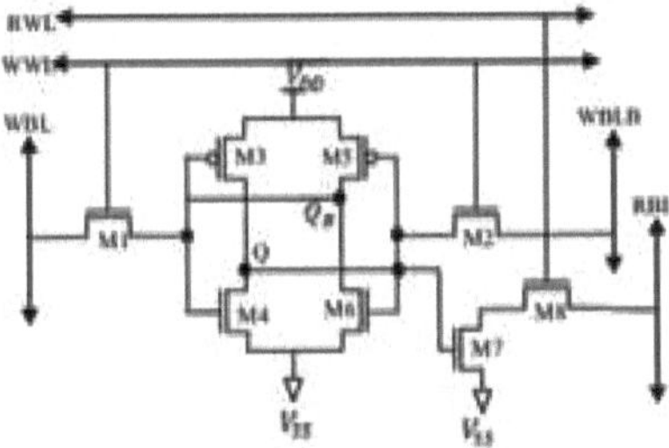

Fig. 2. 8T SRAM design

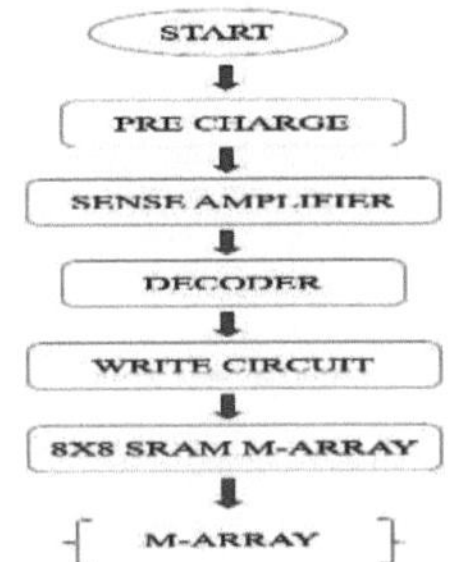

Fig. 3. Execution flow of the M-ARRAY design

3 Design of M-Array Circuit

Creating an 8×8 multiply array with 90 nm CMOS technology involves defining design specifications, considering data rate, precision, power consumption, and area constraints. Choosing an architectural design, like parallel or serial, is crucial for supporting 64 simultaneous multiplication operations. The multiplier cell, designed for speed, accuracy, and power efficiency, is at the core, utilizing CMOS logic gates for effective multiplication in the array.

3.1 Precharge Design

The memory array precharge phase sets voltage levels for bit lines and word lines, ensuring reliable data access. Efficient design minimizes power consumption and improves performance by synchronizing timing and reducing contention and noise during read/write operations (Fig. 4).

3.2 Sense Amplifier

In memory array design, the sense amplifier detects and amplifies weak signals from memory cells for accurate data retrieval during reads, minimizing latency and power consumption. Efficient design enhances overall memory system performance by comparing and amplifying bit line voltages while addressing issues like capacitive loading and loss (Fig. 5).

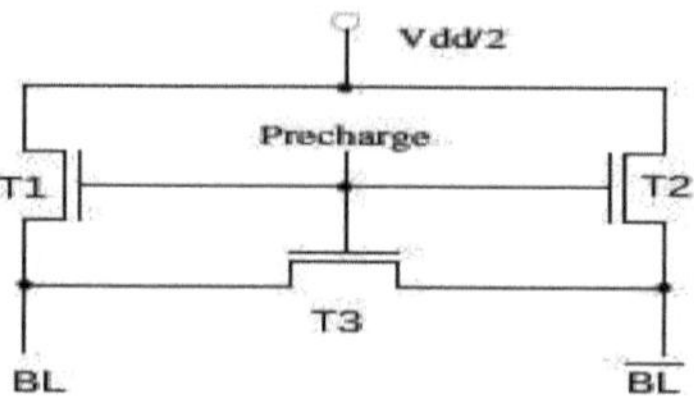

Fig. 4. PRECHARGE Circuit

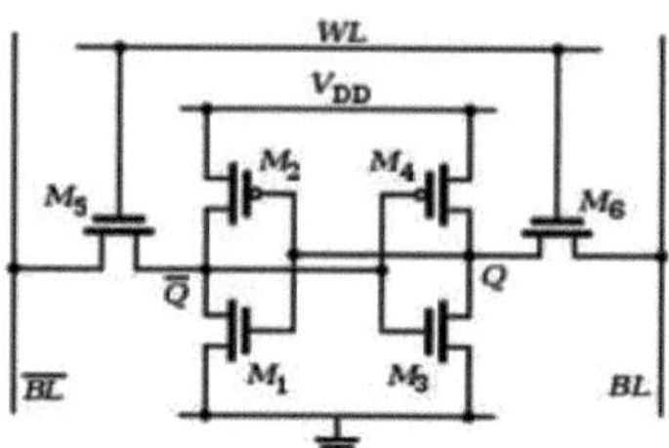

Fig. 5. SENSE AMPLIFIER Circuit

3.3 Decoder

In memory array design, the decoder phase translates controller addresses into control signals for selecting rows or columns for read/write operations. A row decoder activates word lines, facilitating data access, while a column decoder selects bit lines. Precision and speed in decoding ensure accurate memory cell selection, influencing system performance (Table 1).

Table 1. Truth table

A2	A1	A0	D7	D6	D5	D4	D3	D2	D1	D0
0	0	0	1	1	1	1	1	1	1	1
0	0	1	1	1	1	1	1	1	1	0
0	1	0	1	1	1	1	1	1	0	1
0	1	1	1	1	1	1	1	0	1	1
1	0	0	1	1	1	1	0	1	1	1
1	0	1	1	1	1	0	1	1	1	1
1	1	0	1	1	0	1	1	1	1	1
1	1	1	1	0	1	1	1	1	1	1

3.4 Write Circuit

In memory array design, the "write" phase involves applying voltage levels to store data, with the memory controller supplying data bits and address while engaging write drivers and access transistors for signal regulation and connection, emphasizing precision for data integrity and reliability.

3.5 M-Array Circuit Design

Memory array control circuits manage read/write operations in various memory types like SRAM, DRAM, and Flash, encompassing functions such as address decoding, operation control, timing generation, and sense amplifiers with data latches, ensuring precise coordination and reliable performance for efficient data access and storage (Fig. 6).

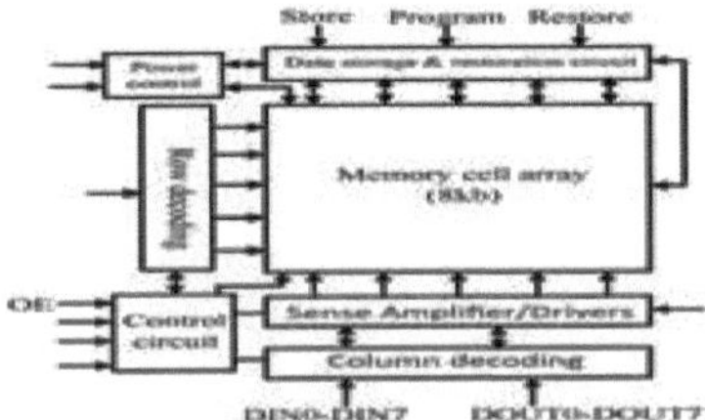

Fig. 6. M ARRAY Circuit

4 Simulation Results

Modern integrated circuits prioritize power efficiency, strategically managing transistor sizes and circuitry to optimize the 8T SRAM cell's performance for contemporary electronic systems with minimal power impact.

4.1 Schematic Diagrams and Simulations

See Figs. 7, 8, 9, 10, 11, 12, and 13.

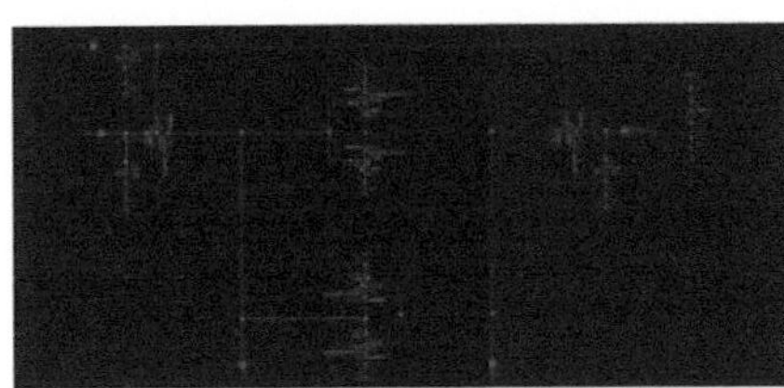

Fig. 7. 6T SRAM Circuit Schematc

Fig. 8. 8T SRAM Circuit Schematic

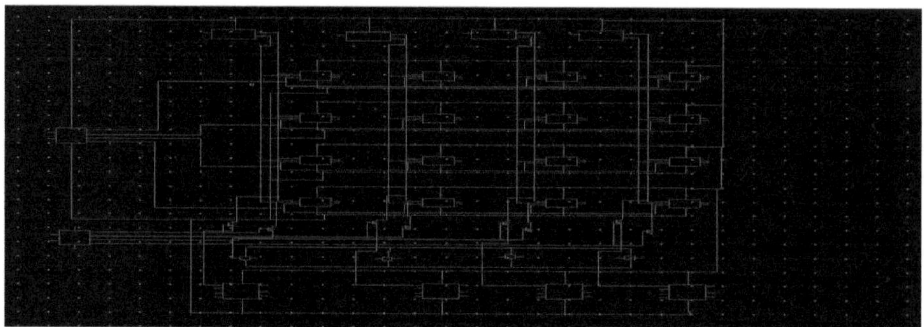

Fig. 9. M ARRAY Schematic

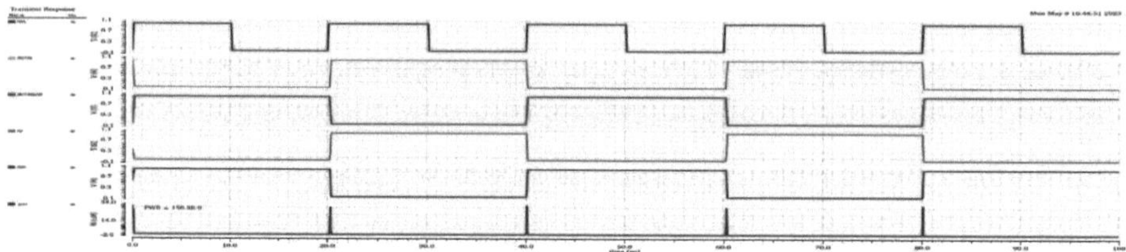

Fig. 10. Waveforms of 6T SRAM

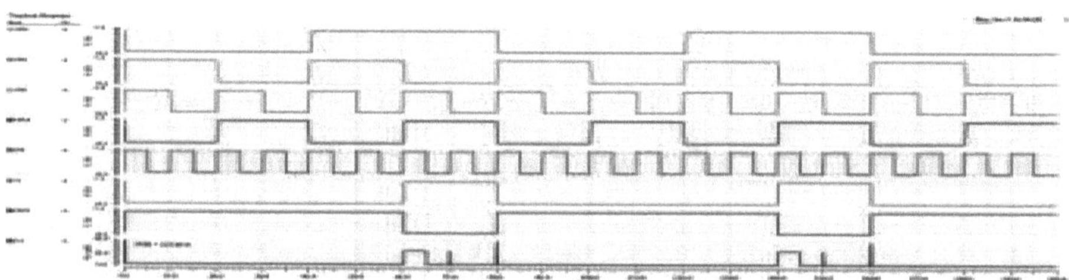

Fig. 11. Waveforms of 8T SRAM

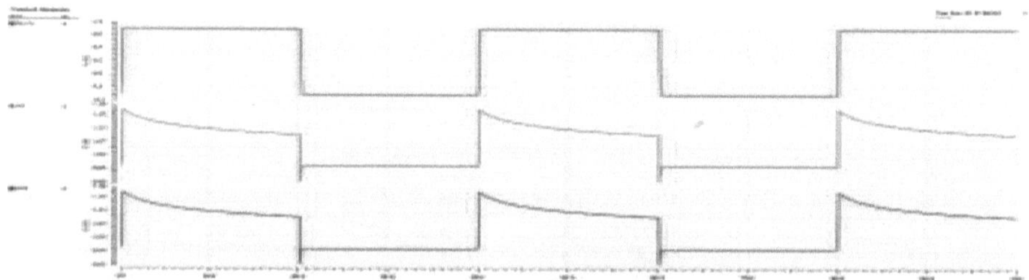

Fig. 12. Waveforms of Precharge

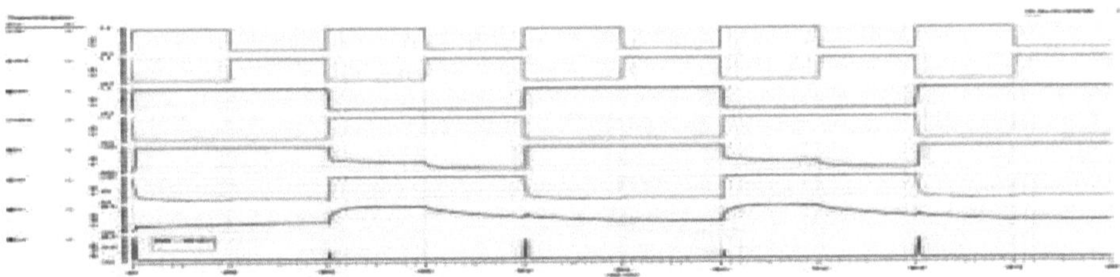

Fig. 13. Waveforms of Sense Amplifier

4.2   Performance Analysis

The passage compares an 8×8 SRAM memory array for moderate needs with a traditional CMOS 6T SRAM cell, highlighting trade-offs in speed, power, and area efficiency based on application-specific requirements (Fig. 14, Tables 2, 3 and 4).

Table 2. Comparative analysis

Aspect	Old Model	Proposed Model
Delay (ns)	10	8
Area (mm^2)	100	50
Power (mW)	10	5

Table 3. Components circuit and outputs

Circuit Component	Output Time (s)
6T SRAM	150.3×10^{-9}
8T SRAM	2.516×10^{-9}
Sense Amplifier	120.1×10^{-9}
Decoder	527.7×10^{-9}

Table 4. Comparison between 8 × 8 SRAM array and traditional

Aspect	8 × 8 SRAM Array	Traditional CMOS
Size	Larger	Smaller
Speed/Access Time	Slower	Faster
Power Consumption	Higher	Lower
Stability/Noise Immunity	Stable	Stable
Integration and Architecture	Complex	Simple
Application	Versatile	Specialized
Design Complexity	Intricate	Basic
Performance-Size Trade-off	Balanced	Efficient

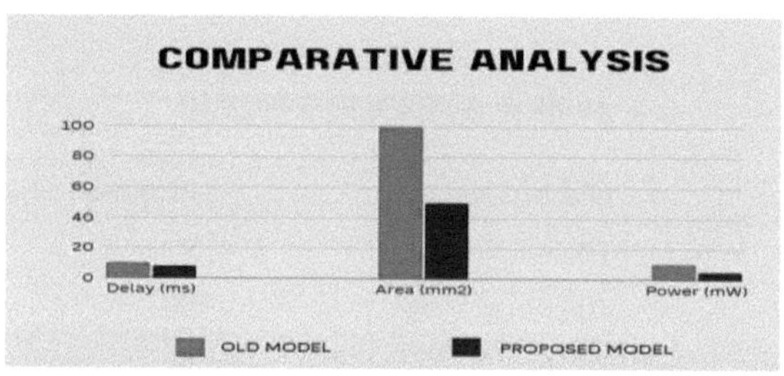

Fig. 14. Comparitive Analysis

5   Conclusion

In conclusion, this research effectively reduces leakage current in 6T and 8T SRAM cells using CMOS 90 nm technology, employing innovative design strategies like reverse-biased FinFETs and power gating. Simulations show superior energy efficiency without compromising performance, demonstrating the potential of CMOS 90 nm for low-power memory solutions and providing valuable insights for future semiconductor processes.

References

1. Kutila, M., Paasio, A., Lehtonen, T.: Comparison of 130 nm technology 6T and 8T SRAM cell designs for Near-Threshold operation. In: 2014 IEEE 57th International Midwest Symposium on Circuits and Systems (MWSCAS), pp. 925–928 (2014). https://doi.org/10.1109/MWSCAS.2014.6908567
2. Turi, M.A., Delgado-Frias, J.G.: Effective low leakage 6T and 8T FinFET SRAMs: using cells with reverse-biased FinFETs, NearThreshold operation, and power gating. IEEE Trans. Circuits Syst. II Exp. Briefs **67**(4), 765–769 (2020). https://doi.org/10.1109/TCSII.2019.2922921
3. Wang, B., Wang, S., Law, M.-K.: On low-leakage CMOS switches. In: 2021 IEEE International Midwest Symposium on Circuits and Systems (MWSCAS), pp. 1–5 (2021). https://doi.org/10.1109/MWSCAS47672.2021.9531780

4. Anandani, D., Kumar, A., Kanchana Bhaaskaran, V.S.: Gating techniques for 6T SRAM cell using different modes of FinFET. In: 2015 International Conference on Advances in Computing, Communications and Informatics (ICACCI), pp. 483–487 (2015). https://doi.org/10.1109/ICACCI.2015.7275655

5. Khan, Q.M., Perdriau, R., Ramdani, M., Koohestani, M.: A comparative performance analysis of 6T and 9T SRAM integrated circuits: SOI vs. Bulk. IEEE Lett. Electromag. Compat. Practi. Appl. **4**(2), 25–30 (2022). https://doi.org/10.1109/LEMCPA.2022.3163963.38

6. Kawaguchi, H., Nose, K., Sakurai, T.: A CMOS scheme for 0.5V supply voltage with pico ampere standby current. In: Dig. Tech. Papers IEEE Int. SolidState Circuits Conf., pp. 192–193 (1998)

7. Pasuluri, B., Kishor Sonti, V.J.K.: Design of CMOS 6T and 8T SRAM for Memory Applications. In: Proceedings of 2nd ICSEC. Algorithms for Intelligent Systems. Springer, Singapore (2021)

8. Reddy, G.K., Jainwal, K., Singh, J., Mohanty, S.P.: Process variation tolerant 9T SRAM bitcell design. In: 2012 13th International Symposium on Quality Electronic Design, 19–21 March 2012, pp 493 - 497, Santa Clara, CA.

9. Pasuluri, B., Kishor Sonti, V.J.K.: Design and analysis of instrumentation amplifier using 45 nm technology. In: Informatica Journal 2021, vol. 32, no. 11 (2021)

10. Colinge, J.-P.: The SOI MOSFET: from single gate to multigate. In: Colinge, J.-P. (ed.) FinFETs and Other Multi-Gate Transistors, 1st edn., pp. 1–48. Springer, New York (2008)

11. Turi, M.A., Delgado-Frias, J.G.: An implemented, initialization algorithm for many-dimension, Monte Carlo circuit simulations using Spice. In: Proceedings of Annual Computing and Communication Workshop and Conference, pp. 56–59 (2017)

12. Muttreja, A., et al.: CMOS logic design with independent-gate FinFETs. In: Proceedings of International Conference on Computer Design, pp. 560–567 (2007)

13. Mutyam, M., Narayanan, V.: Working with process variation aware cache. In: Design, Automation Test in Europe Conference Exhibition, pp. 1–6 (2007)

14. Dhanumjay, K., Sudha, M., Giri Prasad, M.N., Padmaraju, K.: Cell stability analysis of conventional 6T dynamic 8T SRAM cell in 45 nm technology. Int. J. VLSI Des. Commun. Syst. (VLSICS) **3**(2), 41–51 (2012)

15. Kushwash, C.B., Vishwakarma, S.K.: A single-ended with dynamic feedback control 8T subthreshold SRAM cell. IEEE VLSI Syst. **24**(1), 373–377 (2017)

Author Index